797,885 Books
are available to read at

www.ForgottenBooks.com

Forgotten Books' App
Available for mobile, tablet & eReader

ISBN 978-0-484-92090-2
PIBN 10022536

This book is a reproduction of an important historical work. Forgotten Books uses state-of-the-art technology to digitally reconstruct the work, preserving the original format whilst repairing imperfections present in the aged copy. In rare cases, an imperfection in the original, such as a blemish or missing page, may be replicated in our edition. We do, however, repair the vast majority of imperfections successfully; any imperfections that remain are intentionally left to preserve the state of such historical works.

Forgotten Books is a registered trademark of FB &c Ltd.
Copyright © 2017 FB &c Ltd.
FB &c Ltd, Dalton House, 60 Windsor Avenue, London, SW19 2RR.
Company number 08720141. Registered in England and Wales.

For support please visit www.forgottenbooks.com

1 MONTH OF FREE READING

at

www.ForgottenBooks.com

By purchasing this book you are eligible for one month membership to ForgottenBooks.com, giving you unlimited access to our entire collection of over 700,000 titles via our web site and mobile apps.

To claim your free month visit:
www.forgottenbooks.com/free22536

* Offer is valid for 45 days from date of purchase. Terms and conditions apply.

English
Français
Deutsche
Italiano
Español
Português

www.forgottenbooks.com

Mythology Photography **Fiction**
Fishing Christianity **Art** Cooking
Essays Buddhism Freemasonry
Medicine **Biology** Music **Ancient Egypt** Evolution Carpentry Physics
Dance Geology **Mathematics** Fitness
Shakespeare **Folklore** Yoga Marketing
Confidence Immortality Biographies
Poetry **Psychology** Witchcraft
Electronics Chemistry History **Law**
Accounting **Philosophy** Anthropology
Alchemy Drama Quantum Mechanics
Atheism Sexual Health **Ancient History**
Entrepreneurship Languages Sport
Paleontology Needlework Islam
Metaphysics Investment Archaeology
Parenting Statistics Criminology
Motivational

THE BREAK-UP OF CHINA

WITH AN ACCOUNT OF ITS PRESENT
COMMERCE, CURRENCY, WATERWAYS
ARMIES, RAILWAYS, POLITICS

AND

FUTURE PROSPECTS

BY

LORD CHARLES BERESFORD

WITH PORTRAITS AND MAPS

NEW YORK AND LONDON
HARPER & BROTHERS PUBLISHERS
1899

Copyright, 1899, by HARPER & BROTHERS.

All rights reserved.

PREFACE

The break-up of an Empire of four hundred millions of people is an event that has no parallel in history. When I undertook the Mission confided to me by the President of the Associated Chambers of Commerce, I frankly admit that I did not fully grasp the dimensions of a problem the solving of which is only possible by clear thought and decisive action—qualities that have been conspicuously absent from our dealings with China during the late difficulties in the Far East. Although my Report deals mainly with trading and commercial questions, it cannot exclude considerations of high policy, and I am compelled to travel outside the limits originally defined for the scope of my Mission. In framing my Report it is impossible to ignore conditions inseparable from the Commercial Question—viz., matters relating to international, racial, and political complications. The British and American public have been quite bewildered by the controversy which has raged during the last year over the relative merits of the "Open Door" and the "Sphere of Influence."

PREFACE

Investigations on the spot have convinced me that the maintenance of the Chinese Empire is essential to the honor as well as the interests of the Anglo-Saxon race, and I hope that when the British and American people are acquainted with the facts as a whole, they will be similarly convinced.

The Diplomatic and Commercial prestige of Great Britain has been affected by the events in Northern China, but only in a slight degree when compared with the loss of good name involved by forcing concessions from China when she is prostrated by involuntary surrenders to Powers stronger than herself. Hitherto our policy has been to befriend weaker nations. It cannot be said that this policy has lately been followed in the Far East. We have taken advantage of the impotence and distress of the authorities and people of China to advance our own interests, and consequently China has become suspicious of Great Britain; this is not only natural but inevitable.

Our proceedings are certain to encompass the doom of China, and equally certain to produce international strife. Mastery in Asia under a system of "Spheres of Influence" will not be determined by effusion of ink. A straightforward recognition of the principles of freedom, fair dealing, and equality of opportunity which have made our position in the world, coupled with resolution and vigor in carrying these principles out, will not only preserve the integrity of the Chinese

PREFACE

Empire, but will conduce more largely to our interests than the present plan of taking what does not belong to us because other Powers are doing the same. Unless a definite settlement of the problem in the Far East is thought out and brought into effect, war is certain, and the whole civilized world may be compelled to share in the conflict.

No one knows better than myself the inherent deficiencies of this Report. I claim for it, however, the single merit of being an honest endeavor to examine and set forth the conditions under which war will alone be avoided, and will at the same time secure the trading and commercial interests not only of the British, but the whole Anglo-Saxon race.

INTRODUCTORY

I HAVE thoroughly investigated the matters referred to me by the President of the Associated Chambers of Commerce, in his letter to me of August 1, 1898 (*vide* Appendix), and in furtherance of that object I have obtained a very large amount of information connected with trade in China, which I trust will be interesting to the commercial communities of Europe and America.

I have not attempted to give these rough notes of travel any literary style. There has only been time to make a plain statement of valuable facts for immediate use. My professional life has not qualified me to give anything more than what I consider to be a common-sense judgment on the finer issues of financial and commercial questions. I have tried to see the interests of the trader in China through his own eyes, and with my own I have looked for the reasons which he has given me for his statements.

I arrived at Hong Kong 30th September, 1898, and left Shanghai 9th January, 1899. During that time I visited those places in China where British

INTRODUCTORY

communities reside, and wherever there was a Chamber of Commerce, convened meetings, obtained the opinions of the members, and received a number of resolutions (*vide* Appendix).

I enclose copies of these resolutions, together with the names of the places.

With the exception of three so-called armies, I inspected the whole military force of China, and by permission of the generals put the troops through various movements, in order to ascertain their efficiency.

I visited every fort, every arsenal, with one exception, and all the naval and military schools, also the ships of both the Chinese fleets—viz., the Peyang and Nanyang squadrons, and the one dockyard.

A Report on all these matters is enclosed. I have not, however, entered fully into the degrees of effectiveness which came to light, as it would not be courteous to the Chinese Government, who frankly asked me to inspect the whole of their naval and military organization, and to inform them in what particulars they were inefficient or ineffective, and, further, asked me what suggestions I would make as a remedy. But enough will be found in the Report to show that no security at present exists for the future development of British trade in China.

At Peking I was received on two occasions by the Tsung-li Yamen, and visited Prince Ching and his Excellency Li Hung Chang.

INTRODUCTORY

I also visited six of the eight Viceroys of the Great Provinces.

Everywhere the Chinese authorities received me with extreme courtesy and ceremony, the great Mandarins, Governors, Generals, Admirals, Taotais, and all officials treating me with marked distinction. This was owing to a keen appreciation on their part of the power and influence of the trading and commercial communities of Great Britain, which they were aware I had the honor to represent.

Everywhere friendliness towards Great Britain and her people was freely expressed, and considerable interest exhibited as to the Report I should be able to render to the Associated Chambers of Commerce in London.

Although the Mission I undertook was essentially commercial, I found that it was absolutely impossible to ignore political issues. In China commercial and political questions cannot be separated. I have, therefore, endeavored to show in my Report that future commercial success and prosperity depend entirely upon the treatment of the present political situation. In my humble opinion—an opinion strongly supported by every British community in China—the policy adopted by the British Government now will determine the life or death of British trade with China in the future.

As the trading interests of Japan and the United States are identical with those of Great Britain,

INTRODUCTORY

with regard to the future development of trade with China, I travelled home through those two countries in order to obtain the opinions of the various Chambers of Commerce on this important matter.

An account of the result of my inquiries in those countries is herewith enclosed.

I have endeavored to give detailed facts, as personally investigated or seen, in order to illustrate all statements contained in the Report.

In my Report I have confined myself to those points which affect British trade as a whole. Whenever individual industries are touched upon it will be found that other British trading interests are interlocked with such individual industry. I have touched very lightly on statistics connected with Returns of Trade or Trade Reports, such being already in existence either in able Consular Reports, or in the Returns Imperial Maritime Customs China (Statistical Series), or in the valuable report of the Blackburn Chamber of Commerce, 1896–1897.

I have had numerous interviews with Chinese officials on questions connected with British trade and commerce. A summary of such interviews will be found under the names of the localities where they occurred.

No opportunity has been lost on my part of seeking interviews with representatives of all foreign nations holding trading interests in China. Consuls, merchants, engineers, etc., belonging to

INTRODUCTORY

Russia, France, Germany, America, Japan, etc., have been visited, and every effort has been made on the part of your Mission to promote friendly feeling, and to prove that the policy of Great Britain, as expressed in the "Open Door," is not a selfish policy for the British Empire, but one which must equally benefit the trade of all nations.

That the Mission has been successful in promoting friendship is evinced by the fact that, on the evening of the day before I left China, I was entertained by the whole of the Foreign Communities of Shanghai, when a resolution (*vide* Appendix) was passed by these communities proving the respect and interest held with regard to the proceedings of the Mission.

Through all this undertaking I have known that my Report might be seen by two classes of persons interested in China—namely, those who have already invested capital in that country, and those who may be going to invest. I am aware that the interests of those two classes cannot always be identical. I have met the merchant who says "Speak out," and I have met the financier who says "Speak gently." My duty is a simple one—to speak the truth. I have seen men in China representing every class of commercial interest, and have recorded here, as accurately as I could, the ideas they hold, and the reasons which they give for holding them.

The thanks of the Associated Chambers of Commerce are due to the following gentlemen, who

INTRODUCTORY

rendered me most valuable assistance during my travels: Mr. Thomas Jackson, Chief Manager of the Hong Kong and Shanghai Bank, who kindly made all arrangements for my comfort at every place I visited where there was a branch of the Hong Kong and Shanghai Bank.

Mr. W. Cartwright, late Commissioner of Customs, who accompanied me on my journey up the Yangtse Valley, and by his perfect knowledge of the Chinese language, and of the Chinese themselves, largely contributed to the success of my interviews with the Viceroys and other officials.

All H.B.M. Consuls with whom I came in contact, and particularly Consul-General Brenan, Consul Bourne, Consul Fraser, and Consul Hosie.

Mr. C. W. Kinder, Chief Engineer of the Chinese Imperial Railway from Peking, *via* Tientsin, to Shanhaikwan; Messrs. Jardine & Matheson, and Messrs. Butterfield & Swire, who placed their steamers at my disposal whenever opportunity occurred.

The thanks of the Association are also due to my secretary, Mr. Robin Grey, for his untiring energy and hard work during the whole of my travels—work rendered more difficult by the fact that one of my secretaries, Mr. McDonald, nearly died of fever at Hankow, which necessitated my leaving him behind during the most important stages of the journey. The Report would have been rendered before but for this mischance.

CONTENTS

PREFACE

Dimensions of Problem—Impossibility of Ignoring Political Questions—Present Policy Certain to Encompass the Doom of China—War Certain if Continued—Report's Deficiencies and Aims.......... *Page* iii

INTRODUCTORY

Scope of Mission—Report not Literary: Common-sense Judgment on Facts—Convened Meetings of Chambers of Commerce—Visited Armies, Forts, Viceroys, etc.—Everywhere Friendliness to Great Britain—Travelled Home *via* Japan and America—Industries Touched Upon, and Why—Interviewed Chinese Officials and Foreign Traders — Knew Report Might be Seen by Two Classes—Present and Future Investors—Persons to whom Thanks are Due for Assistance...................... vii

CHAPTER I—PEKING

Arrival, and Visits to Foreign Ministers—Invitation to Visit Port Arthur—Visit to Tsung-li Yamen—Prince Ching's Friendliness to Great Britain—Pointed Out that Commercial Communities Wanted Trade, not Territory—No Real Protection for Trade without Reorganization of Chinese Army—Britain, with 64 Per Cent. of Trade, Anxious about Security—British Officers Should be Employed—Other Nations to Help—Tsung-li Yamen Praises Sir Robert Hart— Return Visit of Tsung-li Yamen—Emperor and Empress Agree to Suggestions—Two Thousand Troops to be Drilled in Yangtse Valley—Viceroy Chung Chi Tung Ordered to Confer—Official Interpreter: Why Employed—Interview with His Excellency Yung Lu *in re* Army Reorganization—Pressed to Remain for Further Interviews—Hu Yen Mei's Fears for China—Interviews with Li Hung Chang and Sir Robert Hart—British Prestige Below Russian—British Influence is in Inverse Ratio to British Trade........ 1

CHAPTER II—TIENTSIN

Arrival at Tientsin—Protest of Chamber of Commerce Against "Spheres of Influence"—Trade of Tientsin Increasing—Energy of British Mer-

CONTENTS

chants Responsible for it—Memorandum of British Merchants Complaining of Lack of Policy—Anxiety of Merchants, and Unwillingness to Invest Further Capital—Not Afraid of Legitimate but of Military Diversion of Trade by Russia—Alienation of Chinese Territory would Ruin Trade built up by British—Interview with His Excellency Yu Lu, and the Taotai Li—Helplessness of China—Good Feeling Between British and German Merchants in Tientsin................. *Page* 14

CHAPTER III—TONGSHAN

Particulars of the Shanhaikwan-Newchwang Railway—A Further Extension to Sin-min-thun to Join Russian Line Projected — Interesting Workshop and Locomotive Statistics for Railway Men—Why American Engines are Preferred to English—Automatic Couplings are used—Engines Building in China—Particulars of a Coal-mine at Tongshan.. 23

CHAPTER IV—NEWCHWANG

Arrival at Newchwang—British Merchants' Alarm for Future—Trade of Newchwang Compared with Yangtse Ports—Meeting of British Merchants—Fears of Annexation by Russia—British Concession Wanted—Mineral Wealth of Manchuria—Russian Military Position, and Evasion of Chinese Customs—Nothing to Prevent Russia Marching into Chihli—Letter of Merchants—Reforms Necessary for Opening up Interior Suggested—Merchants' Complaints and Needs—Great Coalfields, etc., in Manchuria—British Consular Agent should be Stationed at Kirin—Ways in which British Trade may be Damaged—It should not be Abandoned—Manchuria a Splendid Country—British Trade Considerable, Russian Nil—Manchuria Russianized would be a Prelude to a March on India—British Capital Invested in Manchuria would Strengthen Our Position—Russia in Manchuria, and Her Railway Material not Paying Duty—Importance of this Exemption to Foreign Bondholders, as it Curtails the Income Hypothecated to Foreign Countries—Russian Flag Hoisted in Manchuria—Treatment of Chinese Peasants—Their Railway, Mainly Strategic, will take Five Years to Complete—Material Being Bought in America—How Railway will Affect Newchwang—Land Dispute Between Russians and British at Newchwang—Treatment of Chinese—British Missionaries' Fears—"Manchuria Russian in all but Name"—Troops Pouring into Manchuria—The Russian Railway Agreement—Open Door in Manchuria Depends on Russian Good-will—Assurances (of no Value) Against Military Strength—Newchwang Key of Position—Customs Revenue at Newchwang Increasing—Foreign Imports—British Trade and Indian Yarn Going Up—English Cotton-Goods Losing Ground in Favor of American—Metals and Kerosene—Russian Oil Sold as American—Exports of Silk—Bean and Opium Trade—Mineral Wealth Very Great, Coal and Gold Found in Large Quantities—Silver-mines in Manchuria—Factories Started—Review of Trade in 1898: Figures not yet Published—Opening of new Chinese Railway Expected this Year... 32

CONTENTS

CHAPTER V—CHEFOO

Arrival at Chefoo—Memorandum of British Merchants—Field of Development in Cotton Goods—Gold and Coal Mines in Province—Complaints of Apathy Displayed by British Consuls—Alarm of Merchants Lest Kiao-chow Should Divert Trade—Shantung: One of the Few Provinces where Railways will Pay at Once—Visits to Factories and Men-of-war—Opposition of Chinese to Machinery...........*Page* 65

CHAPTER VI—WEI-HAI-WEI

Visit to Wei-hai-Wei—Opinion as to Its Naval Capabilities—A Good Mercantile Port, but for Our Consent to Germany Closing the Door.. 71

CHAPTER VII—KIAO-CHOW

Invitation from Prince Henry—Opinion as to Capabilities—Land Regulations at Kiao-chow... 73

CHAPTER VIII—SHANGHAI

Arrival at Shanghai—Anxiety of British Merchants for Future—Disadvantages of New Navigation Laws—Right of Interior Residence Denied—Viceroys Complained of Interference with Provincial Revenue—China Association Meeting—Reasons for Limited Expansion of Trade with China Set Forth—No Complaint Against Imperial Maritime Customs—Treaties Imperfect—Transit-pass System—Intentions of Lord Elgin—Result an Utter Failure—In Many Parts Transit Passes Ignored—Merchants Tired of Complaining—Trade in South Has Shifted from British to French Route owing to French Energy—Right of Residence in Interior Forbidden, which Hinders Trade—China's Necessities Increasing—Tariff to be Revised, but no Reforms Proposed—China Wants Money, but Foreign Lenders Want Security, which China Cannot Offer—A Strong Government in Peking a First Necessity—British Government Ought to Have a Policy—Whether China Remains Intact or be Partitioned, Necessity for Reforms are the Same—Dangers of Partition Policy—Great Britain Should Lead the Movement for Reform—Difficulties Great, but Other Nations Should be Asked to Co-operate—Chambers of Commerce Meeting—Points in Address Affecting Trade—Bank of China Case, Affecting Validity of All Contracts with Chinese—Should be Dealt with Promptly by Home Government—Chinese Officials at Fault—Cotton Trade of Shanghai: Chiefly American in Origin but British-owned—America Increasing Her Interest and Competing Seriously with Lancashire—British Trade not Injured so Much as British Manufacturer—Few American Firms, and 60 Per Cent. of American Trade British-owned and Under Our Flag—Three Interviews with Marquis Ito, Who Supported "Open Door" Policy—Thought Corea Should be Included—Reorganization of Army Neces-

CONTENTS

sary—Interviewed His Excellency Kwei Chun: Conversation *re* China's Condition—Extension of Settlement—French Pretensions and Opposition—Origin of Extraordinary French Claims at Shanghai—Informed Viceroy of Nanking, if French Claims Granted, would Cause Trouble—Disturbances Fatal to Trade would Follow—Dangers of French Policy—French Demands at Paotung—Resolution of Foreign Community—Interviews with Taotai, and also Missionaries—Interchange of Views—French Jesuits in Favor of "Open Door" Policy, and Declared no Difficulties in it..*Page* 76

CHAPTER IX—NANKING

Arrival at Nanking in Chinese Cruiser—Received with Great Pomp—Viceroy Afraid of Disturbances—Distress from Floods and Antiforeign Feelings—Thought Reorganization of Army would Lead to Dismemberment of China—Commercial Understanding would Assist China, but Russia would not Permit—Correspondence with His Excellency on Army Question—Change of Views—Description of Naval and Military Colleges—Money Well Expended: Waste of Money, however, on Naval College in Country with no Fleet—Interesting Letter from the Viceroy Liu Kwen Yi.............................. 106

CHAPTER X—WUHU

Visit to Wuhu—Memorandum in Favor of "Open Door"—Merchants Nervous—Coal in Locality, but Authorities will not Allow it to be Worked... 115

CHAPTER XI—KIUKIANG

Visit to Port—Received by Residents—Principal Export Declining—Mineral Riches, Property of British and Americans, not Allowed to be Worked... 117

CHAPTER XII—CHINKIANG

Visit to Chinkiang—Useful Memorandum of the Chamber of Commerce—Trade of Chinkiang—Success of Transit-pass System Here—Exports Must be Developed—New Inland Navigation Rules Defective—Cargo has not been Conveyed Owing to Defects in Rules—Condition of Grand Canal Bad—Rioting with Connivance of Authorities—British Flag Should be Allowed by Consuls on All British Merchants' Launches—Right of Residence in Interior Necessary to Push Trade—Complaints as to Yangtse Regulations and Preferential Rights—Serious Complaints as to British Consuls at Chinkiang—Also as to Native Officials Who Delay Business to Their Own Advantage—Suggestions by Merchants for Reform of Abuses Complained of—British Prestige at a Low Ebb—Gunboats Wanted on Waterways—Charges Against Consuls Have Some Foundation in Fact—Trade of Chinkiang in 1898 Shows

CONTENTS

General Decrease All Round—Reasons for Such Decline: Insecurity, Scarcity of Capital, and Floods—Factories and Local Trade—Japanese Steamers Subsidized—Second Visit to Chinkiang—Interview with Admiral of Yangtse..................................*Page* 120

CHAPTER XIII—KIANGZIN

Interview with General Li, who was Unhappy About China's Future—He was Afraid Russia would Prevent England from Assisting China.. 138

CHAPTER XIV—HANKOW

Found the British Community Very Anxious as to Future Security, Owing to Rebellions Such as Yu Man Tsup—Origin of Rebellion, which has Lasted Twelve Years—Merchants' Resolution—Weakness of Local Officials—Incendiarism Rife—Importance of Opening up Waterways—New Navigation Law's Defects—French and Russian Seizures of British-owned Property at Hankow, which was Registered at Consulate, but French Tore up Boundary Stones—British Firms Published Protests, but French Consul Absolutely Sold Land—Russian Armed Interference with British on Land Bought in 1862—Consul Feared British Firm would not be Supported by H.M.'s Government—Cases Should be Inquired Into—Hankow Land Certain to Increase in Value—To Exact Compensation from China—Cowardly as She is Powerless—Viceroys would be Glad to See Gunboats on Yangtse—Rapids no Difficulty—Steamers on Yangtse—Nationality and Numbers—Coal-fields and Iron-mines in Hupeh—Visit to Latter at Wong Chi Tong—Tea Business at Hankow Declining—Freight Principally British—Summary of Interviews with Chung Chi Tung, the Viceroy—He was Afraid of Disturbances, as He had not Enough Troops to Quell Them—His Excellency Suggested Employment of American and Japanese Officers for Army Reorganization, but Saw Insuperable Obstacles to his Orders, as to Drilling Two Thousand Men, Especially on Financial Grounds—At a Second Interview the Viceroy Raised Fewer Difficulties—Visit to His Excellency Sheng, Who Thought Russia Too Strong, and China Might Have to Throw in her Lot with Russia—Visit to the Iron and Steel Works at Hanyang—The Rich Province of Hunan Most Anti-foreign in China—Gold-mines with Modern Machinery in Hunan—Accounts of Various Foreign Factories Started in Hankow—Hankow the Chicago of China in the near Future.............. 139

CHAPTER XV—FOOCHOW

Arrival at Foochow—British Merchants' Complaints of Likin—British Capital could be Profitably Employed Here—State of the Min River—Trouble with the Chinese Officials—Friction as to What Constitutes the Area Free from Likin—Interview with the Viceroy Hsü Jung Kwei—His Views on the Provincial Armies System—Visit to the Tartar General Tseng Chee—Finances of Fuhkien Province—Difficulty in Paying Wages at Arsenal................................... 169

CONTENTS

CHAPTER XVI—SWATOW

Arrival at Swatow—Resolution of British Merchants—Officials Afraid of the People—Province Decimated in 1872—Opposition of Natives to Machinery—British *versus* American Goods—Restrictions Fatal to Trade—*Vide* a Railway Proposed Here—No Chance at Present for Development of Trade..................................*Page* 177

CHAPTER XVII—AMOY

Arrival at Amoy—Tea Trade Nearly Extinct Here—Suggestions of Chamber of Commerce for Improving Tea Trade—Imposition of Likin Accounts for General Decline in Trade—Cases Given me of Flour, Brickmaking, and Other Trades Killed by Likin—Salt Monopoly Abuses—Causes of Famine in China Examined : Proved to be Due to Grain not Being Allowed to be Moved—Captain Fleming's Report on Coal Area of Kwangtung—Emigration to Singapore—Respect of Chinese for Queen Victoria.. 182

CHAPTER XVIII—HONG KONG

Arrival at Hong Kong and Interview with Reformer Kang Yu Wei—The Reform Party Crushed, but not Killed, in China—They Favor Extension of Western Trade with China—Reformers not Practical Enough: Theoretically Sound in Views—Opinions of Chinese Compradors and British Merchants—Disturbances Great Drawback to Trade—France in the South—Trade of Hong Kong with Kwangsi and Kwangtung: Tables, Ditto—Chinese Custom House in a British Colony an Anomaly—Its Effect on the Junk Trade—Blockade of Hong Kong—The Opium Trade at Hong Kong—Particulars and Figures—System not Fair to Chinese Government—Memorandum Showing Customs Views on Question of Custom House—Resolutions of Chamber of Commerce, Hong Kong, on this Subject—Views of the Chamber on the "Open Door" Principle—Address from the Chinese Residents at Hong Kong—Humiliating Regulations of British Government—Their Views on Reform...................................... 191

CHAPTER XIX—CANTON

Arrival at Canton—Presented with Memorandum by Merchants—Definition of the Area of the Treaty Port Wanted—Transit Passes and Piracy on the West River—French Claims to Sphere of Influence Unjustified by Amount of their Trade—Reply to British Merchants' Memorandum—Copies of Documents Showing Correspondence between British Minister, Consul, and Chinese Authorities *re* the Area of the Port Exempted from Likin—Piracies on the West River—Account of *Tung Kong* Case—British Launch Boarded, and then Compelled to Tow Pirates—Scarcely a Day but Flagrant Cases Occur which Impede Trade—Forty-one Cases of Piracy Reported by Local Press—

CONTENTS

Officials Should be Made Pecuniarily Liable for Losses—Extraordinary Story of Piracy on a Hong Kong Junk: Two Hundred Dollars Damage Done, and People Thrown into River—Statement of Police as to Condition of Junk After Fight—Case of Piracy on the *Chung On:* Captain Shot and Mutilated After Death by the Pirates—Comparison of English, German, and French Trade in Kwangtung and Kwangsi—French Sphere of Influence would be Detrimental to British Trade—Interview with His Excellency Kwei Yun—Mineral Resources of Province—Effect of Disturbances on the Integrity of Chinese Empire...*Page* 232

CHAPTER XX—WUCHOW

No Time to Visit Wuchow, but Mr. Hosie (Consul) Came Down to Canton—New Navigation Laws Imperfect—Suggestions for a Railway—Chinese Guards of British Consul had One Rifle Between Them.. 264

CHAPTER XXI—CHINESE ARMIES AND NAVIES

Chinese Armies and Navies: Full Account of Each Visited—Reported Position of Russian Troops in Eastern Siberia and Manchuria.... 267

CHAPTER XXII—FORTS AND ARSENALS

Forts and Arsenals—Full Reports of Visits to All but One.......... 290

CHAPTER XXIII—RAILWAYS

Wide Difference between Built, Building, and Projected—Account of those Built—Account of Railways Building, with Nationality, etc.—Account of Railways Projected or Suggested in China—Particulars of Kind of Railways Required in China—We may have to Concede Spheres of Railway Interest.................................... 304

CHAPTER XXIV—WATERWAYS

Antiquity and Convenience of Waterways, but Peculations of Officials Render Useless—The Yangtse River, 3500 Miles Long: Rapids First Navigated by Mr. Little—Account of Distances and Condition of River from Hankow to Ichang—Gorges of Yangtse neither so Difficult nor Dangerous as Supposed—Steamers Required to Navigate Them—Rise and Fall of River—British Civil Engineers Wanted—Probable Cost of Improving Rapids—French Claims to Sphere of Influence in Yangtse Valley—H.M.S. *Woodcock;* Shallow-draught Gunboat on Yangtse—Steamers Badly Wanted for Towing—Account of Grand Canal: Showing its Condition, and how it would Add to Trade of Chinkiang—Account of West River Trade—How French Claim would Interfere with it—Routes Taken to Avoid Likin *via* Pakhoi Instead of Hong Kong—Junks Flying no Flag Nominally Owned by British—Leads to Evasion of Likin—Unfair to Chinese Customs—Differential Treatment

CONTENTS

and Restrictions on West River — British Ship-owner has Direct Interest in Goods to Destination, Merchant has not—Necessity for Securing Equality of Treatment for all Goods—Yellow River: Account of its Changes of Bed—Cause of These Inundations, and Damage They Do—Navigation Difficult, Owing to Lowness of Water and Swiftness of Current—The Wangpoo River—Way in which the Woosung Bar Affects Shanghai — Pei Ho River: Difficulties of Navigation, Cause, and Proposed Remedy—Liao River Closed by Ice in Winter—Shipping at Time of Visit—The Han River—Account of the Big " Bore " —Smaller Rivers Silting Up—Dredges Necessary—Gold in Rivers— Tung Ting Lake and Siang River—Poyang Lake—Roads in China— Suggestions for Reform—Lighting of Peking.............. *Page* 318

CHAPTER XXV—THE BRITISH CONSUL IN CHINA

Merchants Too Hard on Consuls—Defects in System, not in Men—Complaints of Merchants Tabulated—Consuls Themselves Admit Defects— Some Duties of British Consuls Specified, Showing Nature—A Commercial Attaché Wanted—Present Appointment a Farce—Training of Consuls Deficient, and does not Make Them Business-like—Foreign Nations Give Their Nationals Better Consular Support — British Government Must Move with the Times and Assist Merchants—British Subjects Better Recommended by American than by their Own Consul —Charge for British Transit Passes Places Merchant at Disadvantage—Remedies Suggested: More Men, Better Pay, Earlier Retirement.. 348

CHAPTER XXVI—FINANCE AND CURRENCY

Recognizing Difficulty of Subject: Made a Collection of Currency—List of Coins, Etc., in the Collection—Weak Financial Position of China Due to Military Weakness—Revenue Squandered in Expenses of Collection —List of Loans — Guarantees on Railway Loans Bound to Hamper China Later—Why the Mandarins Misappropriate Revenue—Days for Loans Gone—Guides to Investors in this Country—Proposal for Increasing Revenue—How Spheres of Influence would Affect Foreign Bondholders—No Security Without Adequate Military and Police Protection—The Value of the Different Taels in China—Dollars Used— Subsidiary Coinage and Copper Cash — Paper on Relation Between Copper Cash and Silver — Memorandum on Chinese Copper Cash — Reply to Two Questions as to Gold Standard: Is it Possible? and How has Rate of Exchange Affected Price of Commodities? — Reforms Suggested to Improve Finance and Currency—List of Banks in China... 359

CHAPTER XXVII—TRADE, TREATIES, AND TARIFFS

Changed Conditions and Competition Telling on British Trade — New Markets Opening—Machinery Especially Required—Unpublished Re-

CONTENTS

turns of 1898 Trade Showing Net Decrease—Export Trade has Suffered from Disturbances, etc.—Railways will Help British Trade if Chinese Integrity is Maintained—Customs Duties: Request for Increase—British Treaties: Nanking Treaty, Tientsin Treaty of 1858, Principal Articles and Intentions—Sir Rutherford Alcock's Unratified Convention of 1868—Sir Robert Hart's View of Alcock Convention—Chefoo Convention. Principal Articles and Intentions of Framers—Article VII. of Customs—Tariff Opposed to Treaty—New Customs Rules as to Transit Passes—Information not New, but is a Useful Short Summary—Illegal Taxes: Names and Descriptions—Dual Customs Control (Imperial and Provincial) Hinders Trade—Difficulties of Transit Pass System Explained — Merchants' Suggestions to Remedy Abuses—French Firm Action has Benefited British Trade—Salt Monopoly and Land-tax Abuses—The Chinese Side of the Questions Presented—Revision of Tariff: Increase Merchants will Consent to — Reforms Asked as a *quid pro quo*—How Treaty Revisions can be Carried Out Fairly — The Marquis Ito's and the Merchants' Suggestions — Future Trade Prospects — Japan and China Compared — Summary of Points and Necessities of Situation.................................*Page* 389

CHAPTER XXVIII—JAPAN

Invitations to Visit Japan—Arrival at Nagasaki—Machinery the Trade Most Likely to be Developed with Us—Arrived at Kobé and Osaka—Visit to Arsenal and Factories—Iron and Steel Works, Metal Factories, etc.—Meeting of Merchants—Electric Plant at Kioto which Hauls Boats Overland—No Country which Uses Electricity to Such Advantage—Arrival at Tokio—Views of Japanese on "Open Door" Policy—Japanese Think Chinese would Make Good Soldiers—Visits to Military and Naval Schools, and Parade of Troops—Address to Japanese Chamber of Commerce — Interview with Emperor of Japan—Visits Paid to Dockyard and Fleet—Japan Must Have an Export Trade—China Market Nearest............................... 419

CHAPTER XXIX—THE UNITED STATES

Arrival at San Francisco — Visit to Ship-building Works — Address to Chamber of Commerce at San Francisco—Chicago· Visit to Public Institutions, and Speeches Made—Buffalo—Account of Niagara Electric Works—Visit to Washington—Mr. Whitelaw Reid on Philippine Policy—Arrival at New York: Address to Chamber of Commerce—Interest Taken in the Mission in America—Policy of "Open Door" Supported in the States—Question of British Ownership of American Goods—Friendship to Great Britain—American Trade with China More Important than Apparent—Interests of Great Britain and America Identical.. 433

CONTENTS

CHAPTER XXX—OBSERVATIONS

Review of Report—Points out Difficulties and Dangers of Sphere of Influence Policy, and Offers Suggestions for Reforms to Remedy Present State of Affairs..*Page* 448

APPENDIX

Letter Authorizing Mission, and Resolutions of Chamber of Commerce and Other Bodies in China—Summary of Trade Statistics in China. 459

INDEX... 485

THE BREAK-UP OF CHINA

PEKING

The estimated population is 1,300,000

I ARRIVED in Peking on October the 16th, 1898. Having heard that there was some misunderstanding as to my status, it having been asserted that I was an emissary from the British Government, I paid my respects to all the foreign Ministers accredited to Peking, and explained clearly to their Excellencies what position I held. I spoke of the reference given to me by the President of the Associated Chambers of Commerce, Sir Stafford Northcote, which showed that I had been asked to come out to make a report on British trade and commerce, its future development, and what security existed throughout the Empire for such trade and commerce.

During my visit to M. Pavloff, the Russian Chargé d'Affairs, he told me that he would be delighted if I could find time to visit Port Arthur. He also declared his regret that, whereas nearly all essential that China should maintain her integrity. I further added that if, owing to the break-up of China and the necessity of protecting foreign trade, European countries were forced to adopt the policy of "Spheres of Influence," it might possibly cause considerable irritation and unwished-for complications between those countries, but it most certainly would bring about the fall of the Chinese Empire.

Prince Ching remarked that the members of the Tsung-li Yamen quite appreciated all I had said, but asked me how I thought trade and commerce could be better protected than it was at present.

I informed the prince that real and effective protection could be given to property by a thorough and complete reorganization of the Chinese Army as a whole; that the present system of having provincial armies had proved itself, over and over again, ineffective; that a vast amount of property had been destroyed, and that many lives, of missionaries and others, had been sacrificed, all owing to the want of efficient military and police; that these losses of life and property had caused immense inconvenience and expense to the Chinese Government itself; that if a tenth part of the sum that the Chinese have had to pay as indemnity for the loss of life and property had been devoted to military organization, such losses would not have taken place.

I also pointed out that even if the sum supposed

to be devoted for military purposes in the provinces were expended as intended, China would have an army of from two to three hundred thousand men, without a penny of extra taxation being placed upon the people.

Prince Ching replied that he did not think it would be possible to alter the old-established custom and practice of having provincial armies to maintain order in China. I remarked that the Chinese Government had lately had a very excellent illustration of the result of the provincial system when carried out with regard to the fleet. If the two fleets—the Peyang fleet and the Nanyang fleet—had been a national fleet under one commander and organization, it would have been impossible for the Japanese to have obtained the brilliant and easy victories which they achieved in the late war, and China would not now be in the deplorable position, politically and financially, in which she finds herself at present.

Their Excellencies commenced discussing this point among themselves, and I was informed that some of them entirely agreed on this point.

I then suggested that as Great Britain had 64 per cent. of the whole foreign trade of China, she was naturally anxious as to its adequate security, and, being on very friendly terms with the Chinese, it might be possible that the British Government would allow an officer to help the Chinese to put their army in order, if the Chinese Government applied to the British Government for assistance of this description. I further said that I had no authority whatever to make this statement, but in the interests of British trade and commerce, as well as on account of the friendly feelings that I had towards China, I made it as a suggestion, in order that something practical might be proposed to remedy the present unsatisfactory state of affairs.

I reminded the Prince that the Chinese Government had already had extensive experience of the loyalty and utility of British subjects when employed as Chinese servants, and referred to General Gordon, who had been the means of keeping the present dynasty on the throne; and to Sir Robert Hart, who, by his able and excellent administration over the maritime customs, had produced the only certain available asset they possessed in the whole Empire.

Several of the Ministers present here said that, though there might be difficulties, they agreed with my remarks. They also spent some little time in strong eulogies of General Gordon and Sir Robert Hart. I may mention, as an interesting fact, that during the many interviews and conversations which I had with Viceroys and other high Mandarins, they invariably asked me if I knew what Sir Robert Hart's opinion was on the question which we were discussing. This complete confidence in Sir Robert will naturally excite feelings of pride and satisfaction among his countrymen at home.

PEKING

I further remarked that, in the event of the Chinese Government contemplating such an idea, it might be well to invite those nations who had large trading interests with China to lend a few officers and non-commissioned officers to work with the British in the reorganization of the army.

The Prince said that they had already had German officers to drill some of their troops, and also Captain Lang, a British naval captain, to organize their fleet. In both cases the work had been done to the entire satisfaction of the Chinese Government.

Prince Ching repeated that the Tsung-li Yamen thought my remarks very sound, and that they would like to see me again in a few days, when they had had time to think over my suggestions. He said the Tsung-li Yamen were satisfied with the integrity of Britain's motive, that they knew she did not want territory, but would do all in her power to promote trade.

The interview, which had lasted three hours, then closed with the usual Eastern compliments and ceremony.

On October 22d, Prince Ching and some members of the Tsung-li Yamen paid me the compliment of visiting me at the British Legation.

Prince Ching immediately referred to the previous interview, and said that they had seen the Emperor and the Empress Dowager, who considered that the suggestion I had made appeared to be good, and that they recognized it was in the

HIS EXCELLENCY YUNG LU

While at Peking I paid a visit to his Excellency Yung Lu, at present one of the most powerful and influential men in the Chinese Empire.

He conferred with me relative to the interviews I had had with the Tsung-li Yamen. He said the principle of reorganizing the Chinese Army under British and foreign officers and non-commissioned officers was going to be adopted, and that an edict had already been sent to his Excellency Chung Chi Tung. His Excellency Yung Lu was most anxious that I should give him details as to how the principle should be carried out. This I consented to do, after impressing upon him that what I said was my own private opinion, and that all the details connected with such a scheme must be discussed by the two governments, and not by private individuals.

I explained to his Excellency that naturally Great Britain would be anxious to help China, not so much for the sake of China herself as for the sake of British interests with regard to the furtherance of trade.

His Excellency asked me a direct question—whether if China put the whole of her armies under British officers, Great Britain would assist China in any quarrel that might arise between her and any other Power.

I remarked that I would not enter into any political questions, but that the last thing Great

Britain wanted to do was to mix herself up in quarrels which might arise between other countries. I asked his Excellency if I might see the military forces at present quartered around Peking. His Excellency replied that he would be very glad if I would visit those armies which were properly drilled and effective, but that it would be no use my seeing the two armies that were composed of coolies, and were not smart or properly drilled. An account of the armies I saw will be found in another chapter.

Before leaving, his Excellency pressed me to remain longer in Peking, and to see Prince Ching and the Tsung-li Yamen again, with the object of going further into details connected with the organization of the Chinese Army. I remarked that that was impossible, and that if the Tsung-li Yamen thought seriously of the matter, their proper course was not to discuss it with me but with the British Minister.

I also called upon his Excellency Hu Yen Mei, Director of Railways and Governor of Peking, a most energetic and enlightened Mandarin. He professed himself very friendly to the British, and said that when China was opened up by railways it would surely make for the benefit of China and the trade of all nations. He, however, was very anxious as to the immediate future of his country, and said that he earnestly hoped the Chinese Government would shortly create an efficient army, as if disturbances occurred European countries would be very likely to take large slices of territory as compensation for life or losses, which China in her present position was powerless to prevent.

His anxiety was based greatly on what had occurred while I was there. Two of the British engineers, making the line near Fungti, had been badly beaten and shot at by some of the Kansu troops.

While at Peking I paid a visit to his Excellency Li Hung Chang. I found him very old and infirm. The conversation was of no interest to this Report.

I called upon Sir Robert Hart, the Inspector-General of Customs, and upon Mr. Bredon, the Deputy Inspector-General, and had some conversation with them relative to the Customs administration at Hong Kong.

The subject matter of this interview will be found under the chapter of this Report headed " Hong Kong."

Sir Robert Hart expressed an opinion that it would be for the benefit of trade and commerce, as well as of China herself, if she would create an effective military force for the protection of her trading interests.

From my conversation with Chinese authorities, foreigners as well as British in Peking, an opinion was distinctly formed in my mind that British prestige is certainly below that of Russia. I hardly ever made a suggestion to any prominent Chinese official which I thought might tend to the security of Anglo-Saxon trade and commerce, that I was not met with the question, "But what would Russia say to that?" or words to that effect.

The idea is gaining ground all over China that Great Britain is afraid of Russia. Whenever I expressed astonishment at such a thought being entertained, the individual or individuals to whom I was speaking referred to some of the following recent events—viz., Great Britain being afraid to support Japan when Japan was ordered out of Corea and the Shantung Peninsula; the objections which prevailed against Great Britain advancing the loan to China; the Talienwan and Port Arthur incidents, and the Shanhaikwan Railway incident.

A prominent bank official summed up the situation very tersely by saying, "sixty-four per cent. of the whole foreign trade with China is British. There should be a corresponding percentage of influence, but British influence is in inverse ratio to British trade."

II

TIENTSIN

The estimated population is 1,000,000.

TRADE STATISTICS

The total value of trade in 1897 was Hk. taels 55,059,017 (nearly £8,000,000).

The total tonnage of shipping entered and cleared in 1897 was 1,326,663, of which 574,177 was British.

I ARRIVED at Tientsin on the 15th of October, 1898. Soon after my arrival I attended a meeting of the Chamber of Commerce. The chairman, Mr. W. W. Dickinson, a British merchant, opened the proceedings by expressing thanks on behalf of his Chamber to the Associated Chambers of Commerce in London, for having sent a mission out to China to inquire into the state of trade.

This Chamber vehemently protested against what is described as a Sphere-of-Influence policy, and declared that the future trade of Tientsin would be entirely dependent upon preserving the integrity of China, as well as some guarantee for the policy of the Open Door.

They pointed out also that Tientsin is a great trading and distributing centre of North China

TIENTSIN

and Manchuria; it is also the natural outlet for the provinces of Chihli, Shansi, Kansuh, part of Honan, and Northern Shantung, as well as of Eastern and Western Mongolia.

TRADE

The Customs Returns bear testimony to the steadily increasing volume of trade at Tientsin.

But these returns by no means show the full amount of duty paid by the trade of the port, as a very large proportion of the import duty on foreign goods is collected in Shanghai, and goes to swell the returns there.

The amount of duty collected in Tientsin in 1888 was 591,494 taels, about £84,499; in 1897, 973,000 taels, about £139,000; an advance in nine years of nearly 65 per cent.

The total value of imports and exports of Tientsin in 1887 was 32,724,499 Haikwan taels, about £4,674,928. Ten years later, in 1897, the total value amounted to 64,644,211 Haikwan taels, about £9,232,030, being an increase of no less than 99 per cent.

This increase of prosperity has not been obtained without great labor, severe losses to individuals, and many disappointments, suffered almost entirely by the British merchants whose energy opened up the country.

The capital required has been very large, and has up to the present time been increasing. This is borne out by the fact that though eighteen years ago there was no bank at Tientsin, there are now four — viz.: 1. The Hong Kong and Shanghai Banking Corporation, established in 1881; 2. The Deutsch Asiatische Bank, established 1890; 3. The Chartered Bank of India, Australia, and China, established in 1895; 4. The Russo-Chinese Bank, established in 1897.

The amount of capital employed by the branches of these four banks at Tientsin has been estimated at about eight millions of taels, or about £1,100,000.

A very large proportion of cargo arriving and leaving this port is carried in foreign vessels, principally British.

These vessels have to be specially constructed for this particular trade, owing to the difficulties connected with the bar, which makes them very much more costly than ordinary coasting steamers.

BRITISH CHAMBER OF COMMERCE

The British section of the Chamber wrote me the following memorandum, which they desired me to transmit to the Associated Chambers of Commerce:

" The British section of this Chamber has carefully followed the action of her Majesty's Government over matters affecting China for some considerable time, and has observed with constantly increasing anxiety the infringements of the in-

TIENTSIN

valuable Treaty of Tientsin, under which trade has flourished. They consider the existing deplorable state of affairs in North China is very largely, if not entirely, due to the absolute absence of any definite policy, the complete apathy shown to, or the apparently vague idea possessed of, the extent of British and other interests now placed in jeopardy. Protected by the Treaty referred to, we have not hesitated to invest money in China; but in view of the recent violation thereof by China's northern neighbor, we naturally feel that any further development is accompanied by undue risk, and there remains a distinct feeling of unrest and apprehension regarding the safety of capital already locked up."

These remarks appeared to me to be of so startling a character that I asked for some evidence to take home to the Associated Chambers.

Two leading British merchants both personally told me they had capital they were anxious to invest in China, but that they intended to keep it until they saw a definite line of policy proclaimed at home. They both declared that the Shanhaikwan Railway incident had practically shown that the British Government had admitted the right of the Russian Government to interfere in matters of purely commercial enterprise. They stated that the incident had completely demoralized all capitalists in the northern part of China.

These views were supported by the whole British community present.

THE BREAK-UP OF CHINA

Again, the representatives of the Taku Tug and Lighter Company, whose property is worth about £140,000, informed me that though they wanted to invest a large amount of capital in alterations and improvements in the lighter system, the uncertainty which existed as to the Russian position in the North rendered it imprudent for them to invest any more capital for the development of their property.

Several British merchants told me they would not invest any capital in the North, now that Russia has been allowed to secure positions which place her at the advantage of being able at any moment to create circumstances which would depreciate the value of capital invested.

They said that events in the North had produced that want of confidence which was fatal to financial or commercial enterprise and the development of trade and commerce.

The merchants also expressed great fear as to the security of the trade they already possess. The reasons given for their anxiety were the following:

The heavy trade in wool, skins, hides, furs, and bristles, etc., comes principally from Lanchau, on the borders of Tibet and Hsi-ning, farther northeast. These goods come right up the Yellow River, and through two passes, Khaupingkhau and Nankhou. Both these are dominated from Peking. There is no other pass for hundreds of miles to the south of these two. The whole of

TIENTSIN

the trade named, which now comes through these passes to Tientsin, could be diverted to the North by any power dominant in Peking.

The merchants pointed out that building railways will often divert trade, but that would be gradual, and the British would also be building railways in competition; but they look forward with great apprehension to the future, owing to the dominant military position of Russia, which in a few years would enable her suddenly to divert trade.

The merchants impressed on me the necessity of assisting the buying power of the people occupying the scattered and undeveloped northern districts, by giving facilities for the free export of their products. They pointed out how easily a hostile northern power might divert the trade of these districts from the routes of egress already created by Anglo-Saxon traders in Manchuria.

With a fair field and no favor, or the Open Door, the merchants declare that they were perfectly prepared to face any difficulties which they might meet through the diversion of trade by railway enterprise or by legitimate competition.

The merchants protested most vigorously against their interests being sacrificed, as they would be if the Treaty of Tientsin were disregarded and a Sphere-of-Influence policy adopted in its stead.

They explained that nearly the whole of their trade came from the far-off interior, and from the Northeast, and that also in the North and the was Anglo-Saxon energy, enterprise, and capital which had originally made a platform for trade in China, and had given an equal opportunity to the trade of all nations.

III

TONGSHAN

On October 25, 1898, I paid a visit to Tongshan, proceeding thither from Tientsin by the Shanhaikwan Railway. This railway has been engineered and built by Mr. Kinder, a British subject of great ability and energy.

It may be well to give a description of this railway and its intended extension, as the money has been found by a British Corporation. It is the railway that has evoked considerable public interest, owing to the serious misunderstandings which have occurred between the British and Russian Governments with regard to the nature of the securities given by the Chinese Government.

The railway at present is opened for traffic from Tientsin to Chunghouso, forty miles beyond the Great Wall, a distance of three hundred miles, and will shortly be opened to Kinchow, a farther distance of about seventy-six miles.

On the security offered by the Chinese Government, between two and three millions of British capital were subscribed towards the construction of this railway to the port of Newchwang.

The form of the original security was altered altogether, in deference to the vigorous protests of the Russian Government, and it was agreed that those who had subscribed towards the loan should have a lien, not upon the extension of the railway, as originally intended, but upon its receipts, and, further, that the engineer and those connected with the accountant branch should be British.

It has been agreed between the Chinese Government and the British Corporation to make an extension of the railway from Kinchow to Sin-min-thun, a farther distance of one hundred and twelve miles. In addition to this, it is intended to make two branch lines, one of fifty-five miles length, between the junctions fixed on the main line, about ten miles to southeast of Kwangnin and Yingkau, near Newchwang. The other branch line is intended to go to the Nan-Paian coal-fields, from a place called Kaobhaio, about thirty miles to the northwest of Kinchow.

In the future it is intended to bridge the Liao River near Sin-min-thun, and carry the line to Mukden, where it might join the Russian main line to the north, about thirty miles from the Liao River.

The Chinese railway gauge is 4 ft. 8½ in., the Russian gauge is 5 ft.

The total extension of the railway, after the line to Kinchow is finished, will be:

To the Nan-Paian collieries	30 miles
From Kinchow to Junction for Yingkau	45 "
From Junction to Sin-min-thun	67 "
From Junction to Yingkau	55 '
Total	197 '

TONGSHAN

The coal-fields at Nan-Paian are very large, and the coal is of excellent quality. There are also very rich coal and iron deposits in Kwangnin. From the high quality of these deposits, their proximity to the sea, the splendid climate (very similar to Canada), and available labor, it becomes a question of argument whether any other similar deposits in China would be as profitable as these in the immediate future.

I visited, in company with Mr. Kinder, the Tongshan workshops, where I elicited the following facts:

WORKSHOP AND LOCOMOTIVE STATISTICS

Native employés engaged in connection with the Tongshan Railway workshops, about one thousand.

Annual cost of the maintenance of native staff amounts to £11,000.

Foreign staff employed consists of one locomotive superintendent, one accountant, one draftsman, one store-keeper, one shop foreman, one boiler-maker, the yearly salaries of which amount to £1866.

Average construction of rolling-stock for one year:

Various ten-ton cars	146
" twenty-ton cars	216
Passenger cars—	
First-class	10
Second-class	28
Brake vans (eight-wheeled)	10
Cars rebuilt—	
Various fifteen-ton cars	8
" twenty-ton cars	4

THE BREAK-UP OF CHINA

Approximate cost of running the shops per year, including rent to mining company, water, gas, fuel, salaries of foreign employés, wages of native employés and workmen, £14,100.

The approximate value of the Tongshan workshops, with their present equipment of machinery, is estimated at £48,000.

One thousand and fifty square yards comprises the covered area of shops.

The entire area of the works covers seventeen acres.

The total consumption of fuel, as consumed by the workshops, is as follows per annum:

No. 5 quality	. . . .	16 tons.
" 9 "	. . . .	50 "
" 5 dust	. . . .	200 "
" 9 "	. . . .	2234 "
" 1 coke	. . . .	186 "
" 2 "	. . . .	151 "

Statistics for Locomotive Department from Tientsin to Chunghouso, covering a distance of two hundred and thirteen miles.

Locomotives chiefly used—Dubs's, manufactured in Glasgow. The others are Baldwin's (American).

Average per month: thirty-six locomotives running.

Mileage:
Train	. . . .	42,453 miles.
Shunting	. . . .	15,150 "
Construction	. . . .	9,666 "

TONGSHAN

Light . . . . 142 miles.
Total engine mileage . . . . . 67,411 "
Consumption of coal . . . . . 3,681,683 cwts.
"   per engine mile . . 54 "

Working of Engines:

1. Wages of native drivers and cleaners, etc., including overtime . . . . . . Taels 2290 = £324
2. Wages of foreign inspectors and drivers, including overtime . . . . . . " 940 = 133
3. Fuel . . . . " 5225 = 740
4. Stores (foreign and native) " 316 = 44
5. Lubricants (foreign oil and native oil) . . . . . " 750 = 106
6. One-third of salaries of foreign officials, clerks, etc. " 520 = 75

£1422

Repairs to Engines:

7. Materials for repair of engines, with proportion of shop expenses . . . . Taels 1778 = £251
8. Wages for repair of engines, with proportion of shop expenses . . . . " 1578 = 223
9. Stores consumed by steam sheds . . . . " 121 = 17
10. Miscellaneous coolie hire, etc. . . . . " 274 = 38

£529

Total expenditures of Locomotive Department, £1951

EXPENSES PER MILE IN STERLING

1898. October 31st.	ENGINES PER ENGINE MILE					
^	WORKING EXPENSES.				Nos. 7, 8, 9, 10. Total cost of repairs.	Total cost of repairings and workings.
^	Nos. 1, 2, 6. Salaries of foreign officials, native clerks, drivers, etc.	No. 3. Fuel.	Nos 4, 5. Oil, stores, etc.	Total cost of working	^	^
Average per month taken from the working of the past six months.	£ s. d. 0 0 1¼	£ s. d. 0 0 2¾	£ s. d. 0 0 0¼	£ s. d. 0 0 5	£ s. d. 0 0 1¼	£ s. d. 0 0 6¾

During the past twelve months four locomotive boilers were retubed, five locomotive fire-boxes replaced, and two locomotive boilers replaced.

The average life of boiler-tubes in China extends over a period of two years; boilers, fifteen years; fire-boxes, five years.

The oldest engine now running is the "Rocket of China," manufactured by C. E. & M. Co., 1880.

The oldest imported engines are from Stephenson, Newcastle, and came to China in 1883.

I found Mr. Kinder was employing engines of American manufacture—Baldwin's. On inquiring why he was giving up using English engines, he gave me the following facts:

He had applied to several English firms, but they could not deliver according to his specification, either as regards price or time. The English price was £2800, with twenty-four months to deliver. The American engines were only £1850, and four and a half months to deliver.

He said the American engines were not so good, but quite good enough for his purpose. The Americans use steel instead of copper and brass for various fittings, and instead of turning the axle down to get a collar for the wheel, as the English do, they simply screwed a collar on to the axle.

Mr. Kinder was building engines himself, which he estimates will cost £1600 each. I saw the first engine nearly complete. He makes everything at the works excepting wheels and axles. Mr. Kinder's great difficulty was in getting skilled labor.

The couplings used throughout the North China railways are the American automatic coupling, costing £10 per car.

The railway from Peking to Shanhaikwan (300 miles) cost £6000 a mile, everything included—*i.e.*, rolling-stock, workshops, etc.

This line is laid with 85-lb. steel rails as far as Lukowchiao. From Tientsin to Chunghouso it has 70-lb. rails for thirty miles, and 60-lb. rails for the remainder. All of the rails are of Sandberg design and inspection. At present the average age of rails is about five years.

I obtained the above statistics, and have set them out here at some length, because I thought they would be of service at home to those interested in Chinese railway enterprise. The figures give the original cost, outlay, and care and maintenance charges for what is at present the only railway in China, excepting the seventeen miles between Shanghai and Woosung.

COAL-MINE AT TONGSHAN

I visited the coal-mine at Tongshan. The output is two thousand tons a day. It could be more. This mine pays a high dividend now. It was ten years before it paid at all.

There are one thousand men employed. The Chinese make first-rate miners under European foremen. The coal costs from 9s. to 12s. a ton at the pit's mouth.

I saw a new shaft being sunk, which will eventually be from 1500 to 1700 feet in depth. The Germans got the contract for this shaft and all the machinery connected with it, although their tender was £2000 more than any English tender. I was told this was to promote friendly feeling.

I found the following further details connected with this mine:

>   Total output of coal, 1896 . . . Tons 488,540
>   "   "   " " 1897 . . .   " 538,520
>   "   "   " " 1898 (estimated) " 650,000
>   Total output since commencement
>   to end 1898 (estimated for 1898) . " 4,524,119

The above outputs include the Company's mines at Tongshan and Liusi.

TONGSHAN

Proportion of lump coal, about 35 per cent.
" " dust " " 65 " "
Total output of coke, 1895 . . . . Tons 11,136
" " " " 1896 . . . . " 24,097
" " " " 1897 . . . . " 29,428

N.B.—There has been so far no serious attempt made to manufacture coke by European methods.

Average number of hands, between 4000 and 5000, inclusive of surface hands.

There are three shafts in Tongshan—

Shaft No. 1 . . . . 600 feet deep
" " 2 . . . . 300 " "
" " 3 . . . . 1300 " "

now being sunk, to be eventually brought to a depth of 1500 or 1700 feet.

Water pumped 80 to 100 cubic feet per minute.

Liusi Colliery, near Kuyeh, raises about 450 tons per diem; shaft, 300 feet deep.

IV

NEWCHWANG

The estimated population is 60,000

TRADE STATISTICS

The total value of trade in 1897 was Hk. Taels 26,358,671 (over £3,700,000).

The total tonnage of shipping entered and cleared in 1897 was 730,964, of which 363,922 was British.

I ARRIVED at Newchwang November 4, 1898. On landing I was met by a number of the British residents, who expressed themselves most grateful to the Associated Chambers of Commerce for having sent out a representative to inquire into the state of British trade and its future security in Manchuria.

They declared themselves much alarmed for the future, since they regarded Manchuria as really a Russian province, owing to the heavy garrisons of Russian troops scattered throughout the country.

They said that though the Russians might not impose a tariff on goods just at present, they were placing themselves in such a powerful military position that they would be able to do so in the near future.

NEWCHWANG

TRADE

The port of Newchwang is one of the most important in China to the British merchant. British trade has increased there far more in proportion during the last few years than anywhere else.

Butterfield & Swire, with thirty-five steamers, in 1897 made two hundred and fifty trips in and out of Newchwang.

Jardine & Matheson made about an equal number of trips.

Memorandum showing increased value of trade in foreign goods at the Northern as compared with the Yangtse ports during the ten years 1887–1897.

FOREIGN GOODS IMPORTED FROM FOREIGN COUNTRIES AND CHINESE PORTS

	1887.	1897.
Newchwang	2,745,636 taels.	8,995,929 taels.
Tientsin	13,741,010 "	30,212,260 "
Chefoo	4,630,536 "	11,066,410 "
	21,117,182 "	50,274,599 "
	(About £3,000,000)	(About £7,000,000)
Chungking	—	8,443,947 taels.
Ichang	1,955,353 taels.	647,902 "
Hankow	10,528,981 "	17,172,351 "
Kiukiang	3,329,937 "	6,563,311 "
Wuhu	2,094,036 "	3,700,373 "
Chinkiang	9,084,409 "	13,285,419 "
	26,992,716 "	49,813,303 "
	(Nearly £4,000,000)	(About £7,000,000)

When I was there, twenty steamers and over two thousand junks were lying in the river at the port.

It must be remembered that there are only two doors open to the sea for importing trade into the vast province of Manchuria, one is Newchwang, and the other is Talienwan.

Talienwan is closed at present; and, even if opened in the future, is, I am informed, being made so powerful that it could be closed at will.

The backbone of the Chinese coasting trade under the British flag is the Newchwang coasting trade—beans, bean-cake, pease, and kindred stuffs. If Newchwang is closed the whole coasting trade would be very materially affected.

A point to be noted is that the Liao River at Newchwang will allow vessels to load to a draught of 17 ft. 6 in. at neap tides, and 18 ft. 6 in. at spring tides; while at Taku the draught of water is only from 8 ft. to 11 ft.

At a meeting of the British merchants and residents, called in order that they might have an opportunity of laying their views before me, I elicited the following opinions. I would first observe that all the speakers at this meeting, without exception, spoke as if Manchuria had been, or was going to be, annexed by Russia. This is worthy of comment, as these gentlemen reside on the spot.

They declared their wish to be friendly with the Chinese, and to work cordially as traders with them. They unanimously expressed an opinion that with this object in view they would not ask for mining or other rights in place or under conditions which would interfere with Chinese prejudice.

They were most anxious to obtain a concession on the north bank of the river opposite to the town, and, indeed, looking to the increasing value of Anglo-Saxon trade and commerce in this port, this desire appeared necessary and reasonable, more particularly as most of the old concessions granted to the British had subsided into the river.

The concession asked for is the only available bit of ground, and the merchants expressed fears that, if it does not become a British concession, it certainly will become a Russian concession.

The merchants also desired that the east end of the town should be formed into a foreign settlement, with equal rights to the representatives of all nations who might reside there.

The three provinces of Manchuria are known to be very rich in minerals, and the merchants held that they should have the right of working mines in all of these provinces, where any foreigners, or the Chinese themselves, have the right at present.

The valleys have rich alluvial soil, capable of producing immense crops of cereals, and there are extensive forests, besides vast coal areas. Gold was exported to Shanghai in the year 1897 to the value of £300,000. Manchurian coal is decidedly superior to Japanese coal. I have seen both.

They also called attention to the restrictions placed upon the new privilege of navigation on the waterways—*i.e.*, that steamers are only allowed to ply within the area of the port where they are registered, thereby nullifying the advantage that might be gained by a free navigation of the rivers.

The merchants complained that they had no right to take steamers up the Liao River as far as Kirin. They declared Russians had the sole privilege. I think this is incorrect; but, anyway, it should be tested. They also hoped that a British Consul would be stationed at Kirin. Looking to the rapid manner in which events are developing in Manchuria, it would appear reasonable that, for the sake of the interest of British trade, there should be some Consular authority in that vast country—twice as large as France. At the present moment there is not a single British Consul north of Newchwang.

These merchants also complained that the Russians were landing railway material without examination or payment of duty, although the Customs are allocated to pay the service on the British loan.

They appeared to be very anxious as to the future with regard to the large and increasing military forces which Russia continues to pour into Manchuria. As Russia has no trade with Manchuria, other than across her frontier, the merchants considered their trade threatened by such exhibition of military power. They described the proceeding as the practical annexation of the country going on under their very eyes.

They also complained that there was no Russian Consul at Newchwang, which, under the circumstances, appeared to them to invite complications, as no immediate attention could be paid to various difficulties certain to arise under the curious condition of local affairs, that only could be settled by Consular Agents resident in the place.

They also pointed out that there was nothing to prevent Russia marching into Chihli, if she met no more opposition or remonstrance than she has already received with regard to Manchuria.

The British merchants wished me to point out to the Associated Chambers of Commerce that the security of Anglo-Saxon trade in the north of China must rest on something more definite than assurances and promises from a power rapidly placing herself in strong military positions, to which the British Government have offered no counterbalance whatever.

A number of resolutions, embodying the foregoing ideas, were unanimously passed and handed to me for transmission to the Associated Chambers of Commerce. (For copy *see* Appendix.)

About six weeks after my departure from Newchwang I received the following letter, in support of the foregoing resolutions, from the merchants of Newchwang:

sians and others; and would be in a peculiarly favorable position for obtaining prompt redress for any infringement of the Treaty rights of British missionaries and merchants.

"5 and 8. The port of Newchwang is the natural, and has thus far been the actual, outlet and inlet for the trade of the three Manchurian provinces, and of part of Chihli and Mongolia. Its position at the mouth of the River Liao gives it the advantage of cheap water carriage to distribute imports and collect produce for export.

"The freight carried by boats in the summer is borne in the winter by carts, carrying on an average 22 cwt., which take advantage of the frozen ground to bring down loads of beans, oil, maize, millet, and grain, spirits, hemp, leaf-tobacco, and general produce; and taking back to the North cotton, woollen, and silk piece-goods, cotton yarn, raw cotton, kerosene-oil, metals, especially iron; sugar, matches, needles, glass, and other imported goods.

"Besides this, the smaller inland towns on the Liao and its branches, which, during summer, sent produce to and receive imports from this port by river, are, during the winter, each of them the scene of similar activity, though on a somewhat smaller scale.

"This trade has been principally developed by British enterprise. Great part of the imports are of British and Colonial origin, and 50 per cent. of the tonnage employed in the carrying trade is under the British flag.

"The value and volume of this trade is annually increasing, and will continue to increase if no artificial obstacles are interposed.

"But it may be diminished, or entirely destroyed, in any one of the following ways:

"By prohibitory transit dues levied at various points on the principal land and river routes leading to this port.
"By admitting goods free of duty by rail into these provinces.
"By granting a drawback on goods of Russian origin, or passing through Russian hands.

NEWCHWANG

"It is necessary, therefore, to guard against the possibility of such action, by keeping 'open' not only this port, but the whole of Manchuria; for an 'open door' leading to a closed country will be of no more use to merchants than would a Barmecide's feast be to a starving man.

"We append some figures and further facts in support of our contention that our rights in Newchwang and Manchuria should not be lightly abandoned, as if they were of no present or future value.

"The value of the trade in 1897 was 26,358,671 Haikwan taels, being an increase of 3,500,000 taels over 1896, which again was 5,000,000 taels in excess of any previous year. The returns for the current year are not yet made up, but it is an open secret that there is again an increase over the values for 1897.

"If then the trade, under present circumstances, is capable, year by year, of such great expansion, it is natural to suppose that it will increase to an enormous extent when this country, with its great grain-growing areas, mineral wealth, forests, etc., is opened up by railways.

"Why should this magnificent country, with an area of 390,000 square miles, be looked upon as a Russian preserve? What excuse is there for the tendency at home to consider it as such?

"Russia, so far from needing Manchuria as an outlet for her surplus population, has not yet been able to colonize so much as one-half of her own possessions in the north of Asia. As to trade, she has little in the north of Manchuria, and none in the south, except the proverbial cargo of sea-weed, which has duly arrived this year.

"In 1897 British shipping amounted to 181,961 tons, half of the whole. Russian shipping amounted to 713 tons, $\frac{1}{500}$ of the whole.

"From the opening of the port to the present time the foreign resident merchants have nearly all been Britishers, and the foreign-owned land in the proposed settlement and elsewhere is largely in British hands.

THE BREAK-UP OF CHINA

"To carry on the trade, British merchants have invested large sums in land, houses, godowns, wharves, etc.; nor must it be forgotten that, in common with other Treaty ports, Newchwang was opened by the expenditure of British blood and money.

"We also desire to point out the importance, from a national point of view, of not allowing Manchuria to be annexed by Russia, for should Manchuria pass into the hands of that Power, not only would this 'door' be 'closed,' but British interests in China proper would be seriously menaced, and the unopposed absorption of these provinces, with their hardy and spirited peasantry, would inevitably be the prelude of a successful march southwards towards India.

"In conclusion, we trust that you will use your great influence to impress on the British Government and people the importance of British interests in Manchuria, and how seriously those interests are menaced at the present moment.

"We are, My Lord,
"Your Obedient Servants,
"BANDINEL & CO.
"BUSH BROS.
"PRO BUTTERFIELD & SWIRE,
"DAESUTT.
"J. EDGAR.
"To Rear-Admiral the Right Honorable
"Lord Charles Beresford, C.B.,
"London."

With regard to the above observations of the British merchants, it may be well to mention here things which came within my own knowledge.

With respect to Observation 2, the request for a foreign settlement for all nationalities appeared to me to be most reasonable in the interests of equal opportunity, and the "Open Door" policy

NEWCHWANG

for all nations. Newchwang is certain to be the distributing centre for the north.

The Chinese authorities I spoke to on this matter were most friendly, and heartily in sympathy, and promised to do what they could to forward it. The Chinese even went so far as to say that they would grant money to make roads. This great friendliness dates from the Chino-Japanese war, when the British had a Red Cross hospital for the northern Chinese armies, and tended 10,000 of the wounded. In return they built a hospital entirely out of Chinese money at Newchwang. Dr. Daly, a British subject, now manages it. I went over the hospital, and found its arrangements excellent.

With reference to Observation 4, viz., the grant of mining rights, this would unquestionably further the policy of the " Open Door," as it would give all nations a chance of profiting by the development of the enormous latent mineral riches of Manchuria. I, however, pointed out to the merchants that as matters at present existed there was nothing whatever to prevent them acquiring properties in Manchuria, and that the best thing they could do would be to invest capital in Manchuria, so as to give the British Government some right to demand security for vested interests. I showed that there was nothing at present which excluded them from equal opportunity in obtaining concessions in Manchuria.

Again, as to Observation 5, the merchants here, as in all other places, called attention to the restric-

THE BREAK-UP OF CHINA

tion placed upon them by the new navigation laws, which materially interfere with trading progress.

With respect to Observation 6, it appeared to me to be imperatively necessary that there should be a British Consul stationed at Kirin, in order that some official account could be rendered of what the Russians are really doing in Manchuria. At present all accounts come from missionaries or merchants, and, under the circumstances of the case, might be minimized or exaggerated.

As regards the free landing of Russian railway plant, referred to in the merchants' Resolutions given in the Appendix, and in their observations to me, I may say that I myself saw steamers pass the Custom-House and proceed to the Russian landing-place, called Newchiatung, without any examination on the part of the Custom-House whatever. When I was at Newchwang already thirteen large Russian steamers had passed without examination. I questioned the Chief Commissioner of Customs on this point, and he informed me that he had orders from Peking that he was in no way to interfere with these steamers. I was informed that they contained railway material. It would be as well here to mention the exact terms of the contract. They are shortly as follows: The railway is being built by the Russians under a contract with the Chinese Government, nominally *for China*. After eighty years China is supposed to take it over. Russia in the meantime makes the line, advances the cost, and under-

NEWCHWANG

takes its maintenance, working, and protection. The Russians made it a condition of their contract that all material and plant used in the work, and brought from abroad, is to be landed in China free of duty.

Thirty-six thousand tons of railway material, among which were thirty Baldwin engines, have been shipped to Newchwang.

It is only fair to point out here that the Imperial Chinese Railway now continuing its line from Shanhaikwan to Newchwang, under an agreement with a British corporation who have advanced the capital, have also been granted the right of landing their material and plant duty free; but the cases are not practically the same, although they may appear so theoretically. The Trans-Manchurian Railway is admittedly a strategic railway; it is financed, built, protected, and administered solely by Russians, and is supposed to revert to the Chinese in eighty years. The Shanhaikwan Railway is not strategic, but is built to open up the trade of the country; it is financed by a British corporation, built, protected, and administered by Chinese, and is to revert to them when they have repaid the borrowed money.

The exemption of railway materials from duty is a matter of considerable importance to bondholders, in that it affects the value of their security for the loans made to China. Till 1897 there was no railway in China, except that running from Peking *via* Tientsin and Shanhaikwan; the ordinary materials, sleepers, rails, etc., required for this line, it was customary to pass duty free under Government certificate. Whether such a procedure was thoroughly equitable is open to question, seeing that the foreign Customs revenue had been almost entirely hypothecated. The subsequent extension of this procedure certainly seems inequitable. Even under the old procedure machinery imported by this railroad had been required to pay duty, and machinery was held to include locomotives; but towards the end of 1897 the director-in-chief of the Peking-Tientsin-Shanhaikwan Railway, Hu Yen Mei, protested to the Throne against the levy by the Tientsin Customs of the duty on locomotives. He obtained Imperial sanction to everything required, by his railroad being exempted from Customs duty. Since then many contracts have been entered into for the construction of very extensive lines of railroad, and in several of these contracts it is explicitly stated that the duty treatment in regard to materials for the Shanhaikwan line shall apply to materials required for these new lines. The result will be that materials and machinery required for most, if not all the lines to be hereafter contracted, will be exempted from payment of duty. Were the foreign Customs revenue unencumbered, such a system would not perhaps be of much moment, because collection of duty would simply amount to taking money from the coffers of one Government Department to pay it into those of another, but it is a different question to curtail the source of income of the foreign Customs after more than the whole of that income has been hypothecated to foreign countries. On the other hand, some bond-holders may be glad enough to risk this, in order to give facilities for opening up the country.

With regard to the apprehension expressed by merchants as to the increasing number of Russian troops in Manchuria and the addition of military posts, as far as I could gather from those in a position to know, there are about 120,000 Russians in Eastern Siberia and Manchuria.

I was informed that the Russian flag is hoisted at Lunkkin, twelve miles this side of Kinchow. I was also informed that the Chinese flag had been originally hoisted alongside the Russian.

I saw many armed Cossacks in Newchwang, both in the town and along the railway. They were placing a telegraph line in the middle of the main street, the poles of which blocked the traffic.

There can be no question that the Russians are at present in a position of tremendous military advantage in the event of anything occurring which might involve a warm argument as to what was necessary for the proper security of British trading interests.

It is not unnatural for the British merchants to ask why these forces are there, and what they are going to do. British trade with Manchuria is over £3,000,000, with an upward tendency. Russian trade with Manchuria is nil, except a very

For report on this railway, *see* chapter on "Railways."

This railway will pass through Mukden, and have a branch line to Kirin, and will tap the great bean-growing districts in the north and northwest; it also taps the large coal-fields in the neighborhood of Liaoyang, eighty miles north by east of Newchwang (Yingtzu); and if it can get hold of the bean traffic, which now comes by river, the trade of Newchwang would suffer very considerably. With the short branch the railway can either use Newchwang or pass it. This might kill the trade of Newchwang, although it would still be an open port under treaty.

However, the Chinese Imperial Railway, which is to run up the River Liao to Sin-min-thun, near Mukden, from Shanhaikwan *via* Kinchow, should be able to provide the competition necessary to prevent monopoly.

There was some disagreement between Russian and British merchants with regard to the ownership of land in the place where the Russian railway station was to be located.

Some British merchants offered £1 a mou (⅙th of an acre) more for the land than the Russians were prepared to give. The Chinese accepted the British offer, and the land became British, and the title-deeds were registered in the British Consulate. Although these deeds were so registered, the Russians declared the British had no right to the land, and induced the Taotai, the Chinese authori-

NEWCHWANG

ty, to refuse to recognize the sale. A serious dispute was avoided by the promptitude and determination of Mr. Allen, the British Consul, who went to the Taotai's Yamen and would not leave until the deeds were stamped.

I saw land that had been taken from the natives by the Russians at the rate of ten taels per mou. when identical land marching with it was bought by them (the Russians) for 100 taels a mou because it belonged to foreigners.

There is no doubt that the proceedings of the Russians in the neighborhood of Newchwang have been of a very high-handed character. They took their present settlement without leave from anybody, and paid the natives at nominal rates for the land. I was shown where the railway had gone through growing crops without compensating the natives, who were greatly incensed, but were advised to keep peaceful by the authorities.

I have mentioned the foregoing instance in order to add my personal testimony to the statement made by the British merchants resident in Newchwang as to the dominant position of the Russians in Manchuria.

But I wish it most emphatically to be understood that in these remarks, or in any remarks I may make with regard to the present position of Russia in Manchuria, I merely made them as a plain statement of fact, and with no aggravating or irritating intention. My views may be pro-British; they are certainly not anti-Russian.

It would be ungenerous of me if I were not to mention here the extreme kindness, courtesy, and civility with which the Russians treated me at Newchwang.

Dr. Greig, of the Manchurian Protestant Mission, was very much exercised as to the rights of the Protestant Missions in Manchuria and their property. These missions have been established thirty years, they have over forty European agents in Manchuria, and about 10,000 native Christians; they have valuable properties at all the missions, including school and hospital. The hospital at Kirin cost £1,600 to build. Dr. Greig declared that both himself and all his missions looked upon Manchuria as Russian in all but name. He showed that under the Treaty of Tientsin, and by special edict of the Emperor in 1891, his missionaries had a right to reside among the people, to teach the Christian religion and make converts and carry on medical work without let or hindrance.

Dr. Greig had quite lately travelled all through Manchuria. He was extremely anxious as to the future position of himself and his coadjutors with regard to the present military absorption by Russia of Manchuria. I recommended Dr. Greig to refer the matter he had brought to my notice to his Presbytery.

Mr. Sprent, and other missionaries, who know the whole of Manchuria well, informed me that as late as June, 1897, there was not a single Russian at Kirin. At the date when I was at Newchwang,

NEWCHWANG

November, 1898, I was told there was a large established camp.

Mr. Sprent said he had seen parties sent out to survey the mines in Manchuria. He believed the parties were subsidized by the Government.

Since the end of 1897 the Russians have been pouring troops into Manchuria; every month the numbers are increasing. There is feverish activity in the preparations of the railway. Under these circumstances, the future development and security of Anglo-Saxon trade must entirely depend upon the good-will of the Russians.

It is only necessary to read the agreements relative to the Russo-Manchurian Railway and Port Arthur and Talienwan, signed by M. Pavloff on behalf of the Russian Government, and Chang Yin-huan and Li Hung Chang on the part of the Chinese Government, to see how completely and entirely Russian authority is dominant in Manchuria. These papers are to be found in the China Association Report for 1898.

At Newchwang, and generally throughout China, I found the British merchants regarded equality of opportunity—or, as it is expressed, the policy of the "Open Door" as regards Manchuria—as entirely dependent on the good-will of Russia.

The reason they advanced was the interference of Russia with a purely commercial enterprise connected with the Shanhaikwan Railway, in which case the Russians refused to allow an agreement made between a British corporation and the Chinese Government to be ratified. The original agreement was relative to the question of mortgaging a portion of the railway line as security for capital advanced, to build the whole line from Shanhaikwan to Kinchow and down to Newchwang.

As the merchants expressed it, the Door is more effectually closed by determined interference with purely commercial enterprises than it would be by the interposition of a tariff or preferential rate.

The merchants throughout China were most determined in their opinion that, though Russia might keep the door open in Manchuria until the completion of the Siberian Railway, the immense military preparations, the rapidity with which powerful fortifications are being pushed on, can have but one meaning, which is, that when Russia has her hold on Manchuria strengthened, preferential rates will be imposed in favor of Russian trade.

The British merchants begged of me to impress as forcibly as I could upon the Associated Chambers of Commerce of Great Britian, that assurances with regard to the future liberty of trade and commerce in Manchuria were of no value whatever under present circumstances, where enormous military preparations are apparent on one side, with no trade to protect as an excuse for such preparations; while on the other side there is an immense and increasing trade, with no protection or security whatever.

NEWCHWANG

The British merchants further pointed out that if Russia openly annexes Manchuria, Corea is cut off, and entirely at her mercy. Mongolia would easily be absorbed, and the great horse-breeding ground for the whole of China with it. This would give Russia control over the hordes of irregular cavalry that have before now overrun the whole of China, and also give them control of a hardy and stalwart population of many millions, that only need to be drilled and disciplined to make as fine soldiers as any in the world. They also pointed out that if Russia were once in this position there would be nothing to prevent her sweeping down from the north of China to the centre, and from the centre to India, thus paralyzing British trade and commerce. They further expressed a hope that the powerful Associated Chambers of Commerce would demand from the British Government where the line was to be drawn of Russia's advance to the south; and, further, what steps are going to be taken to keep that line intact.

As Newchwang is the key of the position with regard to the question of the Open Door in the future, and as fears are expressed as to the ultimate intentions of Russia, I have entered very fully into a detailed trade report connected with that place.

The settlement at Newchwang (Yingkow) lies on the south bank of the Liao River, and is distant about fifteen miles from the river's mouth.

From the end of November to the end of March, navigation is entirely stopped owing to the river being frozen over, the ice being from seventeen to nineteen inches in thickness, and admitting of heavily laden carts crossing over it.

The trade of Newchwang is almost entirely in native hands, the foreign merchants being no more than agents for the Chinese. The American Trading Company is the only firm which actually imports goods on its own account. There are three British firms; but these are chiefly or (it may be said) wholly engaged in shipping business. During the last ten years the trade has been steadily increasing, and the figures published annually by the Customs show the immense importance of Newchwang as a port of commerce.

During 1895, Newchwang was in the hands of the Japanese, and the value, therefore, of the trade in that year need not be taken into account; but in 1896 the value of the trade was over 22,000,000 taels, and in 1897 it exceeded 26,000,000, showing in one year an increase of over 4,000,000 teals (about £570,000). In 1887 the revenue collected was 405,000 teals, while ten years later it exceeded 568,000 teals, showing a gain of over 40 per cent. when comparing the figures of 1897 with those of 1887. The revenue collected in 1897 was in excess of all previous years, with the exception of 1891, when the collection exceeded 583,000 taels. But while in 1891 the collection was over 28,000 taels on Foreign Opium, the receipts under this head in 1897 were just over 3,000 taels, showing that, notwithstanding the almost total disappearance of Foreign Drug from Newchwang trade, the receipts from miscellaneous goods have steadily improved.

FOREIGN IMPORTS

The trade with foreign countries is confined to Hong Kong, Japan, and Russian Manchuria.

The only article imported from the latter country is sea-weed, which is used as a vegetable by the Chinese. The quantity imported has not varied for many years. The trade with Hong Kong has increased enormously. In 1891, from that colony goods to the value of 304,000 taels were obtained, while in 1897 the value had increased to 1,238,000 taels, showing an advance of no less than 307 per cent.

Formerly Indian cotton yarn reached this port *via* Shanghai; now it comes direct from Hong Kong, a fact which will account largely for the increase.

The chief items which are imported from Hong Kong are cotton yarn, sugar, and old iron.

Japan is advancing fast, the value of the imports reaching 280,000 taels in 1897, while in 1891 it was only 22,000 taels. The principal articles imported from Japan are cotton yarn and matches, and the value of these in 1897 was as under:

Cotton yarn	8,000 piculs.
Matches	224,000 gross.

The greater part of the Newchwang foreign trade is carried on through Shanghai.

COTTON GOODS

The principal items are American drills, American and Indian sheetings, gray and white shirtings, and cotton lastings. Of late years, English-made goods have been losing ground, while American have been advancing:

American drills,	1893	100,000	pieces.
" "	1897	349,000	"
" sheetings,	1893	252,000	"
" "	1897	566,000	"
English drills,	1893	80,000	"
" "	1897	—	"
" sheetings,	1893	71,000	"
" "	1897	10,000	"

Shanghai-manufactured goods are also finding a market here, 11,000 pieces having been imported during 1897. Cotton yarn was first imported in 1882, 120 piculs finding its way into the port. Of this quantity, however, 24 piculs did not find a market here, and had eventually to be re-exported. In 1888 no less than 48,000 piculs were imported, the bulk of it being English-made yarn.

Latterly English yarn has receded and Indian yarn has come to the front. During 1897 the importation of yarn reached 164,000 piculs, over 140,000 of which was Indian yarn. From Japan about 18,000 piculs were received, and of Shanghai-manufactured yarn there were imported 4500 piculs. There were, however, only 700 piculs of English yarn imported.

WOOLEN GOODS

These are of little importance in the trade of this port, the poor natives using wadded clothes during the cold season, and the rich, fur clothing, furs being comparatively cheap.

METALS

The only metals worth mentioning are nail-rod iron and bar iron. During 1897 28,000 piculs of the former and 5500 piculs of the latter were imported. A large quantity of old iron is imported, and is used chiefly for making junk anchors, horseshoes, etc.

KEROSENE

A large quantity of both American and Russian kerosene enters the port each year, the American oil finding much more favor than the Russian. In 1896, 527,000 gallons of American were imported, while in 1887 the quantity exceeded 2,000,000 gallons. During 1897, 15,000 gallons of oil were imported into the port direct from Japan, the oil being entered in the Customs Returns as Japanese oil. The Russian oil does not compare in any respect with the American oil; but to make its sale practicable, Chinese often transfer the Batoum oil to cases which have contained American oil, and thus many are led to suppose that when they have bought a case of oil with the word " Devoc " on it they have obtained the genuine article.

EXPORTS

The staple exports are beans, bean-cake, and bean oil. The other items on the export list are felt, deer-horns, ginseng, skins, and wild raw silk. Deer-horns and ginseng are highly prized by the natives for their medicinal properties, and fancy prices are accordingly paid for them. The increase in the export of wild raw silk merits notice. Ten years ago—that is, in 1887—the export of this article was valued at 647,000 taels, while last year its value was 1,374,000 taels, showing an advance of no less than 112 per cent. Until recent years the bulk of the beans and bean-cake trade was carried on with the south of China; but since the Chino-Japanese war an extensive trade has been carried on with Japan; in fact, Japan has outstripped China altogether, as the following figures will show:

	1891	1897
Exports to Japan	460,000 taels.	5,079,000 taels (about £700,000).
" " Swatow	2,727,000 "	2,438,000 taels (about £340,000).
" " Canton	1,751,000 "	2,338,000 taels (about £334,030).

NEWCHWANG

Beans are sent to Hong Kong and Canton for food, and bean-cake is sent to Swatow for manure.

OPIUM

The foreign product has almost disappeared from the list of imports, the native drug being extensively cultivated all over Manchuria.

MINERALS

The mountains in Manchuria are reputed to be rich in minerals. Copper and lead have been found, and iron-mines exist in the vicinity of the coal-mines near Liaoyang.

The demand, however, for the iron produced is on the wane, owing to the cheapness of the foreign article. Coal is mined in a very primitive way, as the Chinese have no efficient pumping gear, and thus the water stops operations after a certain depth has been reached. There being no waterway near the mines, and the roads being very bad, there is little business done during the summer, but in the winter, when the roads are good, business is brisk, and as many as two to three hundred carts—each cart carrying one ton and a half—are employed every day in carrying coal away from the mines. Some of the coal reaches the port— for foreign use only—the bulk, however, is used by natives in Liaoyang, or round about Mukden. The coal costs about 14*s.* a ton at the pit's mouth.

By the time, however, that it reaches the port its cost is nearly doubled. There are also several coal-mines near Kirin, the coal from which is used by the large arsenal which has been established there.

GOLD

This mineral is found in many of the valleys in Central and Northern Manchuria, the principal valley being that through which the Moho (a tributary of the Amoor) runs. The gold is obtained by the washing process. The Moho Mining Company, who are exploiting the country, have also some stamping machinery, and appear to be doing a large business. The value of the gold exported in 1897 was 2,029,000 taels (nearly £300,000). When the country is opened up and developed, mining will be worked on European lines, and thus in course of time we may expect to find that Manchuria is rich in gold.

SILVER

There is a silver-mine about sixty miles to the west of Hunch'un, where foreign machinery is employed in mining operations; but no information can be procured respecting the mine.

PIGS' BRISTLES

An extensive trade is done in bristles, the value of which during 1897 was 36,000 taels (about

£5000). A fact worthy of note is that the trade in bristles was started by a Protestant missionary, who wanted to find employment for his converts. The bristles are sent from here to Shanghai, and are thence exported to England and other foreign countries.

FACTORIES

In 1868, a steam bean-mill was started here; but, owing to native opposition, it was not allowed to work, and thus the experiment came to an end. In 1896 Messrs. Butterfield & Swire erected a bean-mill, and with satisfactory results, the profit accruing from the making of bean-cake in this way being enormous. The mill is worked by Chinese only, and is practically Chinese-owned.

Other mills are shortly to be erected, and their erection will greatly enhance the importance of Newchwang as an open port.

1898

It is somewhat too early to review the trade of the present year, as the figures for the year have yet to be summarized and examined; but it may be fairly said to have been a year of great commercial activity, and its results will no doubt show an increase over 1897. The port did not open until the first week in April, and thus there was no trade at all to chronicle for the first quarter of the year. In spite of this fact, however, favorable results, as remarked above, may be looked for. Most noticeable in the trade was the enormous demand which came from Japan for Manchurian produce. Instead of British vessels coming in from Chinese ports to load for Chinese ports, Japanese vessels arrived from Japanese ports and loaded beans and bean-cake for Japan again.

The market was completely drained of the staple commodities, and prices went up to fabulous figures. It is not, however, unlikely that the shipments to Japan exceeded the quantity required, and that losses may accrue at the end of the year.

The year will be a notable one in the annals of Newchwang, as being the year in which the railway to connect the port with Mukden in the north, and with Talienwan in the south, was started. The Russians have the railway entirely in their own hands, notwithstanding the fact that the undertaking is styled the "Eastern Chinese Railway." So far, only sleepers and part of the rails had arrived; but the rolling stock was expected in the course of a few days, and the line as far as Haiching should be opened in the spring of 1899.

V

CHEFOO

The estimated population is 32,876

TRADE STATISTICS

The total value of trade in 1897 was Hk. Taels 22,051,976 (over £3,100,000).

The total tonnage of shipping entered and cleared in 1897 was 2,385,301, of which 1,327,559 was British.

I PAID two visits to Chefoo, the first on October 13th, and the second on November 9th.

The British merchants at this place handed me the following memorandum:

"CHEFOO, *October* 15, 1898.

"MY LORD,—We take the liberty of addressing you with regard to the prospects of trade at this port, and solicit your great influence on behalf of vested British and other interests which are threatened here; the opening of Kiao-chow with the prospective railways and alleged sole right of German control in the claimed sphere of influence, which embraces nearly the whole province, being likely to have a very adverse effect on the port generally.

"SHIPPING.—The tonnage entered and cleared last year amounted to 2,385,301 tons, of which about 56 per cent. was under the British flag, and we may mention that after Shanghai, this place claims to be the second in this Empire for the amount of sea-going tonnage visiting the port. The total annual value of the trade amounts to nearly £3,000,000 sterling.

"COTTON GOODS.—There is a vast field for development in this direction, the high price of transport throughout the province enhancing the cost so much that foreign cottons are practically placed beyond the reach of the poorer classes of the province, the population of which is about 30,000,000.

"There are valuable gold and coal mines in the province, and if only concessions could be obtained to work these, the result would be a great boon to commerce generally and would create a demand for machinery of all descriptions.

"The recent opening of inland waterways will be a valuable help, as, under the regulations, foreign-built steamers are now allowed to trade to any of the subsidiary coast ports, but there are no navigable rivers in the province, and unless some cheap inland means of transport can be devised, the trade of the port is bound to suffer. Nearly the whole of the traffic from this port is carried on by pack-mules, which is not only slow and very expensive, but likewise injurious to the cargo carried.

"We would suggest that a concession be obtained for a railway to run from Wei-hai-Wei and Chefoo to Che-nan-foo, with a loop-line branching from Chefoo *via* Lai-Yang, and joining the main-line at, say, Wei-hien. The traffic, we are confident, would be immense, and the benefit to trade generally could not be overestimated. If this could be put in hand promptly, any adverse influence that might accrue from the opening of Kiao-chow would be counteracted.

"We would further ask that our Consuls be strongly urged to look after British interests, and adopt the same policy as is taken up by foreign Consuls, whose eagerness to forward the interests of their nationals is in strong contrast to the apathy displayed by most of our Consuls in China.

"Trusting that you will use your great influence on behalf of the matters above alluded to,

"We have the honor to be, my Lord, your Lordship's most obedient servants,

"A. M. Eckford.
"P. F. Lavers.
"E. E. Clark.
"Henry J. Clark.
"J. P. Wake.
"A. J. Cooper.
"T. A. Cooper.
"J. Silverthone.
"Jas. McMullan.
"A. L. R. Donnelly.
"C. Ornabe & Co.
"Fergusson & Co.
"Gardner & Co.
"T. M. Armstrong.
"A. Parkhill.

"The Right Honorable
    "Lord Charles Beresford,
        "Peking."

I think, perhaps, the merchants were unnecessarily alarmed as to the position the Germans have assumed at Kiao-chow. A country generally works with due regard to its own interests, and it certainly would not be to the interest of German trade, as a whole throughout China, if she eventually carries out a policy of exclusiveness in the province of Shantung.

Kiao-chow has been declared an open port, and when the proposed German railway to Tsinan is finished, development of trade in that part of China is certain to follow, and though it might, under some remote contingencies, inflict damage to the port of Chefoo, still it is certain to increase the volume of trade in China, which will benefit the trade of all nations, but particularly that of the British. With reference to the concession which the merchants suggested should be obtained, I informed them that I did not think there would be the slightest difficulty if a responsible company made application through the British Minister, as since his appointment Sir Claude MacDonald had given his support to every application of a *bona fide* nature. I further said that the clause in the memorandum referring to "the adverse influence that might accrue from the opening of Kiao-chow" did not express the line of policy which was unanimously declared to be the best for Anglo-Saxon trade—*i.e.*, the "Open Door" policy and equal opportunity for all nations, and that Great Britain could not expect to have everything, and as long as the "Open Door" policy was the policy in force in China, British merchants ought to view with satisfaction the efforts of other countries to open up China, and so increase the volume of trade.

I made some inquiries about the resources of the Province.

There is a gold-mine at Chou Yuan, sixty miles from Chefoo, which now employs one thousand men working for Chinese with Chinese capital. The most primitive methods are used for extracting ore.

There is another gold-mine at a place called

Phing-tu worked in the same manner. I could get no particulars about it.

It is one of the few provinces in China where the waterways are not navigable, and, therefore, railways will be a paying interest as soon as completed. All merchandise is carried on mules, or by coolies.

The merchants here declared their trade was suffering through want of security and general uneasiness caused by the recent position taken by Russia in the North.

I found an interesting illustration here of the methods lately employed towards the Chinese Government, which I can only describe as unchivalrous and unmanly to a Government and country in its helpless condition.

A Mr. Fergusson, a British subject, bought a property which included the right of pre-emption to the foreshore, although the foreshore belonged to the Chinese Government.

The Chinese were induced to sell the foreshore to a Russian Company. Instead of arguing out the point in a friendly manner with the Russian Government, the British Government insisted on the Chinese paying 30,000 taels (over £4000) for granting a concession, which, owing to their weakness, they were powerless to refuse.

The merchants here begged me to bring to the notice of the Associated Chambers the importance of getting a concession from the Chinese Government for permission to have right of residence in

At present, Wei-hai-Wei is in no way to be compared in power to Port Arthur, only eighty miles off, at which place seventy guns have been mounted since it passed into the possession of the Russians, while not a single gun has as yet been mounted at Wei-hai-Wei.

It is an easy place for shipping to make, and with some dredging and wharfing might become by far the finest and safest harbor in the North of China.

Mercantile steamers could load and unload safely to leeward of the island at any time or in any wind, though at present there is no breakwater, but as the British have consented to close the door, as far as railway facilities are concerned, it is unlikely that Wei-hai-Wei can ever become a great mercantile port.

One steamer, the *Hanchow*, was fourteen days loading 1800 tons of cargo in a northern port.

Another steamer took forty-eight hours to discharge 100 tons of cargo, owing to the swell at this same northern port. Such delays are very frequent, owing to continual rough weather.

I found the people at Wei-hai-Wei very friendly to the British.

The island is two-thirds the size of Gibraltar. It is the best place in China to build a sanatorium for the fleet.

In the event of the British desiring to help the Chinese to organize their defensive forces, this place would be most suitable for commencing to train them, whether naval or military.

VII

KIAO-CHOW

I RECEIVED an invitation from Rear-Admiral H.R.H. Prince Henry of Prussia to visit Kiao-chow. Messrs. Jardine & Matheson kindly placed a steamer at my disposal for this purpose, and I put into that port 14th November, 1898, on my way from Chefoo to Shanghai. This place would have great capabilities as a mercantile port in the future, provided very large sums of money are spent upon it. A breakwater will have to be built in order to make it a good anchorage and to defend it from easterly seas, and the inside harbor will have to be extensively dredged in order to give sufficient water.

It is not an easy place for vessels to make, particularly in foggy weather.

When the railway is finished from Kiao-chow to Tsinan, Kiao-chow is certain to become a mercantile port.

Some fears were expressed by the merchants at Tientsin and Chefoo that when Kiao-chow became a mercantile port the shipping industries of those places would suffer. I assured them that, in my opinion, if the policy of the Open Door was maintained while railways developed the latest resources of China, there would be ample room for more mercantile ports, and I also pointed out to them that if other nations help by building railways to develop China the volume of trade as a whole would be certain to increase, and with equal opportunities the Anglo-Saxon merchants must benefit.

The Anglo-Saxon merchant, however, need not fear much competition from Kiao-chow if the regulations as to land remain as they were when I visited that place.

The Government owns the land. If it is bought by private individuals or firms, all sales by auction or otherwise have to be registered. Six per cent. is charged on the assessed value of the land, and it is to be reassessed every twenty-five years for the above tax.

If the land is sold at a profit at any time, one-third of that profit is to go to the Government. The Government claims the right, as a safeguard against fraud, to take over any piece of land themselves at the price stated by the seller and purchaser to be the selling price.

To explain: If two men come to register a sale, one to the other, for a piece of land at $10,000, the Government can say to the seller, "Here is your $10,000, less the one-third profit on what you originally expended," and the intending purchaser thus loses his bargain.

The Germans were very actively employed on shore clearing the ground, building barracks, making parade-grounds, and preparing emplacements for guns in the most commanding positions. The place could be made into a very strong naval base, but this would entail a further large expenditure of money, owing to its configuration.

VIII

SHANGHAI

The estimated population is 405,000

TRADE STATISTICS

The total value of trade in 1897 was Hk. taels 101,832,962 (over £14,500,000).

The total tonnage of shipping entered and cleared in 1897 was 7,969,674, of which 4,591,851 was British.

I PAID four visits to Shanghai, arriving there the first time on October 4th.

Shanghai is, perhaps, the most important Treaty port in the Far East for the Anglo-Saxon trader. It is situated at the entrance of the great Yangtse Valley, and from the above returns it will be seen that British trade is largely predominant.

The British merchants here were much interested in the Mission, and resolved to afford the Associated Chambers of Commerce every information in their power. They expressed grave anxiety as to the future, principally based upon the want of security in the provinces, the Chinese Government having no efficient police or military in case of disturbances. Rebellion, they said, was active in the province of Szechuan, and disturbances had already occurred in Hunan, in the Yangtse Valley, owing to which the Chinese merchants were refusing to trade with those provinces. They represented that this would prejudice British trade in the near future. The British merchants also referred to the dominant military position of Russia in the North, which, they said, must ultimately endanger British trade unless some effective counterpoise was created to balance it.

It was again brought to my notice that the new navigation laws, which should facilitate Anglo-Saxon trade, can only partially carry out their intended benefits owing to the uncertainty which exists as to dues, particularly likin and loti-shui. Also that a steamer under these regulations can only carry cargo within the area of the port at which she is registered; she cannot trade to or pass any locality where there is a Customs House.

Such regulations are prohibitory for cargo traffic, and the steamers virtually carry nothing but passengers.

An ocean-going cargo-boat can trade all along the rivers and pass Customs Houses, but boats that are under the new inland navigation rules are not permitted to do this.

To these disadvantages must be added the refusal of the Chinese authorities to sanction the foreigners' right of residence outside the Treaty ports.

In support of the view taken by the British merchants as to their position here, the Viceroys

Liu Kwen Yi (Nanking) and Chang Chi Tung (Hankow) both expressed to me that they were sure there would be disturbances in their provinces. (*Vide* chapters on " Nanking " and " Hankow.") They pointed out that seven collectorates of the likin in their provinces (£750,000) were allocated to pay the interest of the £16,000,000 borrowed on the 8th of March, 1898, from England and Germany. The Viceroy of Nanking further stated that the whole of the additional increase of the salaries of the Customs House officials—viz., £187,500—has been levied on the Shanghai Customs House alone. Both Viceroys declared that the people were complaining that their taxation was being paid to the foreigner, and that it was impossible to levy further taxes, so that the future looked very gloomy. They appeared to welcome the idea of British gunboats on the Yangtse, provided they were sent to assist the Viceroys, and not to undermine their authority.

On October 6th I met a deputation of the China Association at Shanghai, who presented me with a memorandum couched in strong and definite terms. In the discussion which followed, the members gave it as their opinion that there was a general feeling in Shanghai that the Home Government did not support British interests properly, and that their views and opinions were shelved and not attended to for years at a time. They thought the moment had come for a change of policy. The memorandum is as follows:

SHANGHAI

"In view of the interest which is now aroused at home in matters relating to China, it appears to the Committee of this branch of the Association that the opportunity is favorable for the publication of some general expression of its views upon the question.

"There has, in the past, been general complaint of the want of expansive vitality in our trade with China—a complaint which has nowhere been more freely voiced than in China itself by those actively engaged in the commerce of the country. In many quarters, moreover, it has been alleged that the fault lay with the British trader himself. It is not the object of this memorandum to undertake the defence of this charge, but it is merely desired to put forward some statements of what we believe to be the main reasons for the comparative absence of progressiveness of foreign trade with China. The opportunities of the country we, better probably than any one else, know ought to be enormous, whether in the development of existing trade or pushed into the hitherto unexploited field of China's natural wealth.

"We unhesitatingly attribute the limited expansion of trade with China to three main reasons—namely:

(a) The entire absence of good faith on the part of China in the matter of her Treaty obligations.

(b) The absence of security for the investment of foreign capital in China anywhere outside the Treaty ports.

(c) The general apathy and want of knowledge which have been displayed at home regarding Chinese affairs.

"Reasons (a) and (b) hinge on each other, and reason (c) supplies the explanation of the other two.

"To residents in China it seems superfluous to repeat arguments in support of the charge made against the Chinese of bad faith as regards Treaty obligations; but so little seems to be known at home as to the actual conditions under which foreign trade with China is conducted, that a short statement regarding them may be permitted. By Treaty China bound herself to certain regulations for the conduct of her trade, import and export, with foreign countries. A Customs tariff was arranged by mutual agreement, the duties so agreed upon to be collected at the ports which, by Treaty, were opened to foreign trade. The collection of these duties, which was at first in native hands, came subsequently to be vested in the service well known as the Chinese Imperial Maritime Customs, a service managed by Europeans, but with its sphere of operations confined to the Treaty ports. So far as the collection of duties through this source is concerned, there is no complaint whatever to be made; the service, in fact, constitutes China's only honest source of revenue, and forms her main available asset. But beyond this provision for the collection of duties at the ports, the Treaties went further, and aimed at the protection of merchandise, being the subject of foreign trade, in its movements in the interior of the country. It may be at once admitted that the framers of the treaties were very insufficiently acquainted with the loose fiscal arrangements connecting the governments of China's provinces with the Central Government in Peking; and it is this, no doubt, which has been, and is, the main source of the difficulties which have arisen. At the same time, however, the condition of the relations between Peking and the provinces in no way lessened the responsibilities of the Central Government as regards the Treaty obligations which it assumed. The arrangement arrived at in connection with the movement of foreign merchandise in the interior was simply that, on the payment of an extra half duty, transit passes could be claimed from the Chinese Government, under which imports could be moved from the port of entry to anywhere in the interior, and exports could be brought from anywhere in the interior to the port of shipment, exempting them (in the words of the Treaties) '*from all further inland charges whatsoever.*' The wording is clear enough, and the intention of what was meant was put beyond all doubt in a despatch from Lord Elgin (the framer of the Treaty of Tientsin, upon which the Treaties with other countries were based) to the Foreign

SHANGHAI

Office in 1855. Lord Elgin, in writing of the newly arranged transit dues, defines them as 'a sum in the name of transit duty which will free goods, whether of export or import, to pass between port of shipment or entry to or from any part of China without further charge of *toll, octroi, or tax of any description whatsoever.*' And further, in the same despatch he writes: 'I have always thought that the remedy (against arbitrary inland taxation) was to be sought in the substitution of *one fixed payment* for the present irregular levies.' Nothing could be clearer, yet to this day—thirty years since the Treaty of Tientsin was signed—the transit-pass system is an utter failure. It is true that our government has insisted (though largely ineffectually) that the transit pass clears goods *en route* from taxation, but this limited interpretation of the treaty is clearly not what was intended, the wording being that they are freed from '*all further inland taxation whatsoever.*' In many parts of China transit passes are altogether ignored, and in others, where they are nominally recognized, taxes are levied on transit-pass goods (at destination on imports, and place of origin on exports) destroying absolutely the immunity from arbitrary inland taxation which the Treaties provided for. Ministers and Consuls have constantly endeavored to obtain for British trade in China the freedom from arbitrary taxation which the Chinese Government agreed to give. The failure of their attempts can only be attributed to want of support at home, the outcome of indifference and want of appreciation of the interests involved. The result has been that merchants, tired of making futile representations of their grievances, have simply contented themselves with making the best of such trading opportunities as they found open to them. The case is well stated in Mr. Consul Brenan's report, issued last year (1897), upon the 'State of Trade at the Treaty ports in China.' He writes: 'A long and painful experience of thwarted efforts has had such a discouraging effect upon foreigners in China that a condition of stagnation has come to be accepted as in the nature of things.'

THE BREAK-UP OF CHINA

"But if the British Government has allowed the provisions of the Treaties to become a dead letter, other nations have been less complacent with China in their handling of the matter, and it is somewhat humiliating to find the following passage in the report of Mr. Consul Bourne, who accompanied the recent 'Blackburn Mission to China.' Writing upon the trade of Yunnan, Mr. Bourne says: 'Since my visit to this place in 1885, the import trade in foreign goods has almost entirely shifted from the West River route *via* Pose-Ting (*i.e.*, the British route) to the Tongking route by way of the Red River and Mengtzu (*i.e.*, the French route). This revolution, great indeed if the conservative habits of the Chinese are remembered, is entirely due to the energy of the French in vigorously enforcing on the Chinese Government their right to transit passes to cover goods from Mengtzu to Yunnan-Fu.' Again, on the same subject, Messrs. Bell and Neville, the members of the Mission, write: 'There is little chance of any increase of trade (into Yunnan) by the overland route from Bhamo (*i.e.*, the Burmese frontier route), for goods coming this way are subjected to no less than seven different duties, whereas by the Mengtzu route transit passes are recognized, and the 7½ per cent. paid to the Imperial Maritime Customs exempts the goods from any further taxation.' If the French have been able to enforce upon the Chinese Government this respect of Treaty rights, how is it that we, who hold some 64 per cent. of China's total foreign trade, have so entirely failed? A suggested answer is that our failure is the result of our having treated the Central Government of China too seriously; that our Government has believed that the effective way to obtain redress of abuses in the provinces was by representations at Peking: China's war with Japan effectually burst this bubble of belief in the supposed strength of Peking, and has shown, we hope, that the only effective policy with China is that which we employed in our earlier relations with the country—namely, to deal with abuses where they occur, and to face Peking with the fact of grievances already redressed.

"Again, it may not be generally understood at home that

SHANGHAI

the foreigner in China has no liberty of residence for purposes of trade except at the Treaty ports; he may '*travel* for purposes of trade,' but may not establish trading stations anywhere outside the limits of the ports. This restriction as to residence is naturally a hindrance to the development of foreign trade and enterprise in the country, and the point has special interest at the present time in view of the concession recently obtained from China as to freedom of navigation by foreign craft over the inland waters of the Empire. The concession is an important one, but it is practically valueless unless it is accompanied with the right of foreign inland residence; it is an obvious necessity that, for the protection of merchandise transported by foreign craft under foreign control, there must be established up-country stations and depots, where foreigners, or their agents, can reside for the management of the traffic and for the storage and delivery of goods.

"It is the want of security which is the main reason for the stagnation of foreign trade with China, and the dangers of the present situation are not only sufficient to hinder further trade development and extension of enterprise, but are also a serious menace to the trade which already exists. And the danger to-day is greater than it ever has been; the weakness and the corruption of the Peking Government stands confessed; its necessitous financial condition requires more help than ever from the provinces to meet the foreign obligations to which it now stands committed, and at the same time its power over the provincial governments is becoming less and less, by reason of the disaffection which is making itself apparent in many parts of the Empire. What, then, is likely to be the result upon foreign trade in the interior of the country? The revenue of the Imperial Maritime Customs, of which the provinces have in the past received their share, is now practically wholly hypothecated for the service of the foreign loans; concurrently with this the demands from Peking for more money from the provinces are increased; what can be the result other than an increase of inland taxation? As one means of supplying the deficiency in her revenue, China has given notice of revision of the existing Foreign Customs Tariff, but she offers no security for the remedying of the abuses of which we have for thirty years complained; the proposition put forward by Li Hung Chang, during his visit to London in 1896, was merely that the existing duties be doubled—an ingenious Oriental expedient by which foreign trade should be made to bear the expenses of China's foreign loans. Foreign traders in China are generally favorably disposed towards a revision of the existing tariff in China's favor, but they at the same time most distinctly demand that no such concession shall be granted unless full security be given for the protection of foreign trade in the interior against the abuses experienced in the past. It seems plain that such security can only be found in the entire reform of the present corrupt system of Chinese government; the undertaking of such a task, no doubt, bristles with difficulties, and entails responsibilities which will necessarily be complicated by international jealousies; it is, nevertheless, clear that unless the situation be boldly faced, still greater difficulties and still greater international troubles will have to be faced in the near future.

"The necessitous financial condition of China, brought about by the disaster of her war with Japan, and her obligations thereby incurred with European countries, makes it plain that a continuance of her policy of exclusion, and contempt for foreign ways, cannot longer be maintained. Pressure from without, powerfully aided by an empty exchequer within, has already persuaded her rulers that the vast natural resources of the country can no longer be permitted to remain undeveloped, and in consequence there are now put out to the world huge schemes of railway and mining enterprise, for the carrying out of which foreign capital is invited. It may, however, be taken for granted that before responding to the invitation the capitalist will pause to look into the security which is offered; he may reasonably ask: What power has the Central Government at Peking to protect concessions granted in the Provinces? What has been the experience in the past as to China's good faith in the matter of treaty engagements and contracts?

SHANGHAI

What amount of foreign control and supervision is to be allowed in the expenditure of the capital asked for? Is the present prohibition of foreign inland residence to be relaxed in order to enable foreign supervision of foreign inland enterprise? It is clear that in the answering of these questions is involved the further one: Is this much-talked-of opening of China to be made real, or is it a sham? If it is to be made real it is plainly necessary that strong foreign influence must be used to prevent repetition of the chicanery of the past. With a weak Government in Peking, open to be played upon by the jealousies of competing Powers, no security can be looked for, except such as may be found in force; the establishment of a Government in Peking, which is not only strong, but which is in sympathy with the wishes and feelings of the nation at large, is, we believe, a first necessity if China is to be saved from partition. We believe that the teachings of progress and reform have been widely accepted throughout the Empire. It is plain that wholesale administrative and fiscal reform is imperative both for the salvation of China herself, as well as for the security of the foreign capital which she is inviting for the development of her resources. Suggestions as to methods of reform do not fall within the scope of this memorandum; suffice it to say that the practical side of the question has not been neglected by this Association, and it may be fairly claimed that the British Government has received—from its Ministers, Consuls, and Merchants—a sufficiency of facts, opinions, and suggestions from which a definite and resolute policy might long ago have been deduced.

"For the carrying out of schemes of reform it is clearly necessary that there must be some foundation of strength upon which to base action; naturally this ought to be supplied by Peking, the Central Government being made an effective power for the execution of its commands throughout the Empire. For it is plain that, in the absence of a dominating central power—a power strong enough to maintain the Empire's integrity, there need be no further talk about the maintenance of the 'Open Door' and equality of trading opportunity, concerning which our statesmen have said so much. Weakness in Peking must inevitably mean disruption and partition of the Empire, and it may be reasonably suggested that it was through some shadowy conception of this fact, and through an unwillingness to accept the responsibilities of maintaining Peking authority, which brought into being the alternative policy to that of the 'Open Door'—namely, that of the 'Sphere of Influence'; needless to say that the two policies are directly opposed to each other. But whether China be maintained intact, or whether China be partitioned, the necessity for reform remains the same, the only difference being that whereas in the former case the reform measures would emanate from one strong centre, and be applied to the Empire at large, in the latter case they would be applied over restricted areas by the occupants of the 'spheres.' We submit that the jealousies and complications in jurisdictional matters, which must inevitably arise between the different occupants, form a far more serious danger to the general peace than any which is entailed in a bold policy for the maintenance of China's integrity with a central point of strength. Great things may be judged by small, and the dangers of the 'Sphere of Influence' policy are to-day being illustrated in Shanghai, through the claims of one nation to exclusive jurisdiction over parts of these Settlements, in which we maintain the door is open to all.

"We say, then, that the one thing wanted for the development of trade, for the protection of capital, and for the extension of enterprise in China is security, and we say that such security can only be found in the reform of the country, which can only be effected through pressure from without; and we further say that the vast preponderance of British interests in China clearly demands that Great Britain shall lead and guide the movement. We attribute the hitherto neglect of the China question by our Government, and the policy of drift into which we have fallen, to a mistaken estimate of the strength of British prestige in the Far East, coupled with a fallacious belief in the power of China herself; other nations, newer in the field, and comparatively unhampered by traditions of the past, have seemingly been better able to interpret events in the light of common experience, and have found opportunity in our complaisance and inactivity to exploit the situation to our disadvantage. We do not wish to concern ourselves with any imperfectly understood catch phrases such as 'Open Door' or 'Sphere of Influence,' further than to say that Great Britain's sphere of influence should be wherever British trade preponderates, with the door open for equal opportunity to all; this is an ideal which can never be reached without resolute determination on the part of the British Cabinet to *lead* and not to follow in Peking. We do not hide from ourselves the difficulties which must be faced in order to bring about China's reform, and we therefore urge that Great Britain, in leading the movement, should endeavor to obtain the co-operation of other great nations who have like aims and interests with ourselves—that is to say, whose interests lie in commercial development, and who are not aiming at territorial aggrandizement.

"C. J. DUDGEON, *Chairman.*"

Looking carefully into the cases enumerated in the memorandum, I am of opinion that in one or two particulars the statements are misleading. It is not correct to say that the transit passes are "an utter failure." They were so until the present British Minister, Sir Claude MacDonald, went to China; but that cannot be said now, and it is unfair not to recognize his Excellency's efforts and measure of success. The real fault is in adhering to the Board of Trade decision of thirty years ago, recognizing terminal taxation.

On the following day, October 7th, a deputation of the Shanghai Chamber of Commerce (a cosmopolitan body representing all nationalities) presented me with an address (*see* Appendix). A German member declared that the Commercial Mission of Inquiry to China would be for the benefit of the whole community, whether British or foreign. An American member affirmed that the trading interests of England and the United States were identical, and that the American community were very grateful to the Associated Chambers for sending out a mission to inquire into those questions vitally affecting trade and commerce.

Points particularly alluded to in this address:

> (1.) Non-observance of treaties on the part of China, whereby foreign trade and commerce have suffered.
> (2.) Question of tariff reform.
> (3.) Question of necessity for getting Conservancy Board for Shanghai, in order to provide proper harbor accommodation and do away with Woosung bar.
> (4.) Necessity for increasing foreign settlements in Shanghai by means of extension.

These points are of importance to the trade of all nations, but are of especial and particular interest to that of Great Britain, whose trade is in preponderance.

A very important question affecting commercial interests in the future was brought to my notice by the Chamber of Commerce and the China Association. It is the question of validity of contracts made between Chinese and foreigners.

The question is illustrated by the following facts: The Bank of China and Japan was incorporated in December, 1889, with the nominal capital of one million, which was afterwards increased to two millions in February, 1891.

When the Company was found to be doing a profitable business a large number of Chinese bought shares, but before they were allowed to become shareholders they had to sign the following agreement:

"I hereby request you to register me as the holder of .... ordinary shares of the Bank of China, Japan, and the Straits, Limited, transferred to me, and, in consideration of your doing so, I agree to pay the calls in respect of all moneys unpaid on the said shares at the time and place arranged by the directors pursuant to the Articles of Association.

"And I further agree that all questions between me and the Bank shall be decided in accordance with the Law of England."

The bank got into difficulties in 1893, at which time the shares had a liability of about £7 10s. unpaid calls, and it was resolved to call up £1 per share. The Chinese shareholders refused to pay, notwithstanding the agreement they had signed, which was written in Chinese as well as English. This action, and the magnitude of the total sum involved (upwards of £400,000) forced the bank into liquidation and reconstruction. The case was tried before his Honor Tsai Chün, Shanghai

Taotai, and Mr. Byron Brenan, C.M.G., H.B.M. Consul, at a special sitting. Notwithstanding the protest of Mr. Brenan, the Taotai delivered judgment in favor of the Chinese. The question whether a Chinese, having made such an agreement, not in conflict with any treaty, may be allowed to break it when it suits him, is one of grave importance to the whole mercantile community in China. The British Minister, Sir Claude MacDonald, has warmly taken up the case, but the merchants feel that it is the duty of the Home Government to deal effectively and promptly with such a serious matter.

I was informed that the Chinese merchants who had taken shares in this Corporation were anxious to pay the call demanded, but that the Chinese shareholders included several Mandarins and officials, and it was these latter who objected to pay the call. The merchants are afraid to run counter to those in authority.

COTTON

I was informed that there were twelve cotton-mills, built, building, or projected, at the time of my visit to Shanghai. The industry for the moment was dull, owing to over-production and the large import of Indian yarn. From personal observation, I do not think that the Chinese will be formidable competitors in the manufacture of cotton, unless they employ foreign management and foremen. They allow nothing for depreciation and maintenance, but take all available assets to pay interest and to secure high dividends.

In the Yangtse Valley generally the Chinese are learning to make a cheap yarn, which they have been in the habit of importing from Japan and India.

The Japanese and Chinese cotton is too short and fragile in the staple. American and Indian cotton has to be imported to employ the mills, as the Chinese prefer to buy the yarn and make the piece-goods themselves. There is only one mill (Ewo) in Shanghai that makes piece-goods; all the others are devoted to making yarn.

I visited the Cotton Mills in October, 1898. They were only working half-time, and some of the Chinese mills had closed altogether. The piece-goods industry is particularized in this Report owing to the fact that although it appears as English trade in the Imperial Customs Returns, and although it is owned by the British, and has been brought from America in British bottoms, still it is American manufactured, and the producer and original owner were American. The British merchants, however, derive a most important and lucrative trade by transporting this cotton in British ships, and disposing of it to the Chinese. It may be remarked, also, that the Chinese want the American cotton, particularly in the North, because it is made in the width they require, and of the thicker texture required in the cold climate.

THE BREAK-UP OF CHINA

I asked to be supplied with some details for the Associated Chambers relative to cotton imports. I append the interesting Table of Comparisons that I obtained. (*See Table opposite.*)

From this Table, which analyzes China's import trade in cotton goods and yarns (a trade which forms some 40% of the whole), it will be seen that during the last ten years America has increased her interest in the importation of plain goods by **121%** in *quantity* and **59½%** in *value;* on the other hand, the interest of Great Britain and of India in similar goods has decreased **13¾%** in *quantity* and **8%** in *value.*

There can be no question that this competition of America with Lancashire and India (more particularly with the former) will become keener as time goes on. Ten years ago America's interest in the piece-goods trade with China was confined to her exports of surplus domestic goods— that is, of goods manufactured for home consumption, and which were, for the most part, of too high a standard of quality for general Chinese use. The circumstances are now, however, altogether changed, in that America is rapidly becoming an exporting country, and her manufacturers, seeing the advantages which their nearness to the China market gives them, are directly competing with Lancashire for the trade by erecting mills for the special manufacture of goods suitable for the Chinese market. The great difference between the two percentages of increase in quantity and in-

crease in value shows that a considerably lower standard of goods is being made, which is, of course, to meet the Chinese requirement of cheapness.

A somewhat interesting question is: What part are British merchants playing in this development of the American piece-goods trade with China? The point may, perhaps, be conveniently divided into two heads, say:

(1.) *Origin of Goods.*
(2.) *Ownership of Goods.*

As regards "Origin," it is, of course, clear that any increase in America's share in the China trade is so much to the detriment of the British manufacturer. But a wider question is: How does such increase affect British *trade?* This point, I think, must be decided on the ground of "Ownership"; it is clear that if an Englishman buys (say) cowrie-shells in Africa, these cowrie-shells become a subject of British trade as soon as they have passed into his hands; similarly if he buys American piece-goods in New York, these goods in the same way become a subject of British trade as soon as he is possessed of them—the question of *origin* is an entirely separate one.

The point is, how much of this trade in American goods is American-*owned*, and how much British-*owned?* The question is not an easy one to answer, but an approximate conclusion can be arrived at. There are in Shanghai only two purely American firms of standing—*i.e.*, firms engaged

THE BREAK-UP OF CHINA

in the piece-goods trade;* there are also two firms of mixed American and English partnership. These four firms do a large business in American goods, and we will allow that all such business is American-owned; but on the other hand there are numbers of purely British firms engaged in the American trade. I was told that fully 60 per cent of American Piece-Goods are British-owned, while nearly the whole trade is carried under the British flag and financed through British banks. If, then, the table was arranged from the point of view of ownership, it would stand approximately as follows:

	Pcs.	£	Pcs.	£		
and Indian	11,037,745	3,767,700	9,517,098	3,470,200	1.14 dec.	2.1
American, ish-owned .	1,104,565	657,300	2,486,383	1,048,800		
American, rican-owned	769,709	438,200	1,657,588	698,720	115.35 inc.	37.
	12,219,019	4,863,200	13,661,069	5,217,720	11.80 inc.	

1887. British interest in ownership, 91%. American, 9%
1897.   "   "   "   86.61%.   "   13.39%

* The following are the American firms in Shanghai: The American Trading Company (large importers of goods); the China and Japan Trading Company (large importers of goods); Messrs. Macey & Co. (tea only); Messrs. Frazar & Co. (probably do a small business in goods); Messrs. Fearon, Daniel & Co. (large importers; firm half English); Messrs. Wisner & Co. (moderate importers; firm half English); The Standard Oil Company (kerosene-oil only).

SHANGHAI

In other trades than piece-goods America has large interests which are practically all her own, say:

Kerosene-oil. Value, 1887, £330,000; value, 1897, £1,019,400
Flour.   "   "   145,000;   "   "   180,600

She has also a large interest in *Lumber* (total value, 1887, £68,500; 1897, £55,200), and an increasing interest in *Machinery* (1887, £96,300; 1897, £402,000), though the carrying is largely under the British flag.

Before I left Shanghai on the 10th of October, I had three interviews with the Marquis Ito, the late Japanese Prime-Minister. He expressed the greatest friendliness towards Great Britain, and the gravest anxiety with regard to the future of China, as he declared that unless China supplied herself with an efficient military and police, disturbances were certain to occur which would endanger the life and property of the foreigners. Foreigners might be called upon to interfere in defence of their interests, which would eventually lead to the dismemberment of China. The Marquis seemed interested in the suggestion that a commercial understanding should be considered between Japan, America, Germany, and Great Britain, based on the integrity of China and equal trade opportunities for all nations. The Marquis declared that the trading interests of Japan and Great Britain were identical in the East, and said that each country could materially help the other.

THE BREAK-UP OF CHINA

He also declared that a policy such as was suggested with regard to keeping the door open would not be a selfish policy, but would benefit the trade of all nations.

He declared that the Chinese Government was so weak as to have lost all control, and must shortly fall. He agreed that the four trading Powers—Great Britain, America, Japan, and Germany—might, for the protection of trade and commerce of all nations, assist China in the reorganization of her forces with the help of foreign officers and non-commissioned officers. Marquis Ito said he was sure there would be no objection on the part of Japan to a British subject undertaking this reorganization with the combined help of the other Powers, that Great Britain had a good right to do this, owing to the preponderance of her vested interest, and that the British had proved themselves excellent at leading and organizing Eastern peoples. He thought Corea should be included with China as regards the question of the Open Door. He also declared that the whole commercial future of Japan and England depended upon the policy now pursued.

It must be remembered that the Marquis Ito has been all over China, and knows the Chinese better perhaps than any other foreigner. His opinions are, therefore, most valuable to the Associated Chambers of Commerce. He heartily upheld the opinion that an effective reorganization of the military and police forces of the Empire would be a sufficient guarantee for the security of trade and commerce.

The Marquis Ito was out of office, and, like myself, was paying an entirely unofficial visit to China.

Hearing that his Excellency Kwei Chun, the newly appointed Viceroy of Szechuan, was at Shanghai on his way to take up his appointment, I called and had two interviews with him. I informed his Excellency that the Associated Chambers would take great interest in any suggestion he might make for the improvement and development of trade and commerce in the provinces under his control. His Excellency expressed himself in terms most friendly to England, and said he would do what he could to further the development of foreign trade, and to open the country to merchants, manufacturers, and miners. He also informed me that the provinces he was about to administer were extremely rich in coal, iron, and many other minerals, none of which had as yet been opened up. I took the opportunity of pointing out to his Excellency that, unless China very shortly took steps to provide that security, by means of military and police, which it was the right of foreign countries to demand for the protection of their trade and commerce, she was certain to fall to pieces, and in such an event was equally certain to be split up into European provinces. On pointing out to his Excellency that China might save her integrity by asking Great

Britain and the trading nations to organize her forces as a whole, his Excellency heartily agreed with the proposal, saying he wished it could be done, but that such matters rested with the Imperial Government.

I was informed that one of the most prominent Reformers, Huang Chin, had been arrested, and was to be sent to Nanking for execution. Six of his associates had just been executed at Peking. I told the Viceroy that, in my humble opinion, if these political murders continued there were certain to be disturbances in China, and as such disturbances were prejudicial to trade and commerce, it might cause the British to interfere; but that, anyhow, the British public mind would be considerably exercised if these political murders continued. I therefore urged the Viceroy to use his influence to save Huang's life. Huang, I am glad to say, was not executed, but suffered banishment.

The question of the extension of the foreign settlement is one that is intimately connected with the protection and security of foreign life and property in Shanghai. The so-called British settlement is really cosmopolitan, and includes landowning residents of many nationalities. For a long time it has outgrown its limits, and many requests have been sent to the Chinese Government through the British Minister for its expansion. No territorial rights have been asked for, but merely an extension of the municipal control as it exists in the present settlement. The French alone hold aloof from the request for a cosmopolitan extension by demanding an extension of their own settlement. It is worthy of remark that a short time ago the French Consul-General, as *Doyen*, claimed the right to preside over the deliberations regarding matters connected with the cosmopolitan settlement, while the French will not allow any interference whatever in matters connected with their own settlement, over which they claim supreme control. Practically they claim sovereign rights over their own settlement; indeed, they claim that it is the " soil of France." As a matter of fact, the French Treaties with regard to their settlement are word for word identical with the Treaties agreed to by the Chinese Government with other nations. The French have, therefore, no exclusive rights.

The last claim that was made by the French for an increase of settlement in December was for a concession of land in Shanghai, including the old river frontage of the Chinese city, with its newly built stores, warehouses, and wharfage, all lit by electric light, in excellent order, and actively employed, plus another block on the other side of the Chinese city, These two claims, if granted, together with the present situation of the French settlement, would enclose the Chinese city on three sides. The Bund claimed is one of the only Chinese works of this kind in the Empire, carried out on their own initiative. It cost 40,000 taels (over £5000).

The origin of these claims was a demand for compensation by the French Consul-General for a riot and disturbance at the Ningpo Joss-house burial-ground on the 16th of July, 1898. The cause of the riot was a demand by the French for the Ningpo Joss-house burial-ground to be included in a French settlement under French regulations in order to erect a public abattoir. This burial-ground contains thousands of graves of all ages. The French Consul further demanded that all the old coffins in the public cemetery in the Ningpo Guild should be removed by the surviving relatives of the dead, and in future not a single coffin was to be placed in the Joss-house or buried in the grounds. The French Consul-General further stated that it must be clearly understood that when an extension of the Anglo-American (or cosmopolitan) settlement is made, an equivalent extension should be made to the French settlement. With reference to the question of the Ningpo Guild Joss-house, it must be borne in mind that the Chinese pay the utmost reverence to their dead. In fact, it may be said the only religion the Chinese really possess is a devout worship for their ancestors. Besides which Chinese law forbids the removal of graves except with the consent of the relatives.

The riot of 16th of July, 1898, was caused by the French landing armed seamen and trying to take possession of the Ningpo Guild Joss-house ground by knocking down the walls. A mob collected and commenced throwing stones at every foreigner who presented himself. The mob was charged by the French blue-jackets and several volleys were fired, the result being thirteen Chinamen were killed outright and thirty wounded, of whom four died later. It happened that on my arrival at Nanking a French cruiser was lying at anchor opposite the town with the French Consul-General, M. Bezaure, on board. In the course of one of my interviews with the Viceroy, Liu Kwen Yi, his Excellency, after stating he knew the British were friendly to the Chinese, asked me my opinion of the case. I explained to his Excellency, as representing British trade and commerce, that if he acceded to the demands of M. Bezaure, it was only natural a disturbance would be created by the Chinese; that no one knew to what extent a riot in the East, and particularly in China (owing to the intense dislike of the Chinese for a foreigner) would grow. That if a riot commenced, British, American, German, and other cosmopolitan communities would arm their volunteers, and might have to fire on a Chinese mob in defence of their life and property, although they had nothing whatever to do with the origin of the disturbance. The result would be that it would bring the whole of the foreigners on the one side, and the Chinese people on the other; although I was aware the cosmopolitan community referred to was totally opposed to the demands made by the French Consul-General. I also told his Excellency that if he refused the demands, nothing whatever could happen I pointed out that these disturbances were fatal to the interests of trade and commerce, and that I thought it unlikely that the French Government would be so unchivalrous as to make such exorbitant demands; but that what had possibly occurred was that the French Consul-General had exceeded his instructions, an episode common to the agents of all nations in matters of a like character.

On arrival at Shanghai, after my visit to Nanking, I was asked to attend a meeting composed of representatives of the trading communities of Germany, America, Japan, and Great Britain. Having been informed by members of the Shanghai Chamber of Commerce that these French claims were seriously interfering with trade owing to the disquietude in the minds of the Chinese, and also on being asked to give an opinion, I repeated what I had said to the Viceroy, holding that no one section of a cosmopolitan community had any right to take action certain to bring about disturbances which would jeopardize the lives and property of the remainder of such community. As it was known that I was the representative of the British Associated Chambers of Commerce, I think it right to report this circumstance.

The French further demanded an exclusive claim to a large area known as Paotung, on the opposite side of the river from Shanghai city, a locality in which they have no interest whatever. There are warehouses, factories, wharves, docks, and extensive business properties at Paotung, but all owned by British and American subjects. If the French extension took place as the French Consul-General demanded, it would include a quantity of English land registered in the British Consulate.

On the night before the final departure of the Mission from China I was entertained at a farewell dinner. This fact is notable on account of the strongly representative and cosmopolitan character of the hosts, who consisted of the following four corporations: The Shanghai Chamber of Commerce (a body representing all nations), the Municipal Council (ditto), the Shanghai Branch of the China Association (British), and the American-Asiatic Association. This event will, I feel sure, be gratifying to the Associated Chambers. The resolution passed at this dinner was to the following effect:

"That our cordial thanks be tendered to Lord Charles Beresford for the service he has rendered to the foreign communities in China, by personal investigation into the conditions of the various interests we represent."

The speakers to this resolution, representing various countries, all dwelt with complete approval upon the policy of the Open Door.

I had several interviews with the Taotai of Shanghai, who appeared deeply interested in anything that concerns the welfare of British trade and commerce. He was once thought to be very

THE BREAK-UP OF CHINA

friendly to foreigners, but has lately received evident marks of displeasure from Peking, which apparently have modified his views. He had received an intimation that he would be relieved of his lucrative office before the customary time. On my pointing out to him that China must inevitably be broken up into European provinces unless she provided an army adequate for the protection of foreign trade and capital, his Excellency cordially agreed, and said that years ago he had written memoranda advocating an alliance with Great Britain in support of it; but he added that late events had proved that Great Britain was afraid of Russia, and that in the event of China requesting Great Britain to undertake such reorganization, he believed she would decline if Russia peremptorily forbade such a proposal. He also said that he believed most of the Viceroys were strongly of the opinion that if England would consent to reorganize the Chinese Army the Empire might yet be saved.

While at Shanghai, I had several interviews with Christian missionaries of all denominations and nationalities. They were unanimously of opinion that the "Open Door" policy would be the only policy to secure the further development of trade in China; and, further, that pursuance of this policy was the only one which promised success for the future of their missionary work in China.

I visited a French Jesuit Mission at Shanghai,

a most powerful organization that has done grand work in China, particularly in connection with science. There is no community that knows China and the Chinese more thoroughly. I was glad to find that these fathers were enthusiastically in favor of the policy of equal opportunity in China, and the reorganization of her army, to give security to commerce and missionary work. The fathers saw no difficulty whatever in carrying out this policy, as they declared the Chinese were easily governed and led. All the enlightened people were hoping for reform, and the fathers declared it was only the effete system of government that was barring the way.

IX

NANKING

The estimated population is 150,000

I ARRIVED at Nanking, which place it must be remembered is not an open port, December 9, 1898, on board H.I.M.S. *Nanshin*, and received a salute of fifteen guns.

The Viceroy, Liu Kwen Yi, sent the Admiral commanding the Nanyang fleet, Chen Yi, to call on me. He, and those with him, appeared greatly exercised at the presence of the French Consul-General from Shanghai, Monsieur Bezaure, who, I was informed, was at Nanking on board a French cruiser, endeavoring to force certain concessions from the Viceroy.

I had two interviews, of very considerable length, with his Excellency the Viceroy, Liu Kwen Yi. His Yamen is four and one-half miles from the landing-place, and the whole route was lined with some thousands of troops and banner-bearers. On arrival at the Yamen, the Viceroy received me most kindly and courteously. I thanked him for placing the man-of-war at my disposal in order to facilitate the object of my mission, and expressed astonishment at the great ceremony and pomp with which I was received. His Excellency replied that he was anxious to show in every way his friendship for Great Britain.

I explained to the Viceroy the object of my mission, and pointed out that the mercantile communities at home were very anxious as to the future security of Anglo-Saxon trade and commerce in China. His Excellency, like the Viceroy Chung Chi Tung at Hankow, said that he himself was afraid of disturbances in the near future. On my asking him why, his Excellency gave me the following reasons:

1. That the likin collectorates had been taken away from the finances necessary for provincial administration, and were now devoted to paying the interests on a foreign loan: further taxation would be necessary to carry on the government.

2. That the people were annoyed at their taxes being paid to the foreigner.*

3. Because it was necessary to reduce his military forces, owing to want of money.

He added that there were a very large number of poor and homeless refugees coming into his province from the northern part of Kiangsu, flooded out by the Yellow River, and that he had not enough troops to maintain order among them.

I pointed out to his Excellency that, under present conditions, there were two sorts of disturbances

---

* This inference is incorrect. The likin is only pledged as security for foreign loans.

likely to occur in China, either of which would be fatal to the interests of trade and commerce—one was a rebellion against the Government in its present weak condition, and the other a general rising against the foreigner. His Excellency declared that there was no chance of the former, but that if taxes had to be levied in order to provide for provincial administration, owing to deficiencies caused by the new allocation of the likin, he was certain there would be disturbances based upon dislike of the foreigner.

On my suggesting the reorganization of the Chinese Army under British and foreign officers, in order to preserve the integrity of China and provide security for foreign trade, his Excellency at first demurred to such a novel procedure, saying that he thought the old system of provincial armies, if properly organized, was far better. When I pointed out to him that China had been so completely beaten in the late war on account of the independence of her two fleets, the Peyang and Nanyang squadrons, his Excellency considerably modified his opinion.

His Excellency asked me to draw up a memorandum showing what I thought was necessary for a reorganized Chinese Army, as well as details for finance. This I did, and later on I received a letter from his Excellency, thanking me very warmly and intimating that he would memorialize his own Government on this matter.

His Excellency informed me that he was aware

that the Viceroy Chung Chi Tung had been ordered to place 2000 men at my disposal for organization. He said that such a proceeding, if carried out, would lead to the dismemberment of China, as other countries would insist on acting similarly in various parts of the Empire.

He also added that, in the provinces under his control, a short time ago the name of Britain was better respected than that of any other nation, but that now the name of Russia was most feared.

His Excellency took a different view from that of other Viceroys on the question of China asking Great Britain for assistance. He said that Russia would not allow China to do anything of the sort.

His Excellency declared that personally he would like to see the British with greater influence in China, and he pointed out the experience that the Chinese already had of British officials serving as Chinese servants. He mentioned General Gordon and Sir Robert Hart, and said that Chinese people could never repay the debt their country owed to those Englishmen.

The Viceroy thought that a commercial understanding between Great Britain, Germany, America, and Japan would go a long way to secure the integrity of the Chinese Empire in the future, provided none of those countries wished to acquire territory as a *quid pro quo* for their support.

When asked if it was possible that there might be disturbances throughout the Chinese Empire, he said yes, that the whole country was so unsettled by late events it was possible there might be disturbances, but no rebellion. I pointed out to him that in the event of disturbances the prospects of trade would be very bad, and future development impossible for a long time to come, and that if they did occur it would be more than likely that foreign countries would perforce have to adopt a policy known as the Sphere of Influence in order to protect their trade and commerce. The Viceroy remarked that if such an event occurred it would be the end of the Chinese Empire.

The second interview with his Excellency was chiefly taken up with a discussion on the French claims at Shanghai. This I have fully reported under Shanghai. At this interview his Excellency considerably modified his opinion with regard to having provincial armies under separate administrations instead of one army under one administration for the whole Empire. He said he agreed with the arguments I had adduced in the memorandum I had sent him at his request, and that he would memorialize his Government to organize the Chinese Army as a whole under foreign officers. He further said he should represent to his Government that if this was not done the Chinese Empire would fall, as foreign countries could not afford to allow their trade and commerce to be damaged because the Chinese did not provide them with security.

Before I left Nanking in H.I.M.S. *Nanshin*, Taotai Hwang Cheng Yi and Tao Taotai and

NANKING

Mr. Ku and Marquis Seng came to see me, bearing messages of farewell from the Viceroy and a letter containing a private memorandum concerning the reorganization of the Chinese Army, a copy of a communication he was sending to the Government at Peking. The translation would show the very satisfactory result of my mission in this case.

The Viceroy asked me to inspect his army, his fleet, the fort under his command, his arsenal, and naval and military colleges.

A report on the army, fleet, and arsenal will be found elsewhere.

The Imperial Naval College, which I visited, was commenced in the year 1890. There are sixty students, between sixteen and twenty years of age, under an English mechanical engineer. The school is fitted with an excellent workshop, with all tools, machines, and appliances for repairing and making boilers and engines. All these were British made. The students looked cheery and well set up, and were very interested in their work. I was informed by Mr. Halliday, the British instructor, that they are extremely quick at picking up any sort of mechanical engineering. At the end of their five years' study they can all talk English. All the students are sons of gentlemen.

There are carpenters' and joiners' shops also in the school; everything in the whole establishment is in excellent order and ship-shape, and the money expended is well spent. It shows what could be

THE BREAK-UP OF CHINA

done for mechanical trading development of the Chinese if properly directed by a foreigner.

As the Chinese have no navy worthy of the name, it is a curious anomaly that they should have two such excellent colleges for naval officers at Nanking and Tientsin.

I visited the Military College. It was started in the year 1895. There is room for one hundred and twenty students; there were only seventy there at the time of my inspection. They are divided into three classes, according to the status of their knowledge. The first class get six taels, the second four taels, and the third two taels per month, together with their food and clothes. They are all the sons of gentlemen. They remain there three years, and are then liable to be drafted to different armies about the Empire, but most of them go into the Liang Kiang provinces — *i.e.*, those provinces under the administration of the Viceroy Liu Kwen Yi.

I asked to have them put through company formation and other drill — they were very good indeed. They had been instructed by a Chinese officer, who had originally been taught by a German officer.

They had modern Mauser rifles, bought in Germany. They were a remarkably fine, smart lot of young men, aged between sixteen and twenty. Most of them came from Hunan.

It is another instance of what may be done by the Chinese, if properly organized.

NANKING

A part of the Budget is subscribed by the Peking Government. The usual anomaly, always to be found in China, exists with regard to these two colleges. The Budget for the Naval College is a heavy one, though not too heavy for what it turns out. The Budget for the Military College is a very light one. As China has no fleet or dock-yard, it must be waste of money to train naval officers so highly. It would appear wiser to devote the money on military reorganization, of which the Empire is so sorely in need.

I left Nanking in H.I.M.S. *Nanshin*, on 12th December, and received a salute from the Nan-yang Squadron. I proceeded to visit the powerful forts on the Yangtse River at the Viceroy's request.

Shortly after my departure from Nanking I received the following letter from his Excellency the Viceroy, which proves the interest taken by his Excellency in British Trade and Commerce.

Letter from Liu, Viceroy of Nanking,
to
Admiral Lord Charles Beresford.

"A respectful reply to your kind letter. After the honor of your Lordship's visit, when I was so unable to adequately carry out the duties of a host, I must express my sincerest thanks to you that you nevertheless have had the goodness to feel grateful to me, and send me your photograph, which will enable me to always have you near me, as if we were still conversing.

"My heartfelt wish is, that the most friendly relations may

exist between Great Britain and China, in order that when any difficulties may occur we may be mutually helpful in fulfilling your noble idea that China should preserve the integrity of her Empire, while England protects her own commercial interests.

"The fourteen suggestions I had the honor to receive from you regarding the training of troops I have already sent to the Tsung-li Yamen, and to his Excellency Yung-lu, and beg to convey to you my sincerest thanks again.

"Card and Compliments of LIU KWEN YI."

X

WUHU

The estimated population is 79,275

TRADE STATISTICS

The total value of trade in 1897 was Hk. Taels 8,888,361 (over £1,200,000).

The total tonnage of shipping entered and cleared in 1897 was 2,867,485, of which 2,159,307 was British.

WUHU was declared an Open Port by the Chefoo Convention, 1877. It is situated on the Yangtse River, about half-way between Chingkiang and Kiukiang, and owing to its proximity to numerous waterways is certain to become an important trading centre if China is opened up.

The British and American merchants handed me the following memorandum: " In order to help commerce in China, the doors already opened must be kept so, and the whole country, from one end to the other, should be thrown open, so that merchants, manufacturers, miners, etc., can live in any part and transact their business. If this was done, the trade of Europe and America would treble in a very short time.

The British community here expressed themselves as nervous with regard to disturbances in the near future, the people having begun to grumble at the likin being collected by the foreigner.

The British and American communities were anxious that the foreign concession should be extended in area.

There is a large trade in timber from Hunan here, and the rafts do much damage to the front of the present small concession. They often carry away the cables of the hulks lying in the stream. This timber trade is in the hands of the Chinese.

There is much coal in the locality; but I was told that the natives do not work it with any profit to themselves. A Chinese firm have started a mine, with a capital of 22,000 taels (over £3000), but it is not paying. There is a range of mountains about forty-five miles from Wuhu which is full of coal. Some of the properties there have been bought by Americans and English; but unless the obstructive attitude of the local Chinese authorities is overcome there is no chance of this property being developed at present.

On my second visit to Wuhu I found that his Excellency the Viceroy of Nanking, Liu Kwen Yi, had sent his principal provincial officers, Taol Sen Kia, Ku Chih Yen, and Tung Tai, in a man-of-war cruiser, the *Nanshin*, to place the vessel at my disposal for as long a time as I might find convenient. On my embarking on board H.I.M.S. *Nanshin* a salute of fifteen guns was fired. In this vessel I proceeded to Nanking.

XI

KIUKIANG

The estimated population is 53,101

TRADE STATISTICS

The total value of trade in 1897 was Hk. Taels 14,865,563 (over £2,100,000).
The total tonnage of shipping entered and cleared in 1897 was 2,656,552, of which 2,004,298 was British.

KIUKIANG, a port situated on the Yangtse River, near the outlet of the Poyang Lake, is some 185 miles distant from Hankow, and 445 miles from Shanghai.

There is a small British and American community. The principal export is black tea, which is in the hands of two Russian merchants. Another tea is a peculiar sort of green tea, and I was told that the total export is declining.

There was an excellent feeling between the English and Americans, both of whom were strongly in favor of maintaining the "Open Door."

I was received by a deputation of residents, who handed me certain resolutions (*vide* Appendix). They were particularly anxious that a British Consul should be sent to Changsha—a wish that was expressed at many other places that I visited.

To show how little chance there is at present for developing trade by opening up the mineral resources of China, I quote the following case:

A British subject had bought a property in the locality containing coal. His title and register are not contested; they bear the stamp of the Yamen. On this gentleman asking for permission to work the coal, the Taotai of the locality refused, giving as his reason that the working of coal-mines was not provided for in the Treaty.

The people of the district are perfectly agreeable that this gentleman should open up and work the mine. Some of the Chinese themselves are deriving a good income near here by working surface coal.

There is a company composed of English and American residents here, and at Wuhu, who have bought certain mining properties, and are in possession of the Chinese deeds duly executed and stamped by the local native authorities with the official seal. One of these deeds states that the properties were bought for mining purposes, and the other states that the properties may be put to any use the owner likes, yet the senior provincial authority will not allow these gentlemen to work their mines. This is another case which shows how necessary it is, if trade is to be developed, to secure by treaty such rights and privileges as will permit capital to be invested.

KIUKIANG

This port might increase its trade very considerably if light-draught steamers and launches for towing were put on the Poyang Lake and the tributary rivers, which would open up the adjacent district and allow goods to be water-borne from the province of Kiangsi.

XII

CHINKIANG

The estimated population is 135,220

TRADE STATISTICS

The total value of trade in 1897 was Hk. Taels 24,145,341 (over £3,400,000).
The total tonnage of shipping entered and cleared in 1897 was 3,535,739, of which 2,353,702 was British.

CHINKIANG, which was declared open to foreign trade by the Treaty of Tientsin in 1858, is an important city, owing to its position on the Yangtse River and proximity to the Grand Canal. But full advantage of this position is not taken.

An account of the Grand Canal, the present condition of which affects the trade of Chinkiang, will be found in the chapter on "Waterways."

Having asked the Chamber of Commerce at Chinkiang to supply me with a memorandum showing their views as to what they considered necessary for the further development of British trade, in order that I might transmit these views to the Associated Chambers of Commerce, they presented me with the following lucid and practical suggestions, which I append in their entirety:

CHINKIANG

"Memorandum regarding Trade and other matters for presentation to Lord Charles Beresford, C.B., M.P., by the Chinkiang Chamber of Commerce.

"TRADE OF THE PORT

"The value of the trade of the Port for 1897 was Hk. Tls. 24,000,000.

"Revenue . . . . Hk. Tls. 811,000
"Transit Dues . . . . . .   "   197,000

"An important feature in the trade of Chinkiang is the distribution of foreign goods under the transit-pass system.

"Cities in the provinces of Kiangsu, Anhui, Kiangsi, Shantung, and Honan are supplied from this centre.

"The port may claim always to have held the premier position among Treaty Ports in this branch of trade, and of the total transit dues collected last year about 25 per cent. were received at Chinkiang.

"Commencing in 1868, through the energy of a British merchant, when H.M.'s war vessels were at Nanking, the system has year by year continued to flourish, in spite of illegal exactions and not infrequent detentions of cargo *en route.*

"The other branch of the transit-pass system, that by which goods are brought from the interior, influences in no small degree the general exports. The rules in vogue here are peculiar to the port, and are known as 'The Chinkiang Rules.'

"Specially framed to admit of foreigners being interested in native business, the system works satisfactorily, but certain restrictions, the most important of which is the arbitrary limitation of articles, require modification.

"It is a matter for regret that it is the custom of H.M.'s Consuls to minimize the importance of this branch of the system.

"It appears to the Chamber that if China is to take British goods on an increased scale, her export trade must be largely developed, and, with the assistance of inland navigation, this can in no way be better accomplished than by the fostering and extension of the outward transit-pass system.

"INLAND NAVIGATION

"British merchants here having been the first in the field in China to take advantage of this most important concession so ably secured by H.M.'s Minister, prominence is given to the matter.

"After meeting with considerable opposition at the hands of the officials, from the Viceroy downward, permits were granted to run launches in inland waters on the 22d June, 1898.

"The route first selected was to Tsing-kiang-pu, an important trade centre on the Grand Canal, distant some 120 miles north from this port.

CHINKIANG

Later, launches were despatched to Soochow, the capital of the province of Kiangsu, situated at about a similar distance on the southern section of the canal.

" Other routes leading to large marts by adjacent waterways have also been selected and are being worked.

" In all some thirty launches under flags of various nationalities are engaged.

" While it was fully expected the natives would heartily welcome a quick means of transit, the results have exceeded general expectations. During four months, returns give the number of passengers arriving at and leaving the port as 60,000, but these figures are considered under the mark, and probably, with the wayside traffic included, the total number can be little short of 100,000.

" It is an important feature, however, that up to the present time no cargo has been conveyed.

" Trade during the year has, from various causes, been exceedingly dull, but probably the principal reason this branch of the business has not been availed of is the, as yet, incomplete system of rules, the administration of which is not yet effective. Certain regulations regarding duties, etc., are to be published before the end of next January, from which good results are hoped.

" It is to be pointed out that Rule 7 (Regulations [amended], 1898) provided that steamers are only permitted to tow on the Yangtse under special Customs papers, and it is suggested this clause should be struck out.

"Mention should be made of a trial shipment of oil by a British merchant under transit-pass last July, consigned to Tsing-kiang-pu. The voyage lasted twenty-five days, whereas it should only have occupied forty hours. All along the line exactions were demanded, and detentions ensued. At the Huai-kuan barrier, near Tsing-kiang-pu, aptly described as the greatest hinderance to trade in North China, the 'Shroff' in charge was subject to gross outrage, the circumstances of which were reported to H.M.'s Minister. It is clear to all who have made a study of trade in this and adjoining provinces that the administration of affairs at this barrier should form the subject of strong representation.

"It is considered important that pressure should be brought to bear on the officials for the better preservation of the Grand Canal.

"Between Chinkiang and Soochow, in the best season, difficulties in passage are met, and for the greater part of the year launches drawing only three feet are unable to get over shoal parts. The northern section is in a somewhat similar condition, and for want of slight dredging launch traffic will here probably be interfered with for four months in the year.

"As an enormous revenue is set apart annually for the preservation of the Canal, and, in addition,

CHINKIANG

tonnage dues are paid by launches, it is urged that representations be made.

"On the 28th June, 1898, rioting occurred at Yangchow, distant about fifteen miles, and other places in connection with the launches. It was stated that trouble originated with discontented boat people, but it was abundantly proved that the authorities, if not actively abetting, certainly connived at, the attack and pillage on launches and passenger stations.

"H.M.'s Minister, acting with promptitude, arranged for the despatch of a man-of-war to this port, and on the arrival of H.M.S. *Phœnix*, Captain Cochran, with Messrs. Scott and Twyman, had an interview with the Taotai, who at once guaranteed security from further trouble and a speedy settlement of claims for compensation. These latter, although amounting to a quite insignificant sum, are still unpaid.

"BRITISH FLAG

"British merchants complain, and it appears with justice, that they are at a great disadvantage in being prevented from flying the national flag on all launches, whether owned or chartered. It is contended that the chartering of vessels by British merchants should entitle them to all privileges, and at a time when British prestige should be strongly maintained in this region of the Yangtse Valley, and the British flag, as far as possible, be predominant, it is urged that rules bearing on the matter should receive a liberal interpretation at the hands of H.M.'s Consuls.

"EXTENSION OF CONCESSIONS

"It is abundantly clear that the area of the British Concession in Chinkiang, only some 700,000 square feet, is too limited for the purposes of residence and trade, and an extension in the form of a Settlement is urgently required, in order that foreigners may have space for manufactures and the preparation of raw material for export. Regarding the acquisition of sites for residences on adjacent hills, the local authorities have ever maintained a hostile attitude, and it is to be regretted that H.M.'s Consuls are unable to remedy this.

"RESIDENCE IN THE INTERIOR

"As regards the better development of trade in China, having now secured the right to navigate inland waters, the next and most important step appears to the Chamber to be the abrogation or modification of the restrictions relating to foreign residence in the interior.

"In no other manner, it would seem, can foreign trade be so satisfactorily pushed, and goods reach the consumer free of illegal and local exactions. At the present time great obstruction is being offered in certain districts in the province

CHINKIANG

of Kiangsu to the circulation of British goods by an enforced exaction termed 'loti,' or what may be described as a 'laying down tax.' If this is permitted unchecked, the benefits of the transit-pass system disappear. Nothing can better illustrate the necessity of foreigners themselves acquiring the right to reside in the interior and establish their own places of business.

"CHINKIANG AND SOOCHOW

" The canal route between the Treaty Ports of Chinkiang and Soochow should, it is suggested, be thrown open as an international route.

"YANGTSE REGULATIONS

" The proposed revision of the Yangtse Rules and Regulations appears to have been unnecessarily delayed.

" The Chinkiang Pass, a frequent cause of vexatious detention to shipping, should be abolished, and it is suggested that the compulsory payments of duties on foreign goods at Shanghai destined for River Ports should be altered, also that the collection of duties as between the River and Coast should be assimilated.

"PRODUCTS OF MILLS IN CHINA

"An arrangement which appears to have official sanction permits the products of native mills in

Shanghai to be sent into the interior under a Free-Transit Pass, an Import duty having first been paid. The passes are issued at the mills in an irregular manner under the authority of Taotai Shêng.

"As a like privilege is denied by the I. M. Customs to products of the foreign mills, it is urged that the injustice should be represented; considerable quantities of the native goods are going inland here under the above favorable conditions.

"CONSULAR REPRESENTATION

"From time to time this Chamber has felt it incumbent to ventilate this important matter.

"Taking a period of three years to last September, it is found that officials in charge of H.M.'s Consulate have been changed no less than twelve times. Such a condition of things precludes sustained effort to promote the welfare of British merchants. H.M.'s Consuls appear averse to take up mixed cases on behalf of merchants, and, if such are commenced, to press for settlement.

"It is not unusual for matters arising out of flagrant breaches of the transit-pass regulations to hang over for years, the patience of the merchant being thus probably exhausted, in addition to which the transit-pass system suffers in reputation.

"Reference has been made to certain claims by British merchants in respect of the launch riots in

CHINKIANG

June. In spite of H.M.'s Consul having specific instructions from H.M.'s Minister that these claims are to be satisfied, they are permitted to drag on month by month. In a case such as this the entire absence of a firm demand to the officials is, in the Chamber's opinion, all that stands in the way of an immediate settlement.

"NATIVE OFFICIALS

" Here, at Chinkiang, the relations between the Consul and the native authorities appear to call for comment.

" Practically all the business relating to British subjects and Chinese is carried on between the Consul and a *Wei-yuan*, locally styled the ' Foreign Business Deputy.' Some years ago the present incumbent was employed as writer in the British Consulate, from which post he was dismissed.

" With a change of Consul the man was quietly invested with the office above described, partly owing to his knowledge of foreign affairs, but chiefly it would appear as a studied insult to the Consulate. He has since been received by H.M.'s Consul, and in return receives him.

"He systematically delays all business to his own advantage, and at times important matters he is supposed to represent to the Taotai do not go further than that official's permanent secretary— one Wu-shu-ping—the most notoriously anti-foreign Chinese in the port. This man for the past

THE BREAK-UP OF CHINA

ten years has persistently retarded and obstructed every Consular case put before the Taotai; his conduct is now specially noticeable, as the present Taotai is a Manchu, and has had no experience of foreign officials.

"PROSPECTS OF THE PORT

"With railways, in the near future, converging at Chinkiang from the north and the south, combined with the undoubted success which must attend the navigation of inland waters, towards the prosecution of which the situation of this port peculiarly lends itself, the Chamber has every confidence in the future prosperity of Chinkiang.

"CONCLUSION

"The suggestions now submitted for consideration are:

"1. Strict and immediate enforcement of the inland navigation rules.

"2. Right of foreigners to reside in the interior, unfettered as regards trade, and to buy land in the vicinity of Treaty Ports.

"3. Amelioration of condition of certain barriers in Kiangsu, notably that at Huaikuan, on the Grand Canal.

"4. Revision of the Yangtse Regulations.

"5. A more hearty and willing co-operation on the part of H.M.'s Consuls for the

CHINKIANG

furtherance of trade and protection of British interests.

"The Committee of the Chinkiang Chamber of Commerce,

"E. STARKEY, *Chairman.*
"F. GREGSON, *Hon. Secretary.*

"*November* 22, 1898."

The points I should like to comment upon in this memorandum are the following:

The excellent position this port holds with regard to the transit system of foreign goods, owing to the energy of a single British merchant as far back as the year 1868.

A further instance of the energy of the British was shown in the fact that they managed to force their right to run launches on the waterways, notwithstanding the opposition of authority, with triumphant result as far as increase of traffic is concerned.

The incident referred to, which took place on June 28, 1898, regarding riots of Yangchow in connection with the starting of steam-launches, is worthy of great attention, as it shows how British gunboats on the Yangtse would further the development of trade and commerce by assisting the Viceroys and authorities to stop or prevent disturbances, such disturbances being fatal to trade and commerce.

In this Report I have frequently called the attention of the Associated Chambers of Commerce

THE BREAK-UP OF CHINA

to the necessity of placing British floating patrols on the waterways. This will not only secure the development of trade, but it will place the British in the position of being first in the field, a not unimportant matter, with equal opportunity to all.

Moreover, it would not be a selfish policy, as the British gunboats, by giving security, would really help the trade development of all nations.

British prestige was at a low ebb all through China at the places I visited; not one, but every Chinese authority I spoke to continually referred to the fear with which Britain regarded Russia.

The suggestion as to the right of residence being permitted is one of the utmost importance for the development of Anglo-Saxon trade, and has been frequently alluded to in this Report.

With regard to the fact mentioned in the memorandum of the loti-shui tax in Kiangsu, this tax is distinctly against Treaty, and steps should be immediately taken to remove this great obstruction to trade.

With regard to the free-transit pass being permitted for products from the native mill at Shanghai, this privilege has lately been revoked, with the result that one or two of the native mills in Shanghai had stopped working while I was there.

The merchants appeared to me to have just cause of complaint at the unnecessary delay over the revision of the Yangtse Rules and Regulations, but since my departure this matter, I am informed, has been at last settled.

CHINKIANG

The remarks in the memorandum concerning those in charge of H.B.M.'s Consulate at Chinkiang appear somewhat drastic. I found that the Consuls had been changed twelve times in three years, which would probably give good reason for British subjects to complain that their trading interests do not receive that attention which they should command.

With regard to the complaint made by the Chamber of Commerce as to the relations between the present British Consul and the Chinese Official called the " Foreign Business Deputy," I informed those gentlemen that I could not take up this question; that the proper procedure for them, if they thought H.B.M.'s Consul was neglecting their trading interests, was to write a letter of protest to the Consul, setting forth clearly what their complaint was, and to forward a copy of the letter and reply to the British Minister at Peking. This procedure appeared to me to be fair to the British Consul as well as to the merchant.

I found a steady but decided decline in the trade of this port, and asked the British merchants if they could give me a reason for this. They sent me the following memorandum:

"SUPPLEMENTARY MEMORANDUM
"TRADE, 1898

" During the nine months, ending September 30th, there has been a steady decline in the trade of the port.

THE BREAK-UP OF CHINA

"Foreign imports, which may be considered a reliable index, have suffered all round.

Opium . . . . . decrease . .	Taels	150,000
Cotton goods . . . " . . .		1,100,000
Woollen . . . . . "		100,000
Sundries . . . . " . . .		500,000
(£277,000)	Taels	1,850,000

"The value of foreign imports for the whole of 1897 was 13,000,000 taels.

"The transit-pass trade has naturally declined in sympathy, the number of passes issued being nearly 1000 less than during the corresponding period in 1897.

"Exports also show a considerable decline in value, of which, as directly regards foreign trade, silk, hides, and wool may be mentioned.

"Transit passes surrendered for cargo brought from the interior are 750 less than the number for the corresponding period last year.

"In this branch of trade British merchants are at a disadvantage as compared with American merchants, in consequence of exemption of fees."

[This question is thoroughly ventilated under chapter on "Consuls."]

"The factors which, in the opinion of the Committee, have contributed to the decline, may be classed under three headings, viz.:

"(a) Insecurity, owing to political complications.

CHINKIANG

"(*b*) Scarcity of capital.

"(*c*) Floods in Shantung.

"(*a*) Creating serious uneasiness, showing no signs of abatement, and most prejudicial to trading interests.

"(*b*) The scarcity of money, which is very real and apparent, has arisen from various causes, chiefly, however, connected with the political situation.

"1. Extensive withdrawals from native banks by wealthy depositors.

"2. Enforced 'loans' from the wealthy classes by the Government to pay off the Japanese war indemnity.

"3. Further exactions for special purposes at Peking.

"4. Curtailing of current loans to native banks by foreign banks.

"(*c*) The provinces of Shantung and Honan, which take a large portion of goods, have suffered largely from the disastrous Yellow River floods, in which, it is reported, millions of people have lost their lives. Districts are infested by robbers, against whom there is no protection, and it is quite unsafe to move either goods or treasure.

"It should be added that native trade is disorganized by the arbitrary and unreasonable periodical prohibitions of movement of grain; and this in turn reacts seriously on British shipping interests.

F. GREGSON, *Hon. Sec.*

"Chinkiang Chamber of Commerce,

"*December*, 1898."

There is a (large) export from this place of goatskins, silk, hides, and wool.

There are two silk filatures and one albumen factory (German), and a cotton-mill in course of erection, with Chinese capital and management.

Besides foreign trade, there is a large local trade between Hankow and intermediate ports. This is a native trade, but it is carried principally in British steamers. The Japanese have two steamers in this trade. They are at an advantage, being subsidized by their Government. Being small, they are, however, not serious rivals; but I heard that there is to be an increase in their number this year. The Germans are about to start a line of steamers for this trade. The British merchants say that these steamers are to be subsidized also.

The merchants here were of opinion that what was immediately wanted to develop trade was steam-launches for towing in the interior waterways, as that would prevent the obstruction and squeezes at present so easily affected on sailing-junks.

Here again I was impressed with the necessity for patrol boats. The likin collectorate having been allocated for the service of foreign loans, provincial officials, it was said, would certainly attempt higher squeezes to cover deficiencies in finance for provincial administration.

On my second arrival at Chinkiang, on board the Chinese cruiser *Nanshin*, I was received with a salute of fifteen guns, and the principal native

CHINKIANG

authorities visited me. Among these authorities was the Admiral of the Yangtse, Hwang by name, a most intelligent official, a Hunanese. He seemed a thoroughly patriotic Chinaman, and was most anxious for the future of his country. He dwelt particularly on the complete want of organization of the Chinese force during the late war with Japan, and told me that he himself had seen pistol ammunition supplied to men with rifles. On my pointing out to Admiral Hwang the necessity for China to organize her army as a whole if she wished to maintain her integrity, and also that if Great Britain was asked to assist her it is possible she (Great Britain) would consider the question for the security of her own trade and commerce, he remarked that he wished it could be so, but he was certain that Great Britain would never insist on helping China if Russia raised an objection. He also said that he considered that his country had been given away to Russia.

I visited all the forts situated in the locality, an account of which will be found in the chapter on " Forts and Arsenals."

XIII

· KIANGZIN

I stopped a few hours at Kiangzin before proceeding to examine the forts and inspect the troops in that district.

I had an interview with General Li, a very distinguished soldier, who wore the yellow jacket.

On discussing the future security for Anglo-Saxon trade and commerce, he expressed great anxiety. He said that on account of the scarcity of money he had been obliged to disband many of his men, and would have still further to reduce them. He said it would be impossible to impose further taxes, as disturbances would certainly accrue.

He expressed himself as very unhappy about the future of his country, and, on my making the proposal relative to the British helping to put the Chinese Army in order, he said he was afraid it never could be done, that Russia would object, and that England was like an old man with plenty of money, who risks nothing to provoke a disturbance, knowing that he has neither the energy nor the power to protect his riches.

XIV

HANKOW

The estimated population is 800,370

TRADE STATISTICS

The total value of trade in 1897 was Hk. Taels 49,720,630 (over £7,100,000).

The total tonnage of shipping entered and cleared in 1897 was 1,783,042, of which 1,109,853 was British.

I FOUND the British community very anxious as to the future security of Anglo-Saxon trade and commerce in this city, owing to the lack of military and police, both in number and efficiency, in its adjacent provinces. Disturbances had already broken out in the province of Szechuan, and the merchants had received intimation that there would be determined resistance offered to any attempt to develop Anglo-Saxon trade in the vastly rich province of Hunan, through the Tung Ting Lake and tributaries. Although the waterways have been thrown open, there is no direct foreign trade at present with this rich province. The situation in Szechuan is fully explained by a letter which arrived at the British Consulate while I was at Hankow in the beginning of December.

THE BREAK-UP OF CHINA

The following copy of this letter is here appended:

"You have probably heard by this time that Fleming of C. I. M. was murdered 4th November at Pang Hai, 300 li east of Kwei Yung Fu. I only heard the 16th, the wire having taken six days from Kwei Yung Fu here, and even now I am quite without details, though I have little doubt it was the work of a band of brigands who have been pillaging and vowing vengeance on the foreigner in those parts. The bad characters have been much stirred up by Yu Man Tsu's proclamations, and the Kwei Chou officials have been doing *nothing* at all to stop the trouble. You may very possibly be getting news of that part of the world quicker than I, *via* the Yuan River. Where is Wingate? he was to pass that way, and I am very anxious about him. It would have been much safer for him to come this way.

"Yu Man Tsu has gone home to Ta Tsu with his bands, now equal to about 10,000 men, laden with the spoil of all the rich Catholics of Central Szechuan, over 4000 houses burned, including about thirty Mission chapels, over 20,000 Catholics homeless and destitute, and damages *at least* 6,000,000 taels (over £850,000). What is to happen, or how it is to be paid, I cannot tell! At present the rebels are quiet, and are being *paid* by the Cheng Tu officials, who have not taken a step to suppress them, or to prevent pillage and murder. It is a most melancholy affair, and has dealt a blow to foreigners from which they will not recover for years. Of course the matter is not decided at all yet. The rebels may break out again at any moment that the Cheng-tu people do not pay them enough. They have utterly destroyed all the Catholics in Central Szechuan, and will have to begin on the heathen now. Hitherto they have only levied contributions on these latter. The new Treasurer and Viceroy have come at last. The former seems a good man, but he brings no troops, and good troops, used with decision and energy, are the only solution of the question."

It may be interesting to insert here the origin of the Yu Man Tsu disturbances. Twelve years ago there was a dispute about land between Yu Man Tsu, a wealthy Chinese, and a Christian Catholic Chinese. The priest of the locality, Père Pons, took the side of his co-religionist, who won the case. There was very strong feeling exhibited in the locality, because it was given out that the Chinese authorities are afraid to give judgment against a Chinese Christian if the priest of the district takes his part. Yu Man Tsu's son got a few hundred men together, and created a disturbance among the Chinese Catholics. The authorities surprised and surrounded him at a place called Tatsu, sixty miles northwest of Chungking, and cut off his head. Yu Man Tsu, being at the time in prison, was helpless; but on coming out he vowed vengeance against every Catholic Chinese.

When I left Hankow, Yu Man Tsu had a priest called Père Fleury a prisoner. The Viceroy Kwei told me he was afraid he would not be able to quell the rebellion, as if he attempted to do so Yu Man Tsu would cut off the priest's head.

A point of very considerable importance to be noted with regard to this question is, that the whole of the property mentioned as having been destroyed belongs to French Catholic Missions. The province where this piratical devastation occurred is reported to be the richest province situated in the Yangtse Valley. After recent declarations with regard to the Yangtse Valley, there would appear to be a large field for political complications in the event of the French wishing to land troops to protect the remnant of their property.

At a meeting of the British merchants held at Hankow, strong resolutions (*vide* Appendix) were passed, a copy of which I was asked to forward to H.M. Government as well as to the Associated Chambers of Commerce.

The merchants declared that the local Government was quite unable to control the people. This was due to the want of money to carry on administration, owing to seven collectorates for likin being allocated to pay interest on the Anglo-German Loan of March 8, 1898. As a proof that the merchants were correct, within a few days of my arrival at Hankow, late in November, a disastrous fire occurred, which devastated an area of over two miles, burned over 1000 people, and destroyed prop-

HANKOW

erty to the estimated value of £1,300,000. This fire was known to be the work of incendiaries, as the authorities had received warning that the town would be burned in order to create a disturbance, and as a protest against the people's taxes being paid to the foreigner.

Two smaller fires occurred while I was there, also the work of incendiaries.

The British merchants declared that Anglo-Saxon trade and commerce was seriously hampered, as the Chinese merchants refused to do any business under these circumstances, and that future development of trade was impossible. The whole question resolved itself into the want of military and police.

The British merchants here also called attention to the importance of opening up the waterways and tributaries of the Yangtse River, more particularly with regard to the Tung Ting Lake, which is the gate of the rich province of Hunan. To carry out this, it was suggested that a British Consul should take residence at Changsha, the capital of Hunan, a great trading centre on the Siang River.

It was pointed out that, though the opening of the port of Yohchau will be most beneficial to trade, it is not the great distributing centre of the province of Hunan, whereas Changsha is.

They also pointed out that the new navigation laws were to a very large extent nullified in utility by foreigners being denied the right of residence in the country; and, further, by steamboats, under the new privilege, only being allowed to carry cargo within the area of the port of registration.

The British merchants here also dwelt upon the very unsatisfactory position in which British subjects find themselves with regard to the rights of property—*i.e.*, as to land bought outside the British concession and registered at the British Consulate under Chinese title-deeds. The complaints made were relative to the position taken up by the French and Russian authorities in Hankow, who have seized upon properties which not only the registers, but stones delineating the boundaries, prove to belong to British subjects. There is no doubt that British subjects have been deliberately deprived of their property by the action of the French and Russian Consuls.

As this question is creating the keenest interets in all Anglo-Saxon communities in China, it may be well to enter rather fully into it in this Report. The matter is well known to the Minister at Peking and to the Foreign Office. I will report on the case as I found it. The British Companies principally affected were Messrs. Greaves & Co., acting on behalf of various owners, including Sassoon and others, Messrs. Evans, Pugh & Co., and Messrs. Jardine & Matheson.

In March, 1896, the boundaries of the new French and Russian concessions were settled between those two Governments and the Chinese Government. In both these concessions British subjects owned land. Immediately the boundaries of the French and Russian concessions were so settled, all British owners of land within these concessions protested to the British Government against their property being included. The Foreign Office answered through the British Minister in China that "owners of British property could not be included within these concessions without their consent."

The French Consul repudiates the validity of all the title-deeds presented by Messrs. Greaves and Giddes & Co., on behalf of their clients, which title-deeds accompanied their protest against their property being included in the French settlement.

The proofs of the ownership are:

1. Register of title-deeds to be found at British Consulate.

2. Boundary-stones engraved with owners' initials, some of which had been in position for thirty years. These stones I saw myself.

3. The fact that the land has been owned for thirty years, whereas Chinese law gives a title conclusive after ten years' ownership or occupation.

In addition to the proof of British ownership shown by registers in the British Consulate, there were boundary-stones bearing the initials and Chinese name of either the owner or his firm. Some of these boundary-stones have been removed by the order of the French Consul, notwithstanding the protest lodged by the British Consul.

THE BREAK-UP OF CHINA

And yet the Russian and French Consuls have put up their own boundary-stones, in spite of the protest of the British Consul, and absolutely decline to consider any proposal with reference to British-owned property over which their concessions were to extend.

January 1, 1898, the French Consul advertised a sale of land within the French concession. Among the lots advertised was land owned by Messrs. Greaves and Giddes and other British subjects.

Messrs. Greaves immediately protested by publishing the following advertisement:

"Notice.

"The whole or portions of Lots 5, 6, and 7, of the 19 parcels of land on the plan advertised at the French Consulate, Hankow, for sale on the 7th April, is the property of A. D. Sassoon, under a title-deed registered on page 586 of the British Consular Register, measuring 520 feet on river and road, with an original depth of 400 feet, more or less (Chinese measure), part now washed into the river. The owner has not authorized the sale.

"Greaves & Co.
"(Agents for Arthur D. Sassoon).
"Hankow, *March* 27, 1898."

On account of this advertisement Mr. Greaves was refused admittance to the auction-room where his client's property was being sold without his consent. Further, an action for defamation of character was instituted against him by the French Consul, but afterwards withdrawn.

HANKOW

The result of the auction was that the French Consul absolutely sold certain lots owned by British subjects without their consent.

Under such circumstances it will be seen that there are no rights of property, or security for British ownership, in the new French and Russian concessions.

The next case is that of Messrs. Evans, Pugh & Co., who own land in the new Russian concession.

The land was originally bought by this firm in 1862, and registered at the British Consulate in 1864. In 1887 the hide business was commenced on this property, and there proceeded uninterruptedly ever since.

April 4, 1896, the concessions referred to were conceded to Russia and France.

Messrs. Evans & Pugh immediately entered the strongest protest against their properties being included in the Russian concession.

July, 1896, the Foreign Office telegraphed to Messrs. Evans & Pugh, through the British Minister, "British-owned property cannot be included in Russian concession without consent of owner." This message was sent twice—once in March and once in July, 1896.

Between April, 1896, and December, 1898, Messrs. Evans & Pugh forwarded nineteen protests, stating they would not consent to have their property included in the Russian concession. In July, 1898, Messrs. Evans & Pugh received a communication from the Russian Consul warning them that their hide business must be discontinued on January 1, 1898, or it would be prohibited.

On January 2, 1899, Cossacks forcibly interfered to prevent hides being taken into Messrs. Evans & Pugh's establishment, and also seized the hides already in the store and threw them out. On Messrs. Evans & Pugh appealing to the British Consul, and asking permission to enroll special constables for the protection of their property, the British Consul advised them to do nothing of the sort, as he (the British Consul) was afraid the firm would not be supported in such action by H.M.'s Government.

Messrs. Evans & Pugh are perfectly willing to relinquish their hide business in the locality owned by them, provided they are reinstated in some other suitable locality for their trade, and receive compensation for damage to their trade, as well as the claims they will have to pay for not fulfilling certain contracts, owing to their trade being temporarily suspended. An offer has been made to Messrs. Evans & Pugh of a locality, but they were asked to *pay* a very high price for it, and no compensation was named to meet the loss on their enforced removal.

The views of H.B.M.'s Consul on the question are expressed in the following manner. He remarks that both firms had their business premises where they now are previous to the granting of the Russian concession by the Chinese authorities.

HANKOW

It seems unfair, therefore, even if their business should prove to be a nuisance, that they should suffer the severe loss which they will inevitably incur if they are forced to leave their present premises. There is, he continues, absolutely no other suitable site which they can obtain, and any money compensation will be comparatively valueless in view of the certain injury which will be done to their business, even if it is not completely stopped.

Another case of a similar character is that of Messrs. Jardine, Matheson & Co., who bought eight lots of land between October 18, 1862, and March 26, 1864. The registers and deeds of sale of these lots are in the British Consulate at Hankow.

This case is something similar to that of Messrs. Greaves and Giddes, and the Russian Consul denies the validity of the deeds registered in the British Consulate at Hankow.

At present the whole of Messrs. Jardine & Matheson's property, comprising the eight lots which they have owned for over thirty years, is included in the Russian concession, notwithstanding many protests on the part of the firm, and a distinct intimation from the British Foreign Office "that no British-owned land should be included in the Russian concession without the consent of the owner."

In the interest and protection of British property at Hankow, it must be well if the Associated Chambers of Commerce were to ask for the whole of the correspondence on these cases.

THE BREAK-UP OF CHINA

Hankow, in the near future, is certain to be in a position of great wealth and trading interest, therefore land in and about the city is daily increasing in value, and the questions mentioned here seem to require immediate attention.

Although it is true the British have lately been allowed to extend the area of their concession in Hankow city, it must not be forgotten that the Russian and French concessions have not been limited to the city itself, but that they have further obtained a large frontage on the Wuchang side of the river, a property which will be invaluable by-and-by, and of great commercial importance.

The towns of Hankow, Hanyang, and Wuchang may be considered as the gates of nine provinces of China. Hankow is divided from Wuchang by the Yangtse River, and Hankow is divided from Hanyang by the Han River. In case of disturbances these towns could easily be defended by small gunboats.

Some suggestion has been made that the British Government should force the Chinese to pay a heavy compensation for having conceded land to the Russians and French containing British-owned property. This is a cowardly and unchivalrous practice, which has been resorted to lately, under similar circumstances, by all foreign countries with regard to China. China being prostrate, one European power, at the point of the bayonet, demands concessions which China has neither the right to give nor the power to refuse. Immediately, another European power, at the point of the bayonet, compels China to pay heavy compensation for acceding to demands which she had no means to resist. No more effectual means could be invented to undermine the authority of the Chinese Government and disintegrate the Empire.

For the protection of existing Anglo-Saxon trade and commerce on the Yangtse River, and to give security for its future development, it is absolutely necessary that shallow-draught gunboats, similar to those in use on the Nile, should be sent there as soon as possible to patrol the upper reaches of the river above the rapids, the Poyang and Tung Ting Lakes, and the Siang and Han Rivers, the latter in direct communication with the rich province of Shensi. There would be no difficulty or danger whatever, as is generally supposed, in steaming up the gorges above Ichang to Chunking, provided the steamer had speed of from thirteen to fifteen knots. This could be done at any time of year, although the Yangtse River rises in the summer in some places from sixty to one hundred feet. I spoke to the Viceroys, Liu Kwen Yi and Chung Chi Tung, on this matter, and they both told me that they would be very glad to see such gunboats, as they greatly feared disturbances; and, owing to scarcity of money, they had been obliged to discharge many of their troops, and were not paying the others full and fair wages. It might be possible, in order to encourage friendliness, and help authority, to fly the British and Chinese flags on board such gunboats.

Mr. Archibald, an American missionary, said that he had hoped the British would shortly put gunboats on the Yangtse River and Tung Ting Lake, as the American railway from Wuchang to Canton was going to pass right through Hunan, the most anti-foreign province in China. He thought that, unless some such precautions were taken, serious disturbances would arise.

As the country is very disturbed in the province of Szechuan, no delay should occur in sending a gunboat through the gorges; and, as the water is rising in April and May, delay is unnecessary.

The following number of steamers on the Yangtse River were trading between Shanghai, Hankow, and Ichang during December, 1898.

Between Shanghai and Hankow:

    3 Jardine & Matheson.
    3 Butterfield & Swire.
    4 China Merchants.
    4 Greaves & Co.
    2 Japanese.
    2 MacBean.

Total.... 18

Between Ichang and Hankow:

    1 Jardine & Matheson.
    1 Butterfield & Swire.
    2 China Merchants.

Total.... 4

HANKOW

No steamer at present plies higher than Ichang.

When Szechuan, Hunan, and the other provinces bordering on the Yangtse are opened for trade, the present number of steamers will be greatly multiplied.

Two steamers are being built in Germany to be placed on the Yangtse River shortly.

Something has already been done towards the development of mineral wealth in this district by his Excellency Chung Chi Tung, Viceroy of Hunan and Hupeh, who possesses numerous coal, iron, and other mineral fields in the two provinces. His Excellency began by working a coal-mine, and an iron-mine, situated at a long distance from each other. To these he added two blast-furnaces, but placed them, under indifferent management, so far from both the coal and the iron that an enormous amount of capital was lost, and in the end it was found better to hand the whole thing over to a company, which I am told is now working with some success.

I visited the iron-mines, which furnish the blast-furnaces. They are seventy-six miles from Hankow. They are very ably managed by a German gentleman. They supply three kinds of ore—brown, magnetic, and hematite. Some of the ore was very good, yielding from 70 to 75 per cent. of iron. The individual mines would last about six years more at the present rate of progress, but the whole district was filled with similar mines. The mines would pay extremely well if the Chinese managing director was honest. The mines are at Wong Chi Tong.

The German manager could deliver ore at Hanyang at one tael (50 cents) per ton, including care and maintenance and every possible charge. The Mandarin who administers the mine, however, debits the same coal at three taels a ton, and it is not apparent what becomes of the difference.

The whole province of Hupeh is very rich in minerals, but this is the only instance of mineral riches being developed in that locality.

The ore is put on trucks, which run on an inclined plane worked by a steel-wire hawser and an engine. At the bottom of the plane the ore is transferred into railway wagons. It is then taken down to the river by rail, whence it is water-borne, and towed up a distance of seventy-six miles to the furnace at Hanyang. All the railway plant was British.

The tea business at Hankow has been referred to fully in the Consular Reports. The British interest is gradually becoming smaller. The whole business may be said to be Russian; and, in fact, most of the tea bought by British merchants is for Russian account.

Three years ago the Russians started chartering steamers, other than British, to take their tea from Hankow. The venture proved disastrous, and they returned to the firm of Butterfield & Swire to carry their trade.

There was naturally some complaint among the

British merchants at the decline of the tea trade with Great Britain; but they readily admitted that it was a question of demand and supply, and that, owing to the favor shown for Ceylon and Assam tea at home, the Chinese tea had been supplanted. The question resolved itself into one of taste.

British trading interest is, however, well represented in the Russian tea trade, for the freight is at present almost entirely in British hands, and the British companies make many thousands each year by carrying Chinese tea for the Russian merchants to Russia.

British trading interest is further represented in Hankow by the fact that the British flag covers cargoes which are really Chinese. About 1500 tons of shipping a week, covered by the British flag, conveys Chinese trade.

If proper security were given, and the Chinese allowed foreign enterprises for developing mineral industries, it is impossible to calculate what the water-borne traffic of the Yangtse would become. Both Chinese and missionaries, well acquainted with the fact, constantly informed me that the provinces of Szechuan and Hunan contain large areas of very great mineral wealth; but Hunan enjoys no foreign enterprise whatever, and Szechuan has it to only a very limited extent.

Elsewhere I make a proposal of how I think this security might be obtained and these localities developed.

I may mention here that I received the greatest

kindness and courtesy from the Russian merchants resident in Hankow, who took me over their works and showed me the manner in which brick-tea is made.

Their management appeared to me to be quite excellent. Their works were well organized and in beautiful order. The engineer in charge of their works was a Scotsman.

While at Hankow I had two long and interesting interviews with his Excellency Chung Chi Tung, the Viceroy of Hunan and Hupeh. This Viceroy is celebrated for his friendly and courteous bearing to all foreigners, and also for his enlightened views as to the necessity of opening up China by means of developing her great mineral resources as well as by means of improving the system of administration throughout the Empire.

His Excellency, although holding these ideas, is a thoroughly loyal and patriotic Chinaman, with a great affection and devotion for his country.

A summary of the interviews will, I think, be interesting to the Associated Chambers of Commerce.

The first interview lasted four hours. I was received with great pomp, ceremony, and hospitality. I stated clearly to the Viceroy the anxiety felt by the British trading communities generally as to the security of their trade and commerce in China. I also pointed out that, owing to want of security, Anglo-Saxon investors would not be inclined to find fresh capital for the purpose of further de-

HANKOW

velopment of trade in China, a question which concerns Chinese welfare as well as Anglo-Saxon enterprise. With regard to the first question, the Viceroy was perfectly outspoken. He said that he was afraid of disturbances in the provinces under his control; that if disturbances became serious he had not enough troops to quell them, owing to his finances being insufficient; that Likin Collectorates in his provinces, usually allowed for provincial administration, had been allocated to pay interest on loans contracted by the Chinese Government with foreign nations. He questioned the wisdom of this act, as such loans were for the benefit of the Chinese Empire as a whole. The service of the loans, he thought, should be secured by the whole Empire, instead of falling on the Collectorates situated in the Yangtse Valley.

On being asked why he feared disturbances, he said the people had got it into their heads that they were taxed in order to pay the foreigners. This had kindled the latent hostile feeling, always existing among the Chinese towards foreigners.

I asked his Excellency whether, as a patriotic man, he was not nervous as to the future of his country. He replied he was very unhappy about it; that he did not see how China was to save her integrity unless she made some effort herself. I then suggested that if the Chinese Government were to request the British Government to organize the Chinese Army as a whole, the British Government might possibly agree under certain conditions. His Excellency asked what conditions. I replied, conditions embracing matters which his Excellency had already referred to, such as the opening up of China's mineral resources, reformed administration, tariff revision, and fiscal reform, embracing the whole Empire.

Although his Excellency was entirely in sympathy with the proposal that the British should organize the Chinese Army, he asked whether I thought it would be possible to employ American and Japanese officers as well as British. I replied that I saw no difficulty whatever, but thought it an excellent proposition, and suggested that some German officers might be employed as well, as they had already drilled some ten thousand men most admirably. I further pointed out that the British people had no desire whatever to dominate China, either by control of the military or by any other method. That it was to the interest of the great trading nations to maintain the integrity of the Chinese Empire, so that the policy of the "Open Door" and equal opportunity for trade to all nations should be assured. His Excellency asked me to draw up a scheme containing proposals both as regards organization and finance. This I did, and received his warmest thanks.

His Excellency was quite open in expressing his anxiety as to the Russian military domination and position in the North. He said that even if the Chinese asked the British to reorganize the army, and the British agreed, that, in the event of

Russia objecting, which she certainly would, Great Britain would retire from the agreement, as she was afraid of Russia, and had proved this by her actions in the North.

The Viceroy informed me that he had received letters and telegrams from the Tsung-li Yamen at Peking to place two thousand men at my disposal, in order to commence the nucleus of a Chinese army in his provinces drilled by British officers. I informed his Excellency of my interviews, collectively and individually, with the members of the Tsung-li Yamen (which will be found under chapter on "Peking"). His Excellency said he saw two insuperable obstacles to the proposal of the Tsung-li Yamen. They were: First, and most important, the certainty that, if the plan were carried out as proposed with two thousand men in the province under his administration, it would immediately cause other countries to undertake a similar drilling and recruiting of Chinese in localities which other countries were pleased to call their Sphere of Influence. Such action would tend to lead to the dismemberment of China. Second, that the Manchu and Chinese troops could not possibly be placed together to work under one lead, and that he had no power to give orders to the Manchu troops, who were under a separate command and administration. I entirely agreed with his Excellency as to the first objection, but said I did not believe the British Government would undertake the organization of separate provincial armies, but that they possibly might of the Imperial Army as a whole, as British trade and commerce existed in all parts of the Empire. Anyhow, I should have no authority to even undertake the drilling of two thousand men without the sanction of the British Government. The question could not be entered into for settlement between his Excellency and myself; it was one that would have to be settled between the two Governments.

The Viceroy also contended that there would be great difficulties about finance. As I was conversant with the different Budgets for defence for the different provinces nearly all over the Empire, I proved to him that China could have a very efficient army without any extra taxation if the money allowed was spent as intended. A large proportion now finds its way into the pockets of the officials, most of the remainder being wasted in the arsenals in making useless and obsolete war material.

In the second interview, which lasted about two hours, the Viceroy appeared very anxious to know what communications I had had originally with the Tsung-li Yamen, and also what further correspondence I had had with them from Hankow. He was more strongly in favor of a reorganization of the Chinese Army by foreign officers, and raised fewer difficulties. I took particular care to impress upon his Excellency that my suggestions were solely made in the interests of protection of foreign trade and commerce and with regard to their future

HANKOW

development, and that it had nothing whatever to do with political questions.

His Excellency asked me to inspect the arsenal under his control, and to give him my views of the work turned out. An account of this arsenal will be found in the chapter on "Arsenals."

I received while at Hankow two visits from the Taotai Yu; he was in charge of the Chinese Customs. He expressed himself as being very friendly to the British, and hoped that the policy declared by the British Cabinet with regard to keeping the door open to the trade of all nations would be adhered to, as he said it meant a declaration in favor of maintaining the integrity of China. He, however, declared that he was nervous on this point in the future, as he thought that China and the British Government were afraid of Russia.

He brought me letters from the Viceroy Chung Chi Tung concerning my proposed army scheme for providing security for trade and commerce.

While here I twice visited His Excellency Sheng, a Director of Railways of the Chinese Empire, a remarkably shrewd, clever, and enterprising Chinaman. He was much concerned as to the future of the Chinese Empire, declaring he thought it would shortly fall to pieces. He said he had on several occasions in years gone by written memoranda to his Government begging it to take in hand their army and navy, and organize them under British officers. He had pointed out that there would be no danger in this, as the British were traders, and, while wanting a Chinese army to protect that trade, they could not utilize the army for political purposes, as the officers would be Chinese servants, like Sir Robert Hart. He said it was no use taking provincial armies in hand for this purpose, as that might invite other countries to do the same thing, and, if done at all, it should be done as a whole.

His Excellency was very interested in all questions connected with finance, and begged me to use what influence I could with the Associated Chambers of Commerce towards getting a revision of the tariff. I said that I was certain that Britain would entertain no such question unless the whole fiscal system of the country was taken in hand at the same time. Anglo-Saxon trade and commerce is severely handicapped by the present unequal system of the likin and loti-shui taxes, as well as the uncertain time at which these taxes may be enforced.

His Excellency also expressed his opinion that England did not take the initiative in China because she was afraid of Russia. He said: "Many of our people are saying, 'What is the use of thinking about the English to help us; they never do anything; the Russians do something; they are much the stronger nation. It is wiser for us to make friends with them.'" I asked his Excellency if this opinion was held by a large number of the influential Chinese. He said: " There are some who thought it might save their country if China were to boldly throw in her lot with Russia, as by doing so it would certainly be a protection against the predatory action of other Powers. China would certainly break up if the millions of its inhabitants perceived its Government was powerless to prevent any European Government from claiming and annexing any part of the Empire." His Excellency entreated me to remain longer at Hankow, with the object of further discussing the plan of reorganizing the Chinese Army as a whole. I declined to have anything to do with this matter, as the initial step promised by the Tsung-li Yamen to me on October 22, 1898 (*see* chapter on " Peking ") —viz., that the Chinese Government would ask the British Government to undertake the reorganization of the Chinese Army for the protection of trading interests—had not been complied with.

His Excellency thought it might be for the benefit of China if the Viceroys in the Yangtse provinces brought the matter before their Government. His Excellency asked me to proceed to Wong Chi Tong to see his iron-mines, which formerly belonged to Chung Chi Tung, now worked by His Excellency Sheng and a company.

I visited Wong Chi Tong as invited, an account of which will be found on p. 153.

His Excellency Sheng has opened a coal-mine, Tingsham, in Hunan. The coal is very good for making coke, and is used in the iron and steel works at Hanyang.

His Excellency Sheng also invited me to visit

the iron and steel works at Hanyang; the management was under two Belgian gentlemen; a British mercantile captain was in charge of all transport from the mines to the furnaces. The original capital, £750,000, was all Chinese. The works have been in active progress for seven years, originally under British management. There are two large blast-furnaces, both British made, from Tees-side Ironworks, but only one has ever been used. The present output is 75 tons a day. There is also a complete Bessemer plant, which can turn out 80 tons a day. The whole plant was employed when I was there in making rails for the Shanhaikwan Railway, and 120 tons of rails could be turned out in a day. The works employ 1000 hands. The machinery is mostly British. The coal used from Tongshan comes in junks from the Hunan Province, 200 miles away. It is very good, but is only worked with picks and shovels on the surface and by the Chinese. The whole province of Hunan abounds with coal of very good quality, both anthracite and bituminous.

All the outcroppings are within distance of small but navigable waterways.

If the British and Belgian gentlemen were allowed absolute control and management, these works would pay very high dividends. All that I saw showed want of management and waste of money. Sometimes the furnaces are stopped for want of coal, sometimes for want of ore. Often there is a glut of both.

HANKOW

I was told that coal costing 300 cash per ton—*i.e.*, about 7½*d.*—at Hsainghua, is worth 9 dollars, or 18*s.*, at Hankow, a distance of about 400 miles.

I found one company at Hankow doing very profitable business in antimony, junk-borne from Hunan, and two Chinese merchants also doing very well with zinc and copper ore, brought from the same district.

Lead and tin are also constantly brought down from Hunan and Hankow, specimens of which I saw.

If foreigners were allowed to open up this province of Hunan by enterprise and capital, and a royalty was paid to the Chinese Government on the output for each undertaking, large fortunes could be made for the companies, and the Chinese Government would derive a new and extremely profitable source of revenue.

At present the province of Hunan, though very rich and the people very well-to-do, is the most anti-foreign in China. Foreigners who penetrate into Hunan, even with the help of the Mandarins, by means of a military escort, do so at the risk of their lives. This I was told by missionaries and a gentleman who barely escaped.

In the year 1897 an English missionary named Sparham went as far as Hengchau. There has been a French mission in this place for over one hundred years, and Mr. Sparham saw the cross on their chapel, but he was not allowed to land.

A British Consul has just been sent to Yohchau,

THE BREAK-UP OF CHINA

a new Treaty port at the mouth of the Tung Ting Lake—a move in the right direction. Before any steps can be taken to open up Hunan proper, a British Consul should be sent to Changsha, the capital and most important town of the province, on the Siang River, a clear blue-water river, about two hundred and ninety-six miles from Hankow. It is a great rice-distributing centre, rice being much cultivated in the surrounding districts. Tea is also largely exported from Hunan, cowhides and gall-nuts and very good silk.

There are already six small steam-launches belonging to the Chinese plying between Hankow and Hunan. They are principally used for passengers, and sometimes for towing junks.

Silver and gold are also brought down in small quantities.

When I was at Hankow reports came of an extensive gold-field in this province, but the Chinese were very reticent as to its locality. That they are determined to keep foreigners out of Hunan if possible is proved by the following fact: In June, 1898, a company of Hunanese Chinese bought from an American firm enough plant to erect several works for gold-milling. It cost £20,000, and is the newest and most intricate machinery for extracting gold (called the Huntingdon mills), the motive power being centrifugal force. The firm that sent it out wanted to send men to erect it, and put it into thoroughgoing order, but the Chinese would not hear of this. In December last, the firm sent out an American gentleman (whom I met) to see how the mill was going on. The Chinese declared it was working very satisfactorily, but would on no account allow him to go and see it.

The Hankow and Canton Railway is to pass through Changsha, the capital of Hunan. It is certain to be valuable; but if the very large number of waterways in this province were conserved, and their trade protected by gunboats, an enormous trade would be insured.

There were two very profitable albumen manufactories; they were started with foreign capital and in foreign hands, but not British.

There is also a large match factory, doing an excellent business, started July, 1897, with a capital of 300,000 taels — about £40,000 — entirely Chinese capital and management.

There is also a very large trade which goes by the curious cognomen of the "muck-and-truck" trade. It is very profitable, and consists principally of hides, bristles, bones, etc. This trade is nearly all in the hands of the Germans. The British, however, are now beginning to see the importance of this industry.

Another trade is the bamboo trade, from the interior, which comes *via* the Tung Ting Lake.

There is also a trade in wool and feathers.

There is a large trade in foreign goods with Hunan, all in the hands of the Chinese. It is one of the best markets in China for Lancashire

THE BREAK-UP OF CHINA

goods, which would be even more increased if the country were opened up. The goods are all bought at Shanghai.

Hunan fully illustrates the necessity of foreigners having the right of residence if they wish to increase and develop their trade.

There is a cotton-mill at Hankow started by the Viceroy, Chung Chi Tung. It was said to be a paying concern, but there is a great deal of waste and interference on the part of the managing Mandarin. There is no doubt it would pay extremely well if put under the sole management of the able Englishman who is there.

Owing to the geographical position of Hankow, in that it will become the railhead from the north and south, and also that it is the great distributing centre for the whole of the waterways in the heart of China, it is certain in the future to become the wealthy and prosperous place that Chicago has for similar reasons become in America.

At the Viceroy's request I visited the Arsenal and Military School, and inspected his troops. For remarks on these, *see* chapter on " Forts and Arsenals."

XV

FOOCHOW

The estimated population is 636,351

TRADE STATISTICS

The total value of trade in 1897 was Hk. Taels 13,556,494 (£1,900,000).

The total tonnage of shipping entered and cleared in 1897 was 641,795, of which 470,239 was British.

I ARRIVED at Foochow on December 20, 1898. The Committee of the Chamber of Commerce handed me some resolutions, which they asked me to transmit for the information of the Associated Chambers of Commerce. (*See* Appendix.)

The city of Foochow was made an open port by Article II. of the Treaty of Nanking, 1842, but up to the present time only a very small portion of the island Nantai has been regarded and treated as a Treaty Port.

The British merchants complained very warmly of the taxes put upon their trade by means of likin.

The city of Foochow proper, and all its suburbs, are not considered by the Chinese authorities as coming under Treaty Rights.

The merchants claim that all imports, after having submitted to the Custom-House examination and having paid their duty, should be allowed free admission to Foochow City proper and its suburbs.

The city and its suburbs, however, are treated as if they were in the interior, and a heavy likin tax is levied on goods which have to pass between the island of Nantai and the city, a distance of about three miles.

This likin tax being imposed is most detrimental to the progress of trade and commerce in this port.

Some of the British merchants here were engaged in the tea-trade, the staple trade of the port, and pointed out that the heavy likin tax referred to formed an insuperable barrier to competition with the teas of India, Ceylon, or Assam.

The present system of taxation is rapidly diminishing the tea-trade, and if it continues will probably destroy it altogether.

There were six steam-launches running on the River Min between Foochow and Sueykow, but none, that I could gather, running on the Yuenfoo River.

There is no doubt that Anglo-Saxon capital could be profitably invested in steamboats for plying on these rivers were it not for the restrictions to which my attention was called here as at other ports—viz., that a steamer, under the new inland navigation laws, can only carry cargo within the area of the port of registration.

The launches that were running, with one exception, were worked with Chinese capital, management, and crews.

FOOCHOW

The question of the state of the River Min was brought to my notice. I observed that it was silted up very considerably, and I was informed that the silting is rapidly becoming worse. This impedes trade, as steamers cannot come up the river to load or discharge at the settlement, and even steam-launches are often delayed, owing to insufficiency of water, which prevents them running between the settlement and the Pagoda Anchorage. The Anchorage is nine miles from the settlement, and the settlement about thirty-four miles from the sea.

From what I saw of the Min River, I should say that if its conservation is not taken in hand very soon between the Pagoda Anchorage and the settlement, water-borne traffic will soon be suspended.

The people have been allowed to run out fishing-stakes, enclose banks, dump down rubbish and ballast, until there remains only a narrow winding channel, which at spring-tides gives barely eleven feet.

At the middle ground below Pagoda Anchorage and above the Kimpai pass, the river has shoaled two feet in the last seven years.

Another great hinderance to business brought to my notice is the existence of a board of International Trade, which consists of the Tartar General Tsung Chee and two Taotais.

All international business is intrusted to these gentlemen by the high authorities. As they have no regular status, the local officials pay little or no heed to their "requests": they are not entitled to give orders.

The British Government has never formally recognized this Board, but in practice the Board constantly intervene between the British Consular authority and the Viceroy.

It can easily be imagined what a very different effect an order under the Viceroy's seal, such as given at Canton, Wuchang, or Nanking, etc., has on a prefect or magistrate, compared with a note from two Taotais making a request. This method of conducting business has already produced friction between the Consular authority and the Viceroy, and the length of time it occupies is unquestionably adverse to the interests of trade.

On going to the British Consul in order to get proof of this, and representing to him that anything he could tell me with the object of helping forward the development of Anglo-Saxon trade and commerce would certainly be interesting to the Associated Chambers, he allowed me to see the following letter, which was written to the Nantai likin office:

"By Article II. of Nanking Treaty. Foochow is one of the cities and towns open to trade where only the just dues and duties promised by the Treaty are payable on foreign trade. Such dues and duties are simply the import and export duties. Your office, however, proposes to interpret the city of Foochow into the foreign hongs along the south bank of the river two miles from the city gate.

FOOCHOW

"Moreover, the object of British merchants in importing foreign goods is to sell them to Chinese, and the framers of the Treaties understood this, and provided a tariff accordingly. Your office, however, proposes to make the import duty a charge which merely enables goods to be landed into a British hong—a contention obviously inconsistent with the wording and meaning of the Treaties."—July 12, 1898.

The Consul's efforts are to extend the area exempted from the likin. At present the area only consists of the British hongs mentioned in the letter.

While at Foochow I paid a visit to his Excellency the Viceroy Hsü Jung Kwei. He received me with great ceremony and honor.

After the usual formalities common in China, I informed his Excellency that I was entirely unofficial and non-political, and that my mission was to report on the prospects of British trade and commerce, to suggest what I could for its future development, and to inform the Chambers of Commerce what security existed for its development. His Excellency expressed his friendship and good feeling towards Great Britain. I pointed out to his Excellency that this feeling was thoroughly reciprocated at home, that the earnest wish of the British people was that friendly relations should be maintained, and that such relations were necessary to develop and extend trade and commerce, the great interest of the British people. His Excellency said that the good-will of England had been clearly proved, and that she was the only Power that had not tried to annex a portion of the Chinese Empire, and he hoped that she would endeavor to keep the Chinese Empire in its integrity. His Excellency further said that he thought China should have an army, in order that she might defend herself. I suggested that if China were to ask the four Powers who at present hold her foreign trade to help her to reorganize her army, I thought it very possible the four Powers might accede to that request, under certain conditions. His Excellency asked what the conditions were. I replied, reform of administration, alteration of taxation, and free permission to open up the great latent resources of the Empire by means of promoting industries with foreign capital, and other reforms necessary, in order that the modern requirements inseparable from the development of trade and commerce should be complied with.

I pointed out that the present system of provincial armies was inadequate, extravagant, and totally ineffective, and referred to the China-Japan War as an illustration of the disastrous results of having such disjointed organizations under various Viceroys.

His Excellency seemed to be of the opinion that the provincial system was best for China, because it had lasted for so many years. When I pointed out to him the excellent services rendered to the Chinese Empire by Sir Robert Hart, in his cosmopolitan administration of the Maritime Customs, which was not provincial but Imperial, his Excellency seemed to modify his ideas, saying that was very true, and that if it answered in one department it was quite possible that it might answer in another. After some considerable conversation, his Excellency went so far as to say he would memorialize the Central Government on the matter. His Excellency asked me if I would inspect his troops, and visit the dock-yard and forts, that he would make all arrangements to send me in his launch down the river to the forts, and also send high officials to conduct me over them. He asked also if I would write to him and tell him what I thought would make them more efficient. This I did.

His Excellency appeared anxious about the future of his country, but not to such an extent as other Viceroys that I had visited. He had only been one month in office.

After visiting the arsenal (*see* "Arsenals"), I called upon the Tartar General Tseng Chee, who entertained me most hospitably. His Excellency is in sole charge and in command of this arsenal, and it was by his permission that I was enabled to go over it. I spoke to him about the condition of the arsenal at some length, pointing out the waste of money going on in that establishment. I also told him that, in my opinion, it was no use for China to think of committing the extravagance of having a fleet, at any rate at present, and that she ought to devote her attention to organizing and making an efficient army for police purposes throughout the Empire, in order to give that security which would invite foreign nations to develop their trade and commerce with China. His Excellency asked me if I would write him a detailed description of what I thought was necessary in numbers to make an efficient army, and also if I could make some calculation as to its probable cost. This I did, and received a warm letter of thanks in return. The General was most intelligent and interested, and very friendly in all he said. Later on I went with the General to inspect his troops.

It came to my knowledge that the finances in this province are in a very bad way, and there had been considerable difficulty in finding funds to pay the authorities at the arsenal. As a matter of fact, although they ought to have been paid on December 1, 1898, they were not paid until December 23, 1898.

XVI

SWATOW

The estimated population is 40,216

TRADE STATISTICS

The total value of trade in 1897 was Hk. Taels 28,398,001 (over £4,000,000).
The total tonnage of shipping entered and cleared in 1897 was 1,917,027, of which 1,655,864 was British.

Before going to Hong Kong I visited Swatow. The European community, including missionaries, is about two hundred.

Swatow was first opened to foreigners by the Treaty of Tientsin in 1858.

At a meeting held by the British merchants a resolution was confided to my care for transmission to the Associated Chambers of Commerce. (*See* Appendix.)

The staple trade of Swatow is sugar, but it does not appear to be increasing to any extent.

There was a good tea trade, but that is rapidly declining.

There is a bean-cake factory, which I was told was paying very well.

The people all round Swatow have always been of a very independent character, and the authorities have never been able to impose taxes to the same extent as they have in other parts of China.

A short time ago an attempt was made by the authorities to increase the likin tax, and a new likin house was erected. The people immediately pulled it down.

The officials in this locality are afraid of the people, and they cannot enforce unjust demands, as they have no troops whatever. The result is that the likin tax is really less than the two-and-a-half per cent. charged for transit passes, and, except for cotton-yarn, I could not gather that the transit passes are used at all. Whether it is owing to the independent character of the people about here or not I cannot say, but there are very few representatives of authority in the country adjoining. At the town of Chao-Chao Fu, about thirty miles distant from Swatow, where there is a population of over one million, the whole constituted authority is represented by one fourth-class Mandarin and four Yamen runners or police. The people there are now perfectly orderly, and far better off than in most places in China. The reason appears to be found in the fact that between 1870 and 1872 a General Fan was sent from Peking with troops to quell some disturbances between the clans which exist in this province, who had been fighting for some time.

SWATOW

He decimated the whole province, and they are now only just beginning to recover.

I found many reports and beliefs current as to the mineral resources of this province (Kwangtung), but no foreigner has prospected or made any report on the subject that I could discover, excepting Captain Fleming of the Royal Engineers.

Some eight years ago a Chinese company was formed, and the money subscribed to open up some mines, but a story got about to the effect that all the women would be barren if machinery was introduced and the country opened up. The mining projects were in consequence abandoned.

In contradistinction to Amoy, the natives make their own salt. Although salt is a monopoly, the authorities are unable or unwilling to enforce the law in regard to it. There is a large fishing industry at Swatow, and as they make the salt themselves it is very profitable.

Most of the British merchants here appeared very satisfied with things as they are. Their business is principally shipping industry. There were some steamboats running up the river to Chao-Chao Fu and San-Ho-Pa.

Only one steamer has been added since the new navigation laws came into force, owing to the restrictions so frequently referred to in this Report.

There is a very large trade between Swatow and Newchwang, 90 per cent. of which is carried in British bottoms.

THE BREAK-UP OF CHINA

British piece-goods hold their own with American piece-goods here better than they do in the North; but all American goods are brought in British bottoms, and are British-owned at time of importation.

It was pointed out to me by the British merchants that a railway would be certain to pay if constructed from Swatow to the native city of Chao-Chao Fu, about thirty-five miles distant. The line would be easy to make, as it would run over very flat plains and not cause an expensive outlay. There is a very heavy trade between the two places, and at present the whole traffic is carried by water on a river that is always shallow, and in the dry season (the winter) falls to ten inches. All trade has to be carried on in sanpans.

I asked them why, if the proposal was so clearly a good one, they did not subscribe the capital and ask for a concession. I was informed by Mr. Monroe, who is the head of Bradley & Co., that Messrs. Jardine & Matheson had already surveyed the country as far back as 1888, and found out the practicability of the scheme. A year ago Messrs. Bradley & Co. applied to the Chinese authorities at Canton for permission for themselves and some Chinese friends with Chinese capital to construct the railway. They got no direct reply, but were given to understand that there is determined opposition to the scheme.

Another similar case, showing the restrictions

fatal to the development of trade, was brought to my notice. The same firm, Messrs. Bradley & Co., in 1892, were instrumental in floating a scheme to provide the town of Swatow with fresh water, of which it has none at present, save what is drawn from the river, which is brackish and muddy. The money required was all subscribed by local Chinese, the surveys were made, the land bought, and everything ready, when the scheme was wrecked owing to the opposition of the people in the neighborhood. The reason for the opposition was never discovered. The Taotai, at that time, was actually in favor of the scheme, but he gave way, declaring openly that he feared the people.

As matters are at present, there does not seem much chance for any substantial development of trade in this locality.

XVII

AMOY

The estimated population is 96,370

TRADE STATISTICS

The total value of trade in 1897 was Hk. Taels 12,973,616 (over £1,800,000).

The total tonnage of shipping in 1897 was 1,727,251, of which 1,417,135 was British.

ON my way from Shanghai to Hong Kong I visited Amoy, a port situated upon the island of Haimun, at the mouth of the Pei Chi River.

This port was first opened to foreign trade by the treaty of Tientsin in 1858.

I met the Amoy Chamber of Commerce and received from them some resolutions for delivery to the Associated Chambers of Commerce. (*Vide* Appendix.)

I found that, about twenty years ago, tea was the great trading interest of Amoy, but it has declined so considerably that it is a mere question of time before it is completely extinct. The reasons given me were, the competition of the Assam and Ceylon teas.

When I was there, there was a certain amount

AMOY

of tea in the hands of tea merchants which they told me they did not think they had a chance of selling. I asked if anything could be suggested to improve the rapid decline of this export, and I was given a copy of some suggestions made by the Amoy General Chamber of Commerce to the Commissioner of Customs in 1896, of which the following is a copy:

AMOY GENERAL CHAMBER OF COMMERCE.

Extract from a communication to the Commissioner of Customs, Amoy, dated 18th February, 1896, in reply to his request for the Chamber's views:

"The decline in the export of Amoy Oolong is owing to the competition of Formosa Oolong, and also to the steady deterioration of its quality year by year. It is quite possible that the quality might be improved, and that Amoy Oolong might again recover a good portion of its lost position; but this Chamber is of opinion that such improvement can never be done by the Chinese alone, and I am therefore unable to offer any suggestions that would be of assistance to you in framing instructions for the guidance of teamen in the interior.

"I can, however, with the fullest confidence, recommend your urging upon the Imperial Chinese Government the adoption of the following five suggestions:

"1. The obtaining of qualified gardeners from India or Ceylon to superintend the reorganization of the Tea Gardens, and to instruct the native Chinese in the most improved methods of cultivation.

"2. Improved methods of preparation by machinery, etc., inland, with the right of foreign supervision.

"3. Collection of likin to be made at the port of export.

"4. Combined export duty and likin not to exceed the Japan tariff.

"5. Articles used in the manufacture and packing of tea to be taxed as lightly as possible, and a drawback to be allowed in lead used as packing material."

However, from the remarks made to me, I do not think there seems much chance of the tea trade being reinstated in the near future. Formosa tea comes through Amoy, and this trade has not been appreciably hurt by competition with Ceylon. Nearly all the Formosa tea goes to America. I could not find that there was any tea exported for the Russian trade from Amoy.

It will be observed that this is one of the first places I visited where statistics show that trade has declined. I endeavored to find a reason for this, and elicited the following facts: The merchants were loud in their complaint relative to the imposition of the likin tax around Amoy. It was so heavy that no European goods got farther into the country than twenty miles. After

AMOY

that distance local taxation made them too expensive.

I was informed also that local taxation either prevents industries being started, or kills them when they are started.

On asking for an instance, Mr. Cass, one of the leading merchants of the place, told me that he had started some flour-mills for the Chinese, but that the local taxation soon killed them.

Europeans are not allowed themselves to put up mills owing to the law forbidding right of residence. If the foreigner, as on this occasion, put up mills for the Chinese, the Chinese are so heavily taxed that they cannot continue the business. In the case I have mentioned, Mr. Cass was a loser as well as the Chinese. The example shows how British trading interests are affected adversely under the present system.

Another case in connection with Mr. Cass came to my notice. There is most excellent clay for brick-making near Amoy. Mr. Cass and some Chinese wished to put up some brick-making machinery, but the Chinese officials, on being applied to, said they would protect the old-fashioned plan of hand-made bricks. If they had been permitted to put up the machinery, Amoy could have developed an enormous trade in bricks.

Another trade that has been killed at Amoy is the salt fish trade. Although the Chinese could themselves make any amount of salt, the salt monopoly is rigidly enforced by the authorities; the consequence is they have to import salt fish from Singapore at a much larger price than they could preserve it locally. It will be seen in the chapter on "Swatow," that in that place they salt their own fish and so possess a thriving industry, officialdom not being so powerful in that locality. The importation of salt is prohibited by treaty, and is a Government monopoly. The result is that the cost of home-made salt has become so great, owing to extortions, exactions, and squeezes, that it is a fact that if salt could be imported, and 50 per cent. duty put upon it, it would still sell under the price paid for home-made salt, and even then give the Government a good and sure source of revenue.

I would remark that the salt monopoly, in increasing the price of food, is a tax on the poor and not on the rich, and there can be no doubt that it has an effect on the stamina of the Chinese. From what I could gather, the insufficiency of salt in their food is undoubtedly the cause of the prevalence of much preventable disease.

While the importation of salt is prohibited, salt fish is allowed to be imported under the treaty tariff of 5 per cent. *ad valorem*. Almost all the salt fish eaten in the province where Amoy is situated is imported from abroad. The coast teems with fish, and if the salt monopoly were removed a new trade would spring up.

With regard to the constant famines which take place in China, I found here what may perhaps be

AMOY

considered an ample reason for the recurrence of these disasters.

Grain is allowed to be imported freely from abroad, but it is not allowed to be moved from one district to another without special permit from the Chinese Government.

Mr. Gardner, who was British Consul at Amoy when I was there, and who before that had been consul on the Upper Yangtse, gave me some interesting details proving the prodigality of the present system. He remembered rice being two dollars a picul at Changchou and Chuan Chou, places about thirty miles from Amoy, when rice was three dollars a picul at Amoy, but authority would not allow rice to be sent from one place to the other.

The growers of rice in the district, only having their own neighborhood as a market, naturally grow the exact quantity they think will be required, and scarcity of rice in the district is a gain to the grower because it sends up the price.

If a crop fails over an extensive portion of the country, there being no surplus of other districts to supply the deficiency, a famine is the result.

Mr. Gardner told me that the Upper Yangtse, after the summer floods, like the Nile, deposits a rich alluvial soil, on which heavy crops of wheat can be grown without manure or tillage. The seed is simply thrown on the receding water. Yet, owing to the prohibition to export grain, this does not add to the wealth of the Yangtse Valley.

Mr. Gardner told me he had himself seen whole fields of ripe, golden corn wasted, either by driving cattle into the fields or by cutting down the eared blades and using them as fuel.

Such maladministration, which inevitably produces poverty among a very large section of the people, is one of the many causes which hinder the development of our trade with China. The Chinese can only buy our goods if they have money to pay for them, and alteration and administration even in this one particular would produce a permanent relief to the people of whole districts, increase their happiness and contentment, and provide them with money to enable them to buy many of those foreign goods which, under altered circumstances, would become necessaries of their existence.

The merchants informed me that wheat could be grown in great quantities in this province; but I have already pointed out that restrictions would not make it worth the while of any grower to embark in such an enterprise.

The province of Kwangtung is rich in coal and iron. Captain Fleming, of the Royal Engineers, as far back as the year 1882, prospected and reported finding a coal and iron district within forty miles of Amoy. The area of the district was over fifty miles. Owing to the passive resistance of the authorities, no one has been able yet to make a start and develop these latent resources.

If the right of residence was conceded, there

could be no doubt that large, profitable, and growing industries would soon be the result. The name of the district where the minerals are to be found is Ankoi.

A small rail or tram would be necessary for only a distance of twenty miles to a place whence the minerals could be water-borne.

I was told that the Japanese are trying to get hold of these mines, if they can manage to get the necessary concession.

All the points brought to my notice at Amoy with regard to the difficulties of developing trade were entirely due to the obstinate conservatism of the officials.

The likin tax was perhaps more irksome at this place than any other that I visited. The limit of the transit passes is really the limit of traffic, and that limit is a very confined area. The merchants told me they never knew where they were with regard to likin taxes; the dates for payment and the amount to be paid were continually being altered. In this province the likin tax has the extra disadvantage of existing under many other names.

I found that under the new navigation laws (inland waterways), twelve new steamers had been started, six of which were under the British flag.

About 100,000 Chinese emigrate annually from Amoy to Singapore, of whom about 50 per cent. remain. Whether or not it is on account of the treatment the Chinese receive at Singapore, I do not know; but the feeling towards the British at

Amoy is of the most friendly character. On the occasion of the Jubilee of Her Majesty Queen Victoria, the city of Amoy was gratuitously decorated by the Chinese community.

As an example of the confidence in the British displayed by the Chinese, before the Japanese occupied Formosa some of these Chinese invited Mr. Bruce and Mr. Cass, two British merchants of Amoy, to go to Formosa to give advice to the people. Upon their recommendation the Chinese gave up their arms.

XVIII

HONG KONG

The estimated population is 246,880

TRADE STATISTICS

The total value of trade in 1897 was £50,000,000.
The total tonnage of shipping entered and cleared in 1897 was 15,565,843, of which 8,268,770 was British.

ON my arrival at Hong Kong on September 30th I found there the leading Reformer, Kang Yu Wei, who had just arrived in a P. & O. vessel, escorted by a British man-of-war.

Hoping to be able to get the views of the Reform Party on the possibilities of the opening up of China and the consequent development of trade and commerce, I asked Kang Yu Wei to come and see me. He came under police protection, $10,000 having been offered for his head. In an interview which lasted some considerable time, Kang Yu Wei intimated to me that the great object of the Reform Party was to introduce Western ideas, that if China did not herself introduce reforms suitable to modern requirements, it was inevitable that she would crumble to pieces, and her Empire be divided among the nations of the earth, that the strongest sentiment in the minds of the Reform Party was patriotism, that their object was to keep China an Empire and to support the dynasty, but that neither was possible unless China saw the necessity of adapting herself to Western ideas. He said his Majesty the Emperor was entirely in accord with those sentiments. He said that the Reformers had entreated the Emperor to get the assistance of Great Britain to enable his Majesty to carry out these alterations in the system of their administration, without which China's condition would be hopeless and helpless.

On asking him why he mentioned Great Britain more than other countries, he replied that China had known Great Britain longer than any of the other Great Powers, that her trade with China was larger than any of the other Powers, and therefore it was to the interests of Great Britain herself to help China, and that the British were honest traders, and that the Chinese could trust them. Also that in the wars that had occurred between Great Britain and China in the past, Great Britain had always behaved in an honorable and chivalrous manner both during war-time and in the moment of victory.

I asked Kang Yu Wei what position the Reform Party was in at that moment. He replied, "Completely crushed, but not killed," and that it was certain to assert itself again in the near future.

The danger was that China might break up before the patriotic Reformers had time to bring about those changes, which were necessary if China was to continue an Empire.

I asked him who were the Reformers who had been publicly executed on September 28th. He said that there were six, one of whom was his own brother. All six were gentlemen of good birth and education, and highly cultured. Kang Yu Wei himself is one of the best known scholars in China. He said that reforms in the East invariably required martyrs, and that if China was not broken up posterity would honor the heroic patriotism of those six men, who had sacrificed their lives in the cause of Reform.

I asked Kang Yu Wei whether, if the Reform Party had come into power, they would have opened up China to the trade and commerce of the world. He said certainly, as that would have made China richer, and strong enough to keep herself an Empire.

He gave me a long list of patriotic men who would look upon Reform with favor. I asked him if he could give me a reason why so many prominent men were in favor of Reform, as the general opinion in Great Britain was that those who wished for Reform in China were very few and far between. He replied that those who were educated, and who really understood the question, were quite assured that without Reform the Chinese Empire, which had lasted 4000 years, must most certainly crumble to pieces.

I reminded Kang Yu Wei that there were 430,000,000 of people in China, and asked him if he could give me an opinion as to whether there were a large number in the country in favor of Reform. He answered that he did not think so at present, as the people did not understand, but many educated and patriotic men who were in favor of Reform had been showing the people that if the changes they advocated were brought about, the country would be very much richer, and taxation made equitable. I asked if he thought disturbances were likely to occur; he said he did not think so for the moment, as the execution and degradation of leaders of Reform had for the present checked its progress; but that the doctrines laid down as necessary for the preservation of China were certain to be supported with increased energy before very long.

There were many other topics on which Kang Yu Wei touched, but as they were purely political, and had nothing to do with commercial matters, they have no place in this Report.

I was exceedingly impressed by the evident loyalty and patriotism of Kang Yu Wei, and his unselfish devotion to his country. There could be no doubt of his earnestness. It was with very great regret that I came to the conclusion that the Reformers had been very unmethodical, and used too much haste in their efforts to serve their country, and had thus defeated their own ends. They had been pushing reforms before preparing

HONG KONG

the way. Theoretically, all that they urged was quite sound, and manifestly for the good of their country; practically, they had made no arrangement or organization for carrying their theories into effect. I pointed out to Kang Yu Wei that the usages, characteristics, laws, and systems which had ruled in an Empire for thousands of years could not be revolutionized in a few months by an occasional edict from Peking. Kang Yu Wei acknowledged the truth of this.

I lost no opportunity of ascertaining the views of the compradors attached to the great mercantile houses in China with reference to the Reform movement. These men are among the best educated and most intelligent of the Chinese gentlemen; they are also fully conversant not only with the affairs of their own country, but with Western ideas of civilization and progress. I found several of them very outspoken in their opinions as to the necessity for Reform; they all were of opinion that the Reform movement had been pressed forward too quickly, and without the organization necessary to insure its success.

My second visit to Hong Kong was on the 25th of December, 1898.

During this visit I received a number of Resolutions passed by the Hong Kong Chamber of Commerce, a copy of which will be found in the Appendix.

There are no complete official returns of the Imports or Exports, owing to the absence of Customs, Hong Kong being a free port; but the value of the trade of the port is estimated at about £50,000,000 per annum.

The China Association also gave me a number of Resolutions, which are to be found in the Appendix.

I found the British merchants in Hong Kong very nervous as to the future position of British trade and British influence in China. They were as strongly opposed to the policy described as Spheres of Influence as the whole of the other British communities I conferred with during my journeys in China. They declared that the late policy of the British Government had voluntarily acknowledged the exclusive rights of Russia and Germany. By the action of her Government, Great Britain had acquiesced in a policy of Spheres of Influence, the exact counterpart of the Open Door policy so determinedly supported a short time ago by the members of the Cabinet. The merchants were of opinion that the Russian, German, and French Spheres of Influence were recognized. They pointed out that the policy described as the "Open Door" is the only one under which there can be reasonable hope of the future prosperity and development of British trade in China. They held, however, that it was no use declaring for such a policy unless means were taken for carrying it out, and insuring its success and continuance. They also gave me as their opinion that, even if the policy of the Open Door was insured, some means must be taken for removing all chance of disturbances in the country beyond the area of the open ports; that the great drawback to the improvement of trade, increase of manufactures, and development of industries was the revenue system in China; but that this vital question could not be taken in hand until the security for trade which the British merchant had a right to demand was reigning throughout the Empire.

The merchants laid stress upon the position occupied by France in the South. They declared that Great Britain ought to indicate clearly that the immense amount of British trading interests in the provinces of Kwangtung and Kwangsi were such as to make it impossible for her ever to allow under any conditions prohibitive tariffs similar to those put on in Madagascar and Indo-China.

Assuming that British trade means:

(1) Trade with Hong Kong.
(2) Trade with other places in British ships. I asked the British merchants to give me some detailed proofs as to the trade existing between these two provinces (Kwangsi and Kwangtung) and Great Britain, in order that the Associated Chambers of Commerce might see the reasons for a demand couched in such strong terms.

I was supplied with the following Tables:

THE BREAK-UP OF CHINA

TRADE IN BRITISH SHIPS TO TREATY PORTS IN KWANGTUNG AND KWANGSI, 1893–1897

Name of Treaty Port	1893 Tonnage British	1893 Tonnage Total	Value of Trade with Ports other than Hong Kong Imports	Exports	Total
Swatow .	1,575,966	1,767,390	751,819	1,126,282	1,878,101
Pakhoi .	—	128,271	27,468	—	27,468
Haihow .	45,740	361,478	488,431	19,566	507,997
Canton .	2,696,829	3,135,983	59,419	—	59,419
Wuchow .	—	—	—	—	—
Samshui .	—	—	—	—	—
Total .	4,318,535	5,393,122	1,327,137	1,145,848	2,472,985

British Tonnage . . . . = 80%

80% of Value of Trade . . . . . . = 1,978,388

Hong Kong Trade, other than Junks—
    Imports . . . . 18,667,110 ⎫
    Exports . . . . 25,078,440 ⎭ = 43,745,550

Hong Kong Trade, Junks—
    Imports . . . . 18,937,126 ⎫
    Exports . . . . 21,001,594 ⎭ = 39,938,720

HONG KONG

TRADE IN BRITISH SHIPS TO TREATY PORTS IN KWANGTUNG AND KWANGSI, 1893-1897.—*Continued*.

Name of Treaty Port	1894 Tonnage British	1894 Tonnage Total	Value of Trade with Ports other than Hong Kong Imports	Exports	Total
Swatow .	1,521,246	1,673,692	411,522	1,435,805	1,847,327
Pakhoi .	—	86,006	—	—	—
Haihow .	51,196	436,188	292,878	12,627	305,505
Canton .	2,826,459	3,370,935	27,430	—	27,430
Wuchow .	—	—	—	—	—
Samshui .	—	—	—	—	—
Total .	4,399,901	5,566,821	731,830	1,448,432	2,180,262

British Tonnage . . . . = 80%

80% of Value of Trade . . . . . . = 1,744,209

Hong Kong Trade, other than Junks—
    Imports . . . . 18,949,753 ⎫
    Exports . . . . 26,418,756 ⎬ = 45,368,509

Hong Kong Trade, Junks—
    Imports . . . . 19,665,908 ⎫
    Exports . . . . 18,765,289 ⎬ = 38,431,197

THE BREAK-UP OF CHINA

TRADE IN BRITISH SHIPS TO TREATY PORTS IN KWANGTUNG AND KWANGSI, 1893–1897.—*Continued.*

Name of Treaty Port	1895 Tonnage British	1895 Tonnage Total	Value of Trade with Ports other than Hong Kong Imports	Exports	Total
Swatow .	1,560,630	1,812,382	1,988,618	1,581,273	3,569,891
Pakhoi .	2,780	100,546	—	—	—
Haihow .	52,950	389,228	29,617	20,563	50,180
Canton .	3,035,340	3,632,634	3,208,612	7,680	3,216,292
Wuchow .	—	—	—	—	—
Samshui .	—	—	—	—	—
Total .	4,651,700	5,934,790	5,226,847	1,609,516	6,836,363

British Tonnage . . . . = 80%

80% of Value of Trade . . . . . . = 5,469,090

Hong Kong Trade, other than Junks—
    Imports . . . . 20,544,099 ⎫
    Exports . . . . 25,086,550 ⎬ = 45,640,649

Hong Kong Trade, Junks—
    Imports . . . . 22,678,090 ⎫
    Exports . . . . 25,041,325 ⎬ = 47,719,415

HONG KONG

TRADE IN BRITISH SHIPS TO TREATY PORTS IN KWANGTUNG AND KWANGSI, 1893–1897.—*Continued.*

	1896				
Name of Treaty Port	Tonnage		Value of Trade with Ports other than Hong Kong		
	British	Total	Imports	Exports	Total
Swatow	1,755,468	2,129,311	733,504	1,669,095	2,402,599
Pakhoi	—	186,262	2,314	2,096	4,410
Haihow	65,058	538,496	1,067	34,836	35,903
Canton	3,021,533	3,696,999	712,917	—	712,917
Wuchow	—	—	—	—	—
Samshui	—	—	—	—	—
Total	4,842,059	6,551,068	1,449,802	1,706,027	3,155,829

British Tonnage . . . . = 75%

75% of Value of Trade . . . . . . = 2,366,871

Hong Kong Trade, other than Junks—
    Imports . . . . 21,025,663 ⎫
    Exports . . . . 24,221,370 ⎬ = 45,247,033

Hong Kong Trade, Junks—
    Imports . . . . 22,565,590 ⎫
    Exports . . . . 24,606,390 ⎬ = 47,171,980

THE BREAK-UP OF CHINA

TRADE IN BRITISH SHIPS TO TREATY PORTS IN KWANGTUNG AND KWANGSI, 1893-1897.—*Concluded.*

Name of Treaty Port	1897 Tonnage British	1897 Tonnage Total	Value of Trade with Ports other than Hong Kong Imports	Exports	Total
Swatow	1,655,864	1,917,027	572,764	2,100,974	2,673,738
Pakhoi	—	113,732	53	3,917	3,970
Haihow	56,672	547,560	8,742	18,616	27,358
Canton	3,000,571	3,718,064	207,763	1,234	208,997
Wuchow	41,402	52,188	23,432	—	23,432
Samshui	84,158	98,984	112	—	112
Total	4,838,667	6,447,555	812,866	2,124,741	2,937,607

British Tonnage . . . . = 75%

75% of Value of Trade . . . . . . = 2,203,205

Hong Kong Trade, other than Junks—
    Imports . . . . 24,807,430 ⎫
                                    ⎬ = 52,967,376
    Exports . . . . 28,159,946 ⎭

Hong Kong Trade, Junks—
    Imports . . . . 23,024,493 ⎫
                                      ⎬ = 39,991,611
    Exports . . . . 16,967,118 ⎭

HONG KONG

SUMMARY

	Hk. Tls.
Average Estimated Value of Trade in British Ships with Ports other than Hong Kong	2,752,352
Average Estimated Trade with Hong Kong *not* including Junks	46,593,823
Average Trade with Hong Kong in Junks	42,650,584
Average Estimated Value of British Trade	**91,996,759**

A comparison of British and French trade is to be found in the chapter on "Canton."

THE BREAK-UP OF CHINA

IMPERIAL CHINESE CUSTOMS IN A BRITISH COLONY

The question connected with the position of the Chinese Custom House at Kowloon has for some considerable time been exercising the minds of all British merchants at Hong Kong. The matter has now reached a more acute stage owing to the recent extension of the area of the colony, which makes Kowloon British property instead of Chinese.

The existing arrangements were made in the year 1884, at the request of the Chinese Customs, in order to protect Chinese revenue, particularly against the opium farmer. The arrangements were as follows:

The Custom House was to be officially at Kowloon, in Chinese territory. All documents were dated from that place. As a matter of fact, the Customs House is really in Hong Kong, where all business is done.

The name of the Customs House Agent is put over the door, but officially the place is not recognized as a Customs House proper.

The following points in connection with this question were brought to my notice by the British merchants at Hong Kong:

That the original reason for permitting the Chinese Customs to establish themselves in and about Hong Kong was the collection of opium revenue. Now the Chinese Customs not only collect the duties on opium for Chinese Imperial purposes, but also general duties on goods and merchandise inside the area of the British colony for the provincial as well as the Imperial Governments.

They declared that the Customs have practically blockaded Hong Kong, and the system employed is such as to offer considerable obstruction to the development of trade by native traders, principally brought about by illegal search without warrants in British waters. There is great difficulty in proving such cases, because native evidence only is available on the British side, while on the Imperial Chinese Customs side European evidence is always to be obtained in the person of the officer commanding the Customs launch.

Since the year 1884 the European trade has increased in tonnage from 6,859,274 to 12,124,599, but the merchants point out that this increase is not so much due to development of trade in the towns, villages, and country districts of China as to increased development of the trade with Japan, Formosa, and the Treaty Ports. They point out that the Customs House system has kept the junk trade almost stationary, it having only increased from 3,375,188 in 1884 to 3,441,295 in 1897.

The Inspector-General of Chinese Maritime Customs has lately requested official recognition of the Chinese Customs House at Hong Kong, which up to now has only been allowed to exist in the colony on the understanding that the Hong

Kong Government reserve the right to cancel the arrangement. They complain that the fact of having a Chinese Custom House on British soil is an anomaly which would not be permitted in any other colony, and that the absurdity and irritation of such a system would be well exemplified by placing a Customs House within the lines at Gibraltar for collecting Spanish Customs dues. The merchants were very distinct in stating that they wished to do nothing unfriendly to China, and to prove this they are prepared to guarantee the opium revenue, and to take every precaution that the Chinese revenue should not suffer by the change. This they were willing to do, although they were aware that it would inflict a loss to the colony of about £38,000 a year—the sum paid by the opium farmer as rent to the Hong Kong Government.

I made it my business to find out the opinion of the Chinese traders themselves as to shifting the Chinese Customs House from British to Chinese property, and as far as I could gather they were unanimously in favor of such a change. The two Chinese members of the Legislative Council of Hong Kong—Dr. Ho Kai and Mr. Weityuk— were both in favor of this proposed change. It is, however, proper to add that I could get no evidence that the junk masters and Chinese merchants had actually complained of the Chinese Customs House being on British territory.

It may be interesting for the Associated Cham-

HONG KONG

bers of Commerce to have some details respecting the opium farm. I visited the farm on December 31, 1898, and saw the manner in which the opium was prepared. The present opium farmer has a contract with the Government for three years at a rent of £3100 a month. He sells an average of eight to ten tins of opium a day. The tins are about 9 in. by 6 in., and contain about £30 worth of opium, thus making from £7200 to £9000 a month. The trade would appear a very lucrative one.

The opium farmer is known to be the largest smuggler of opium into the country. If he did not smuggle he could not afford to pay the large rent demanded by the Government.

Thus, indirectly, the Hong Kong Government derives a revenue by fostering an illegitimate trade with a neighboring and friendly Power, which cannot be said to redound to the credit of the British Government. It is in direct opposition to the sentiments and traditions of the laws of the British Empire.

Having given clearly the opinions of the British merchants in regard to this important question, I made it my business to find out the opinions of the responsible authorities in charge of the Imperial Maritime Customs of China.

Through their kindness I was able to obtain what may be said to represent their views of the question.

They are as follows:

Memo. regarding Chinese Customs at Hong Kong—Kowloon.

1. Hong Kong to formally recognize Kowloon Commissioner. His duties to be specified. Facilities for carrying them out to be given.*

2. Opium landed to be stored under Colonial Bond, only to be allowed to leave with Colonial permit and Customs counter-signature.

Customs to have right to examine go-downs, etc., in company with Colonial officer at all reasonable times.

3. Colonial officer to specially supervise opium farmer's operations, jointly with Customs man. Farmer to report to Colonial officer all opium (prepared) intended for shipment, with destination, etc.

4. Munitions of war not to be shipped on junks without Colonial permit, countersigned by Customs.

5. Customs vessels to have national status. No seizures to be made on vessels under way within Colonial waters. Where questions of seizure in doubtful waters arise to be jointly investigated.

* Establishment to be known as "Kowloon Customs." Presence in Hong Kong admittedly by favor of British Government. Commissioner to be Englishman. Whole arrangement liable to withdrawal if head of Chinese Customs Service not an Englishman. Great Britain may appoint an officer (?) Consular or Colonial to reside in Kowloon. Chinese officer appointed to Kowloon not to be under a certain rank; name to be submitted to Hong Kong Government before appointment.

6. Hong Kong Government to assist Customs by its officers to carry out Hong Kong law, and not Chinese revenue officers; and they may be rewarded.

7. Hong Kong Government to legislate as may be necessary to give effect to this understanding.

8. China to give trade facilities in certain directions—*e.g.*, in issue of transit passes, inland water navigation, direct trade with West River ports of call, and in other directions where same may be possible.

9. Arrangement to be liable to modification after certain named time or specified notice.

I also received the following resolutions, passed unanimously by the Hong Kong General Chamber of Commerce, September 1. 1898:

> "1. That the Custom Offices be no longer permitted to collect duties in the colony or its waters.
>
> "2. That all opium arriving in the colony be accounted for either through the agency of bonded warehouses or otherwise.
>
> "3. That the Government do all in their power to protect the Chinese revenue, more especially with regard to the opium farmer.
>
> "That the revenue stations and revenue cruisers be removed beyond the limits of British territory and British waters."

The British merchants have represented, over and over again, that the Chinese Customs arrangements for collecting revenues at Hong Kong work seriously to the injury of legitimate trade, that it interferes with the freedom of the port, and that it is a great impediment to the general development of the trade of the colony.

Both sides, the British community and those representing the Chinese Maritime Customs, seem anxious to adjust their differences in a friendly manner. On the side of the Chinese Customs the authorities work in the line which they consider best for the interests of the Government they serve. On the British side, the merchants have clearly pointed out that the present system is harmful to the interests of British trade. At the same time it must always be remembered that the Customs Service is not regarded with any great affection by the merchants of any country. If the Associated Chambers thought wise to press this question forward, there can be no doubt that a satisfactory settlement would shortly be arranged, and Anglo-Saxon trade and commerce materially benefited.

Before I left Hong Kong Mr. Gray called a meeting of the Chamber of Commerce, of which body he is Chairman. A summary of the speeches made at this important meeting may be interesting to the Associated Chambers of Commerce of Great Britain. The members desired me to thank the Associated Chambers of Commerce for having sent a Mission to China to inquire into the state of British trade and commerce. They said that such an inquiry was imperative for British inter-

HONG KONG

ests under the present condition of affairs in China. They declared that every one interested in trade in China must regard the Open Door principle as essential to its existence. They pointed out that, notwithstanding all the efforts of Consuls and Chambers of Commerce, British treaties with China were deliberately flouted in the matter of provincial exactions; and that trade could never expand as long as it was burdened by indefinite inland taxes. They also desired me to request the Associated Chambers of Commerce to use their influence to have the commereial clauses of the Treaty of Tientsin carried out in their entirety.

In the Appendix will be found a copy of Resolutions passed at a meeting of Chinese merchants and traders resident in Hong Kong, held at the Chinese Chamber of Commerce Rooms, on Sunday, January 22, 1899.

I received the following address from the Chinese merchants at Hong Kong after my return to England in March, 1899, and place it in the Report to show the Chinese view of the situation in China:

"To Rear-Admiral Lord Charles Beresford,
    C.B., M.P.:

"Your Lordship,—We humbly crave your Lordship's permission to address to you a few remarks on the China question, both in its political and commercial aspects, for the satisfactory solution of which, with noble self-denial and characteristic energy, you have travelled to the Far East, and, while there, have spared neither time nor trouble in making personal observations and gathering useful information. We, together with the leading Chinese merchants and residents, should have approached you during your brief sojourn in Hong Kong, but we were prevented from so doing by two considerations, one of which was that your Lordship's already limited time was completely occupied with important public and social functions in connection with the British and foreign communities; the other was of a far more serious character, and, we venture to think, deserves the earnest attention of your Lordship and of the British Government and Parliament, especially at the present juncture in China. It was the hidden cause of many apparently inexplicable instances of the backwardness of those Chinese who have been accorded the distinguished privilege of becoming subjects of the mightiest and most glorious Empire the world has ever seen; it has prevented their co-operation with the British authorities in all international questions between the British and Chinese Empires. It is nothing less than the dread of the Chinese mandarins, and the total absence of protection from the British Government, that has hitherto kept the British-born or naturalized Chinese from taking openly any intelligent interest or active part in the political and commercial relationship between these two great nations. For some reason or other the Consular Authorities representing the British Government in China have persistently refused recognition and protection to British subjects descended from the Chinese race who happened to be in Chinese territory, or travelling for commercial or social purposes, and they are left to the tender mercies of the Chinese officials, who have thus golden opportunities for filling their pockets or paying off old scores.

" This policy on the part of the British officials concerned is as enigmatical to us as it is contrary to the practice of the Representatives of other European Powers—such as the French, German, Russian, Portuguese—and American, and even the Japanese, who each and all afford the fullest measure of protection to their Chinese subjects in the open ports or the interior of China. The rule of every British Consulate throughout China appears to be to make the granting of protection to Great Britain's Chinese subjects a matter of extreme difficulty, if not of impossibility. They make irksome and, in many instances, impracticable regulations, and insist upon some stringent and almost impossible conditions. By these means they effectually block the claim of protection by the great majority, if not all, of their Chinese subjects.

" As an example, we may mention the rule of distinctive dress, where it is provided that a British Chinese subject claiming British protection must cut off his *queue* and change his long-accustomed mode of dress. What the effect of such a rule on the Chinese would be we can safely leave to your Lordship to imagine, and we need only add that no other foreign nation in China has thought it fair or wise to impose such conditions on their Chinese subjects. The excuse put forward for these unusual proceedings on the part of the Consular Authorities is the fear of international complications. But, as yet, we are not aware of any single case where serious complications have taken place, if we except the numerous troubles connected with foreign Christian missions. On the other hand, even though some insignificant international friction might be caused by extending protection to Anglicized Chinese, would that not be outweighed by the many resulting advantages to British prestige and influence? After this, your Lordship will not be surprised to learn that the Chinese in Hong Kong, or elsewhere, being British subjects, should prefer silence to healthy discussion, reserve to active participation, crafty device to manly determination, equivocal support to loyal co-operation. The close proximity to the main-land, the frequent calls of duty or pleasure to the interior, the utter corruption, and squeezing propensities of the native officials, their revengeful and arbitrary spirit, the close espionage exercised upon the natives by the Chinese Government, together with the want of protection from the British Authorities, must account for all that seemed cold and indifferent in the Chinese respecting topics of momentous and international interest.

"Notwithstanding this, however, your Lordship's important Mission to the Far East and your recent public utterances have aroused universal and intense interest among the Chinese, especially those who are residing in the open ports or under the ægis of the British flag. The policy of the 'Open Door,' so ably enunciated and advocated by you, met with their cordial approval and support, as being the only means whereby Great Britain's commerce in China can be preserved and extended, the Chinese Empire kept intact, and her tradal and political relationships with other foreign nations improved. This policy, simple and effective though it be, will, we apprehend, be opposed by the many who deem it to be national glory when a new territory is acquired and a Sphere of Influence gained, utterly disregarding the dangers and evil consequences that such acquisition may involve. We have, however, the greatest confidence in your Lordship, and we are assured that the great British public and leading statesmen will readily listen to the wise advice of one whose name is a household word, ability unsurpassed, courage indomitable, judgment unbiassed, public spirit loyal and enthusiastic, and whose discernment, aided by personal experience and observation, is true and unclouded. The issue in the hands of such an advocate will and must be successful in spite of all the opposition that may be interposed.

"We believe the active support of the United States of America, of Germany, and of Japan can well be counted on, as their interests are identical with those of Great Britain, and they cannot hope to gain any material advantage by the disintegration of China and the restriction of trade in that Empire. We are certain also that the Chinese will yet fully appreciate the manifold benefits of this 'Open Door' policy, and will do their utmost to assist in its maintenance. They cannot fail to understand that the integrity of their own country, nay, their very existence as a nation, depends upon the firm adherence to this principle. The development of their commerce, industry, and natural resources is equally dependent upon its being upheld by the strongest and freest of all nations. Besides, the Chinese people, having great aptitude and inclination for trade, have naturally at all times a particular leaning towards England, the greatest commercial nation in the universe. In addition to this, the justice and liberty that characterize the British laws and constitution, the perfect and impartial protection which Great Britain affords to all who dwell or trade under her flag (with the one exception already alluded to), make her a favorite with the Chinese, so that whenever England should give a clear indication that she will carry out the policy recommended by your Lordship, she will not find the Chinese behindhand in tendering their support and adherence.

"But what support could China give and of what

value is her adherence to this policy? Very little, indeed, we admit. As has been pointed out, she has no army or navy worth recognizing as such. She is nearly rent asunder by internal dissensions and rival factions. Her officials are the most corrupt and notoriously incompetent; her revenue is ridiculously insufficient, and already overcharged with payment of interest on foreign loans; her land is infested with rebellious bands and lawless mobs; her people are ignorant and full of prejudice and pride. All these evils, and many more which we at present forbear to enumerate, wellnigh render the carrying out of this policy on her soil a matter of impossibility, and seem to force upon the mind of every casual observer the conviction that nothing but actual partition would solve the problem of her future destiny. This, however, was never our opinion, and we are exceedingly glad that your Lordship, after careful study on the spot, is in accord with us.

"Great Britain requires in China the 'Open Door' and not a 'Sphere of Influence,' and China needs radical reform and not absorption by any foreign Power or Powers. But it is quite apparent immediate reformation must be inaugurated. Without reformation the administration of the Chinese Empire will speedily become impossible; partition will become inevitable; and Great Britain will have no choice but to join in the international scramble for 'Spheres of Influence.' It is also clear that without external aid or pressure China is unable to effect her own regeneration. For obvious reasons—personal gain and aggrandizement—those who hold high office, those who constitute her ruling class, do not desire Reform; those in humbler life, forming her masses, wish Reform, but are powerless to attain it. In this predicament we venture to think that England, having the predominant interest in China, and being the country most looked up to and trusted by the Chinese, should come forward and furnish the assistance and apply the requisite pressure. This, we are aware, may be objected to as being a too stupendous task, and beyond the strength of Great Britain; on the other hand, we believe she has the resources to enable her to undertake the work, and when we recall the magnificent successes achieved in India and in Egypt, and other parts of the world, we are confident that even greater successes will crown British effort and energy in China.

"We agree with your Lordship that China, in order to maintain her integrity and the 'Open Door,' and to protect property and capital sunk in her vast territory, must have an effective army and police; but we humbly submit that, before these desirable objects could be attained, some reform in other directions should be effected. We have not forgotten yet what became of the Ever-Victorious Army under General Gordon, or the end of the once formidable fleet under Admiral Lang. We have heard from your Lordship's own lips what ridiculous things have been done in the Arsenal at

Foochow, which has been established for a great number of years under foreign direction, and has cost the Chinese Government immense sums of money. We also remember your remarks upon the forts and magazines at Canton and elsewhere in China. Your Lordship has found, as a matter of fact, that certain sums of money set aside by the Chinese Government for particular objects were discovered to be wofully deficient after having passed through the hands of the native officials, whereas, if properly applied, these sums would have been sufficient for the purposes for which they were allocated.

" These facts, and many more, support our contention that China requires something much more urgently than an effective army and police. Supposing it is possible to furnish China to-morrow with a well-disciplined army and a perfectly organized police, we are quite certain that neither force will be maintained in an efficient state for a year and a day. China's corrupt Government and her peculating officials would starve out either or both of the forces. History will repeat itself. It has been pointed out to us that Turkey, although her Government is as bad as, if not worse than, China's, has been preserved to this day by having a good army and a passable navy, and that if we wish to maintain the integrity of the Chinese Empire a large and well-disciplined army is indispensable. But, in our opinion, something else must first be done in order to lay the permanent foundation of a truly useful army, navy, and police. If we are to have a reformation at all in China, let it be a thorough one. Let us begin at the very root. We should be very sorry indeed to see China in the position of Turkey, bad as her condition is already. Even with her army and her navy, China would be the continual 'sick man' of the Further East; she would be the bone of contention among the European Powers, the frequent cause of international dispute or even of war. She would become the scene of atrocities, massacres, and bloodshed, and the centre of the most abominable and corrupt governments. In fact, she would be, as it were, a festering sore in the sight of the civilized world. Rather than this, for humanity's sake, we would prefer to see China partitioned at once, and good government introduced by the dividing Powers. National death is preferable to national dishonor, corruption, and degeneration.

"The urgent reforms before others we would like to recommend for China's adoption are two in number: First, a system of adequate salaries to her officials; and secondly, a thorough overhaul of her system of collecting her inland revenue, her taxes, and crown rents. We recommend further that if China be unable or unwilling to undertake these absolutely necessary reforms, Great Britain, either single-handed or in conjunction with some other Power, should render China substantial assistance, and, if need be, apply firm pressure on the Central Authorities at Peking.

HONG KONG

"We earnestly assure your Lordship that from our intimate knowledge of the Chinese and the Chinese Government, their nature and their ways, it will be absolutely impossible, failing reform in these two particulars, to accomplish any improvement upon her condition; to uphold the policy of the 'Open Door'—by which we understand the maintenance of the integrity of China, the freedom of trade and commerce within her territories, without restrictive or protective tariffs, and the common participation by all foreign nations alike in all the privileges, rights, and concessions obtained by any one of them.

"Permit us, my Lord, to give you some facts in connection with the wretched pay of the Chinese officials and the evils resultant therefrom. It is well known to all of us that a high mandarin in the capital of China, of Cabinet rank, does not get by regulation any more than £50 a year as salary. In addition to this, however, he has certain allowances, which may possibly make up his whole emoluments to about £200 or £250 per annum. Upon this pittance he is expected to keep up his position, his family, his retinue, his staff, secretaries, advisers, etc., besides entertaining guests and colleagues. In point of fact, he requires from ten to twenty times the amount to meet all his expenses. A Viceroy in the provinces has a more liberal salary. He gets as his yearly official salary about £100, and allowances amounting to about £900 to £1200 more; but, unfortunately, he has to defray out of these sums all his ya-men expenses, including stationery, etc., salaries and food to his secretaries, writers, and A.D.C., his body-guards and general retinue. In addition to this, he has to entertain his innumerable guests, and send his annual tributes to the various high officials in the capital, to say nothing of supporting his high station, his numerous family and relations. As a matter of fact, to meet all his expenditure, he would require no less than £10,000 or £15,000 per annum. A General in the army or an Admiral in the navy gets less than £400 a year as salary, and out of this is supposed to pay for his own personal staff. From these high magnates downward, the Chinese officials are underpaid in the same proportion, until one gets to the lowest grade — the petty mandarins, whose official pay is scarcely better than that of a well-paid Hong Kong coolie, and the soldiers and sailors, who receive four to ten shillings a month, subject oftentimes to various unjust deductions and squeezes by their superiors.

" These generalizations will show your Lordship that such underpaid officials, both high and low, cannot help but resort to a regular system of corruption and peculation, and, in the struggle for official existence, honor and honesty are impossible. The more fortunate and less scrupulous among them amass fabulous wealth, while those endowed with a little more conscience have to be content with a mere competency, and the upright mandarin, if such has an existence, is forced to retire after a short experimental career. From this it can readily be seen why an adequate sum of money set aside by the Government for a definite object is found to be insufficient at the end, or why a sufficient sum of money having been expended, no satisfactory results can be obtained; or why a handsome amount having been paid for superior articles of modern manufacture, the most inferior and antiquated objects are bought in substitution.

"In short, your Lordship, ask any independent Chinaman you meet with, and he will tell you the same story—namely, that when a sum of money passes from the Imperial Board of Revenue successively through the various channels to its destination, like a well-known musical scale, it gradually diminishes and becomes beautifully less. With such a system in vogue, how can China expect any reform? All the mandarins in power would naturally oppose any measure for reform tending to take away their illegitimate though, under the circumstances, quite necessary gains. How can she expect her officials to refuse bribery and blackmail when proffered to them by friends or foes? How can she expect to have a true return of her revenue, and recover the seven-tenths of it which annually goes into the pockets of her officials? How can she hope to create and maintain a well-disciplined army and an adequate navy when the necessary funds set aside for these purposes are liable to diminution by successive peculations and illegal deductions? How can she inaugurate and accomplish her public works, such as the different arsenals, docks, and the embankment of the rivers, when the necessary expenditure is subject to the same unfavorable influences? How can she make a satisfactory settlement about her likin taxes in their various forms, such as loti-shui, cho-li, etc., when a great majority of her officials look to these sources to eke out their income and supplement their meagre salaries? And, finally, how can she proceed with her railways, open her mines, promote her industries and manufactures, increase her commerce, and develop her resources generally, when every official in her kingdom is bent upon making money out of the public funds and revenue, and is resorting to dishonest practices of every description to enrich himself at the expense of the State and its humble subjects.

"With the reformation of this unhappy state of officialdom in China, it will be possible for competent and honest men to enter her service and to discharge, honorably and well, the various functions intrusted to them. It will then be easy for her to commence public improvements with some hope of success. Now, as things are, the largest purse will win the day, either in the civil, military, or political arena; and such a condition will not suit, in our humble opinion, the honorable, frank, and straightforward policy of Great Britain, whereas, on the other hand, it helps the less scrupulous policy of rival Powers. Besides, the reformation in this particular direction will receive the general approval and support of the Chinese, and, we venture to think, of the Chinese officials themselves, most of whom are not without some sense of rectitude. With this reform well in hand, the way would be clear for the next. All opposition from the officials and their underlings having been overcome by the raising of their salaries, it will be easier then to put China's revenues in order.

"The revenue system of China is notoriously bad. The total revenue received into the Imperial Treasury scarcely represents three-tenths of what is levied by the officials throughout the country. A detailed analysis of the financial arrangements of China would occupy too much time and space, but we refer your Lordship to the admirable pamphlet written by Consul-General Jamieson on 'The Revenue of China,' submitted to Parliament in 1897. In this pamphlet Mr. Jamieson has not exaggerated the amount actually collected by China's officials. Rather has he under-estimated the total, and yet from his work your Lordship will learn that the revenue of China should at least be from three to four times its present amount. This fearful peculation by the Chinese officials, together with the evil habit of the Chinese authorities to 'farm' out some of the sources of revenue to minor officials or regular 'farmers,' renders the Chinese revenue system truly a formidable obstacle to the improvement of international commerce, the increase of local trade and industry, and the development of all her natural resources. Unless the financial arrangements are first reformed, it would be useless to attempt anything for the improvement and advancement of the Chinese Empire. If China could be persuaded by a little gentle pressure from Great Britain to place the collection of her inland revenue, crown rents, and taxes, in the hands of a competent establishment, somewhat after the fashion of the Imperial Maritime Customs, it would prove the salvation of China as a nation.

"We will not trouble your Lordship with the other reforms which are more or less necessary to China in her present condition, such as the training of an efficient army, navy, and police, the opening of technical and scientific schools, the placing of competent and properly trained men in charge of her Government departments requiring special and technical knowledge, the opening of all her internal waterways and towns to trade, the speedy and economical construction of her railways, and the opening of her mines, etc. But we will be content by addressing you in regard to what we consider to be the root and origin of all her political and commercial evils.

"To sum up, we would strongly urge upon your Lordship, and through you the great British public, that this is the time for prompt and decisive action in China; that the best policy for Great

HONG KONG

Britain and China alike is the 'Open Door' policy as understood by us in the sense as above described; that this policy, good and sound though it be, requires careful application and bold determination for its enforcement; that previous to, or concurrent with, the carrying out of this policy, the reorganization of China's fiscal system is absolutely essential; that Great Britain, either alone or along with other Powers, should exercise firmness in getting the Chinese Government to intrust the collection of her revenue to a collectorate similar to the Imperial Maritime Customs; that before this is done (or simultaneously) the Chinese officials, both high and low, should be assured of adequate salaries and pensions commensurate with their various positions in the Government service; that while these reforms are on the way the British Government should assist the Chinese authorities in maintaining order within her territories; and that all other reforms should gradually be introduced hereafter as occasion demands or permits.

" Before we close this letter, we would respectfully bring before your Lordship a matter of some considerable importance, although not generally recognized. We refer to what we consider to be an effective means for the extension of British interests and influence among the Chinese and the promotion of British commerce throughout the Empire of China.

" We think that there is a mighty force available for the British Government, a force which has been hitherto lying dormant and undeveloped — either willingly neglected or perhaps never dreamed of. That force is the unchallenged commercial acumen of the Chinese. By a proper system of organization and greater encouragement to British subjects of Chinese parentage, they can be made an arm of strength to Great Britain commercially, and that proud position which she has held in China can yet be maintained despite the rivalry and underhand schemes of her enemies. We humbly suggest that Britain's Chinese subjects be sent to the interior to occupy every possible source of trade and to act as commercial scouts or living channels of communication to the different Chambers of Commerce. Well organized and instructed to make inquiries within their tradal spheres or to penetrate further, if need be, into the interior or any special region, these intelligent merchants may perform wonders and help to maintain the commercial supremacy of Great Britain. It may be stated as an irrefutable fact that, wherever the goods may come from, whether Britain, Germany, France, America, or Japan, they ultimately reach the Chinese market through those Chinese merchants who know exactly what is needed and the best mode of supplying the people's wants. They act the necessary part of middle-men between the foreign merchants and the large mass of native consumers. They can visit places where Europeans would only arouse suspicion; they can extract information where foreigners would only close the natives' mouths. Where Chinese of the interior would willingly interchange views with British subjects of Chinese parentage and Chinese dress, foreigners would have to be content with vague and evasive answers given grudgingly and with circumspection.

"With the support and good-will of these British subjects of Chinese parentage, with the removal of the likin barrier and other obnoxious Customs' regulations, British goods, assisted by superior carrying powers, can supply the Chinese market, and there would be such a ramification of British commercial interests in the whole Chinese Empire that China, in its entirety, would become a complete sphere of British influence, which, as Great Britain is a nation of free-traders, may be considered as synonymous with the 'Open Door.' We are hopeful of seeing the day when Great Britain will emerge from this commercial and political conflict with untarnished lustre and unsullied glory.

"In conclusion, we beg to offer your Lordship our most sincere thanks and the thanks of all the enlightened Chinese for the personal interest and trouble you have taken in the Chinese question; for your lucid enunciation of the policy of the 'Open Door,' and for your strong support of the same, which, if maintained, would not only be beneficial to Great Britain and other nations, but would confer lasting benefit upon China herself; and, lastly, for your kind reception of this address, imperfect as it is. On your Lordship we place our implicit reliance, knowing as we do that you will champion the cause of commercial and political freedom and liberty with the most distinguished ability and success.

"We have the honor to be,
"Your Lordship's humble, obedient servants,
"Ho Kai,
"M.B., C.M., Aberdeen; M.R.C.S. England; Barrister-at-law, Lincoln's Inn; Senior Member of Legislative Council representing the Chinese.
"Weityuk, J.P.,
"Junior Member of Legislative Council representing the Chinese.
"Hong Kong, *January* 20, 1899."

This address shows the deep interest, not unmixed with anxiety, with which the great Chinese trading community view the present and future condition of their Empire. There are many points in the address worthy of comment, but I will select the following:

The statement with regard to the position of those Chinese who have become British subjects is not generally known, and, I submit, calls for the earnest attention of the Associated Chambers. It cannot add to the prestige of the British Empire, nor can it improve British trade and commerce, if

HONG KONG

this state of affairs is allowed to continue. There can be no possible reason why a Chinese who becomes a British subject should not enjoy all the privileges and advantages which are available to any other British national. Why should a Chinaman who wishes to become a British subject be compelled to submit to what he considers degrading and humiliating regulations a bit more than those other nationalities and creeds who wear the dress of their people, and who form the larger proportion of the millions who are proud to be the subjects of the Queen of England?

The Chinese merchants appear to think that the first reform necessary is to pay the Chinese authorities proper salaries. As things are at present, even if this were possible, I fear the squeezes and corruptions would not be less. The idea that a reorganized army would be as incompetent and inefficient as the present, if left to the Chinese themselves, I entirely agree with, but if organized by foreign officers with a system of public accounts, both economy and efficiency would soon take the place of extravagance and decay. No reforms, such as a proper system of collecting revenue or a better system of administration, can possibly be brought about in a country so hopelessly corrupt as China until the first and initial step is taken of giving authority to those powers which only an effective military and police can supply.

XIX

CANTON

The estimated population is 1,600,424

TRADE STATISTICS

The total value of trade in 1897 was Hk. Taels 49,934,391 (over £7,100,000).

The total tonnage of shipping entered and cleared in 1897 was 3,718,064, of which 3,000,571 was British.

On the 29th of December, 1898, I arrived at Canton. Canton is the capital of the province of Kwangtung, and is situated on the Chu-kiang or Pearl River.

At a meeting of the British merchants at Canton I was given the following Memorandum and asked to convey it to the Associated Chambers. The merchants informed me that the development of British trade and commerce in this port would be assured, provided that the disabilities from which that trade and commerce were suffering were removed.

Their Memorandum is very clear and to the point, and is here inserted:

CANTON

"CANTON, *December* 29, 1898.
" Rear-Admiral Lord Charles Beresford, C.B.:

" MY LORD,—You have been good enough to express a wish through her Majesty's Consul to receive during your visit here the views of British firms trading in Canton concerning the general course of trade, and of any disabilities, etc., from which British trade is suffering.

" The Chamber of Commerce here being a cosmopolitan body, the British merchants having their headquarters in this place, the agents of British firms represented in Canton have conferred together, and are agreed to impress upon your Lordship the desirability of—

" 1. A definition of the area of the Port. The Treaty Port of Canton was doubtless in the original Treaty intended to comprise the city of Canton and its suburbs, including the suburbs of Honan and Fa-Ti.

" However, in the Chefoo Convention drawn by Sir Thomas Wade, in Section III., Clause 1, was embodied that, subject to ratification later,

> "'The ground rented by foreigners (the so-called concessions) at the different ports be regarded as the area of exemption from likin,'

although by the additional article signed in London, 18th July, 1885, it was expressly stipulated that this should be reserved for future consideration.

"The introduction of this point, and its non-settlement, have greatly restricted the rights accorded to British subjects by the Treaty of Tientsin.

"The consumption of British goods would, no doubt, be much increased if British merchants were allowed to sell same in the city of Canton and its suburbs without likin being levied.

"Of late years a likin boat has been moored opposite the Foreign Customs shed, and likin has been levied on all goods brought there, to pay the duties regulated by Treaty.

"2. TRANSIT PASSES.—The energetic action of H.M.'s Minister, and of the Consuls acting on the spot, has done much to clear away the obstructions which the Chinese provincial authorities have raised to the free transit of goods under these passes.

"It is to be hoped that an opportunity may present itself of pressing for an open transit pass, freeing goods to any point in the two provinces, without declaration of destination.

"3. PIRACY.—The last few months piracy on the West River and its environs has been rife, and many native merchants bringing down silk, cassia, matting, and other produce from the different districts to Canton, for delivery under contract to foreign merchants, have suffered serious loss of both property and life. There is also constant delay in carriage, owing to native craft being afraid to travel at night or without escort.

CANTON

"It would be well to impress upon the Chinese Government that British subjects, and those employed by them, should be protected from such losses and from violence of this sort.

"4. FRENCH SPHERE OF INFLUENCE.—It lately been put forward in certain newspapers and other publications that the French Government have come to regard the provinces of Kwangsi and Kwangtung as already marked out, under certain eventualities, as a sphere of French influence. We, the British merchants in Canton, venture to protest most strongly against such an assumption being admitted by our Government.

"Broadly speaking, the foreign trade of these two provinces has been composed principally of British goods for many years, combined with a good percentage of German and American goods.

"As regards the exports, which are principally—

"Raw silk, waste silk, tea, cassia, essential oils of aniseed and cassia, matting, canes, etc., it may be interesting to your Lordship to know, approximately, to what a small extent France has participated in this trade in some of the principal exports given in tables attached.

"We can only consider that the claim made by the French in some quarters to the bulk of the silk trade is based on the fact that the silk is principally exported to Lyons, but the trade is not, as is shown, in French hands.

"It will be seen that, if the statement of French influence is allowed by H.M.'s Government to pass without vigorous protest, the whole of a most important export trade, and a valuable outlet for imports, might eventually come under French influence, when the trade itself is principally in the hands of British merchants. The pretensions of the French Government have no support given to them, either by the importance of their trade, which is very small, or by the number of nationals engaged in it.

"5. Preferential Duties.—Attention should be drawn to the fact that British-owned steamers have not been able to obtain their fair share of the carrying trade in this and the West River, owing to the preferential duties accorded by the native authorities to native bottoms, and it is probable that a successful carrying trade, on the newly opened West River, will not be possible until the duties are equalized.

"We have the honor to be, my Lord,
 "With the highest respect,
  "Your Lordship's
 "Most obedient humble servants,
"Dundonald & Co.
"Rowe & Co.
"Herbert Wemys.
"T. E. Griffith.
"Reiss & Co., per Fredk. Jalings.
"Jardine, Matheson & Co., per F. J. Schürch.
"Shewan, Tomes & Co., per E. M. Smith, Jr.
"P. pro Butterfield & Swire, J. R. Greaves."

CANTON

It appears extraordinary that so simple a question as a proper definition of the area of the port cannot be settled.

The question has always been an open one from the early days of the original Treaty of Nanking, and since the year 1885 it has been under consideration. As it is a matter which so directly and intimately affects the conditions of British trade, it would appear that enough time has been given for consideration and that something definite should be decided upon.

Being satisfied that the Associated Chambers would wish for full particulars on this question, I applied to the British Consul for information, and got a copy of some interesting documents, which I here insert. They show how far this matter had proceeded at the time when I left Canton. It will be observed that his Excellency the Viceroy is still anxious for further consideration on this all-important matter, although fourteen years have already been expended in this indefinite manner. Perhaps the publicity given to the question in this Report may hurry on the settlement of a point so essential to the development of Anglo-Saxon trade.

Under the existing Chinese regulations there is not a single foreign store or shop allowed in the city of Canton. The following is an explanation of an attempt on the part of the British Consul to test a case with regard to our treaty rights:

[Copy.]
From H. B. M. Minister at Peking to Consul.

"Peking, *August* 10, 1898.

"Sir,—It is scarcely necessary for me to inform you, in reply to your despatch No. 24 of June 21st, that Messrs. Banker & Co. are clearly entitled under treaty to establish a shop in the city of Canton, and in carrying on the business of such a shop, to exemption from all duties and exactions that are not authorized by treaty. As foreign goods imported into Canton are free, so long as they remain within the limits of the port, from all taxation except the tariff duty, Messrs. Banker & Co. should resist any attempt on the part of the Chinese authorities to levy likin on such goods within the Chinese city.

"If likin is levied in contravention of the treaty, or if Messrs. Banker & Co.'s business is interfered with, it will become your duty to give them every lawful assistance and to exercise the utmost vigilance in defence of treaty privileges. I am, etc.,

(Signed) "Claude M. MacDonald.
"R. W. Mansfield, Esq., H.M. Consul, Canton."

[Copy.]
From Consul to Viceroy.

"H.B.M. Consulate,
"Canton, *December* 12, 1898.

"Your Excellency,—The Treaty of Nanking in Articles II. and X. opens the city of Canton to foreign trade, and provides that foreign goods shall pay to the Imperial Maritime Customs import duty which shall free them in the port, whence they may be conveyed into the interior on payment of transit dues.

"The British firm of Banker & Co. has now petitioned that they have opened a shop in the city for the sale of piece-goods, and I have now the honor to request that your Excellency will issue instructions to your subordinates that the goods of Messrs. Banker & Co. are not to be in any way molested on their way from the steamer wharves to their city shop; nor can any duty beyond the Customs import duty be levied on these goods so long as they are in the port or city of Canton, whether while in the hands of Banker & Co. or of those who purchase goods of them.

"I have received special instructions from H.M. Minister on this subject, and should any of the officials under your jurisdiction disregard treaty rights and unlawfully detain or seek to levy likin or other charges on these goods, such officials will assuredly be held responsible for all loss or injury to business which the British merchant may sustain thereby.

"I have, etc.,
(Sd.) "R. W. Mansfield,
"H.B.M. Consul.
"To H.E. Tan,
"Viceroy of the Two Kwang Provinces."

THE BREAK-UP OF CHINA

[TRANSLATION.]

VICEROY TAN TO CONSUL MANSFIELD.

"KUANG HSU, 24y., 11m., 4d.,
"*December* 16, 1898.

"SIR,—I have the honor to acknowledge receipt of your despatch of the 12th inst., informing me that Banker & Co. had opened a shop in the city for the sale of piece-goods, and requesting me to instruct my subordinates to the effect that Banker & Co.'s goods are not to be in any way molested on their way from the steamer wharf to the city shop, nor can any duty be levied on them so long as they are in the city or port of Canton, whether while in the hands of Banker.& Co., or of those who purchase goods from them.

"In reply I have to state that the 3d section of the Chefoo Convention provides as follows:

"'With reference to the area within which, according to the treaties in force, likin ought not to be collected on foreign goods at the open ports, Sir Thomas Wade agrees to move his Government to allow the foreign concessions at the different ports to be regarded as the area of exemption from likin; and the Government of China will thereupon allow Ichang in the province of Hupei, Wuhu in Anhui, Wenchow in Chekiang, and Pakhoi in Kwangtung, to be added to the number of ports open to trade.'

"A consideration of the meaning of the wording of the above shows that, as in former treaties, there

CANTON

was no express provision with regard to the area within which foreign goods are exempt from likin, therefore Sir Thomas Wade agreed to move his Government to agree to regard the concessions at the various ports as the areas of exemption from likin, and in return China added four more treaty ports to the existing number; thus the exemption from likin only obtains within the concessions, and does not obtain without them. With regard to this point there is not the slightest doubt.

"In the present instance, the action of the British merchant, Banker, in opening a place of business in the city, is clearly not permissible according to treaty, and I must therefore request you to at once direct him to forthwith either close or remove his shop, so that complications may be avoided. This is of the utmost importance.

"I have," etc.,
(Seal of Viceroy.)

[COPY.]

CONSUL MANSFIELD TO VICEROY TAN.

"H.B.M. CONSULATE,
"CANTON, *December* 19, 1898.

"YOUR EXCELLENCY,—I have the honor to acknowledge your Excellency's despatch of the 16th inst., to the effect that the action of Banker & Co., in opening a place of business within the city, is clearly not permissible according to treaty.

"Your Excellency refers to Section III. of the Chefoo Convention, but you do not appear to be aware that an additional article to that Convention was signed on July 18, 1885, in which it is expressly stated that the section your Excellency quotes requires further consideration, and shall be reserved for further consideration between the two Governments. Until such further consideration, therefore, the Treaties of Nanking and Tientsin, which declare the city and port of Canton open to foreign trade, must be carried out in their integrity.

"I had already, before I wrote to your Excellency, referred the matter to H.H. Minister at Peking, and his reply was as follows:

"'Banker & Co. are clearly entitled, under treaty, to establish a shop in the city of Canton, and, in carrying on the business of such a shop, to exemption from all duties and exactions that are not authorized by treaty. As foreign goods imported into Canton are free, so long as they remain within the limits of the port, from all taxation except the tariff duty, Banker & Co. should resist any attempt to levy likin on such goods within the port.

"'If likin is levied in contravention of the treaty, or if Banker & Co.'s business is interfered with, it will be your duty to give them every assistance, and to exercise the utmost vigilance in defence of treaty privileges.'

"Such being my instructions, I am obliged most respectfully to inform your Excellency that I have communicated them to Banker & Co., and that any attempt to levy likin on his goods, or to interfere with his business, will oblige me to institute claims against any Chinese official who may make such an attempt.

"I have, etc.,
(Sd.) "R. W. Mansfield."

[Copy.]
From Consul to Banker & Co.

"H.B.M. Consulate,
"Canton, *December* 21, 1898.

"Sirs,—The Viceroy having replied, raising objections to your opening a shop in the city, I have again written to him that you are within treaty rights, and that I am so instructed by H.M.'s Minister.

"You are therefore at liberty to open your business as soon as you please. The business must be conducted in a perfectly *bona fide* manner, and must be confined to your own firm, and not be on behalf of Chinese unconnected with it, that there may be no ground for complaint. As long as this is the case you may rely upon me to protect your treaty rights, which are that the goods dealt in by you are free from all taxation between the steamer and your shop, and also when they have passed into the hands of your customers, so long as they remain within the city of Canton. You can give a guarantee to your customers that you will meet all claims for taxation, and you will at once report to me any attempt to seize or levy likin on them in the area I have named. I presume the authorities have the right to examine the goods, if they so desire, on the way to your shop, to prevent smuggling of opium or contraband, but should this be done in a wilfully vexatious manner, you will report to me.

"I am, etc.,
(Sd.) "R. W. Mansfield.
" Messrs. Banker & Co.,
"Hong Kong."

[Translation.]
Viceroy Tan to Consul Mansfield.

"Kuang Hsu, 24y., 11m., 11d.,
"*December* 23, 1898.

"Sir,—I have the honor to acknowledge receipt of your despatch of the 19th inst." (quoted at length) "with regard to the question of the establishment of foreign places of business within the city.

"I find that the additional article to the Chefoo Convention contains the following provision: 'As regards the arrangements proposed in Clauses 1 and 2 of Section III. of the Chefoo Agreement, it is agreed that they shall be reserved for further consideration between the two Governments.'

"Thus the additional article only provides that the arrangements shall form the subject of further consideration. It says nothing about making the original Chefoo Agreement null and void, nor does it provide that, until the arrangements shall have been finally decided on, action shall continue to be taken in accordance with the Treaty of Nanking. Therefore it naturally follows that the original Chefoo Agreement cannot be wiped out.

"Furthermore, ten years and more have elapsed since the additional article was agreed to between the British Government and the former Minister, H.E. Tseng, and I have not heard of foreign merchants opening places of business in the native cities at the various treaty ports, which is a clear proof that the original Chefoo Agreement still holds good as of yore.

"In the present instance, as our respective Governments have not yet come to a definite understanding, I cannot consent to the establishment of places of business by foreign merchants outside the concession.

"I have a further observation to make. As concessions have been established, it follows that the correct procedure is for the foreign merchants to reside and transact their business within the concessions. This facilitates their being completely protected, and Chinese and foreigners can secure the blessing of mutual peace.

"Were the foreigners to live among the natives one could never be certain that some trifling cause might not lead to a serious quarrel. In the interests of a lasting friendship between our countries, I feel it to be my duty to discuss the question thoroughly.

"I have the honor to request you, with a view to the avoidance of further complications, to direct Banker & Co., for the time being, either to remove or close the shop which they have opened in the city, and to defer further action until our Governments shall have decided upon a mode of procedure.

"I have long been familiar with your Minister's, Sir Claude MacDonald, reputation for mildness and uprightness, and I am sure that his views will coincide with mine, so I hope that you will kindly communicate my views to him.

"I have," etc.

(Seal of Viceroy.)

[COPY.]

FROM CONSUL TO VICEROY.

"H.B.M. CONSULATE,
"CANTON, *December* 29, 1898.

"YOUR EXCELLENCY,—I have the honor to acknowledge your Excellency's despatch of the 23d instant, with regard to the question of the establishment of foreign places of business within the city.

"I have the honor to observe that from the moment that it was decided between our respective Governments that Clauses 1 and 2 of Section III. of the Chefoo Agreement required further consideration, the question treated by these clauses had to remain as it was before the Chefoo Agreement was drawn up—that is, on the lines of the Nanking and Tientsin Treaties.

"As I have already observed to your Excellency, I applied to her Majesty's Minister for instructions before taking any action in Banker & Co.'s case. His instructions to me, which I have had the honor to quote, are explicit, and your Excellency knows that it is the duty of a subordinate to carry out the instructions of his superior.

"I trust that your Excellency will not therefore deem it an unfriendly act on my part if I say that I am unable to comply with your request, and that I have instructed Banker to open his shop, and act in accordance with the provisions of the former treaties. I would, on my side, ask your Excellency to give instructions that his business be not interfered with. If, when our respective Governments have further considered the question, it is agreed that the terms of Clauses 1 and 2 of Section III. of the Chefoo Convention should come into force, it will then be for me to inform Banker & Co. that their goods, while outside the British concession but within the port of Canton, are liable to payment of likin.

"I have the honor to be,
"Your Excellency's most obedient humble servant,
         (Signed)   "R. W. MANSFIELD, Consul.
"His Excellency Tan,
   "Viceroy of the Two Kwang Provinces."

The British Minister declares in clear and emphatic language that under Treaty there is a right to establish a shop in the city of Canton.

The Viceroy declares that under Treaty this right does not exist.

At Wuchow, some 100 miles up the West River, there are foreign shops in the town and suburbs because the whole place is considered an open port, there being no settlement or concession; whereas at Canton, where there are foreign concessions, only the area of such concessions counts as the open port, and immediately outside their limits likin is levied.

The merchants here were much exercised in their minds at the frequent piracies which had occurred lately on and about the West River.

I obtained from the British Consul and other sources full accounts of the piracies which actually occurred at and about the time I was in Canton. The accounts speak for themselves as to the audacity of these pests to trade and commerce. The merchants told me that at the present time piracy is worse than it has ever been known before in this locality, and is enormously on the increase in the district round Canton. Forty-one instances became public last year, but many more cases occur which never become known, owing to the terror native boatmen have of the pirate's revenge. It is causing immense delay in the delivery of goods, as Chinese in charge of cargo-boats will not travel at night.

CANTON

[COPY]

"PIRACY ON THE 'TUNG KONG' LAUNCH, FLYING THE BRITISH FLAG AT KONG MUN ON THE WEST RIVER — CONSUL'S LETTER TO HIS EXCELLENCY THE VICEROY.

"YOUR EXCELLENCY,—I have received the following petition from the Kwong-wan Steamboat Company of Hong Kong:

"On the 31st October, at about 7.10 P.M., the steam-launch *Tung Kong*, flying the British flag, and the property of the Kwong-wan Steamboat Co., Limited, was at Kong Mun in the San Ui district on the point of returning to Hong Kong. As the anchor was being weighed a number of Chinese, who had boarded the launch at Kong Mun ostensibly as passengers, terrified the master and crew by pointing fire-arms at them, and compelled them to take the launch to a place near the Ma On Shan, which is situate near a stream called Ma Kau, which is the boundary dividing Kao Tsun and Hai Chou, and also the district of Hsin Hui, from the district of Shun Te.

"When the *Tung Kong* had arrived inside the Ma Kau, three snake-boats came alongside, and from these about fifteen more pirates boarded the launch, making in all about thirty pirates on board at that time. The pirates then robbed the passengers of baggage, goods, and effects to the value of about $3000, and these things they transferred to a large cargo-boat of a kind similar to those seen at Kong-moon, and which was estimated to be between two and three hundred piculs in carrying capacity. On board this cargo-boat there appeared some fifteen more pirates, who assisted those on board the launch in transferring their booty; and, after the stolen goods had been put on board, the pirates compelled those in charge of the launch to tow the cargo-boat until about 11 P.M., at which time the launch was allowed to return. In addition to stealing the articles above mentioned, the pirates also took two revolvers, four rifles, and about four hundred cartridges, the property of the Kwong-wan Steamboat Co., and about $200 from the compradore's room. The Company also fears that the pirates intend to attempt to extort money from the owners of the launch, for at the time of the piracy one of them said: 'We know that the owners of this launch are making money, and when we send them a letter they had better obey it.'

"It is believed that Ko Chun and Hoi Chou are the resort of a large and desperate band of robbers, and I have to request that your Excellency will take vigorous steps to root them out. I have the honor to observe that during the past few years piracy and robbery by violence have increased to a very great extent in the Kwangtung waterways. Scarcely a day passes but some flagrant case of the kind occurs, and trade is thereby most seriously affected. It is difficult to avoid the conclusion that the local authorities are negligent of their duties. In the present instance a vessel bearing the British flag has been taken possession of, its captain and crew threatened with fire-arms, and some thousands of dollars' worth of property robbed. Cases of this kind in the territory of a friendly Power cannot but be detrimental to cordial relations, and I feel it my duty to report the present state of things to my Minister.

"If the magistrates of districts allow robbers to collect in bands of many tens and commit depredations with impunity, they are unfit for their position and should be removed.

"I feel sure that your Excellency, who cannot be ignorant of what is going on, will agree with me in this, and that you will lose no time in instituting a vigorous campaign against the organized piracy and robbery which are now constantly occurring.

"I have, etc.,
  (Sd.) "R. W. MANSFIELD, Consul.
"To H.E. Tan,
 "Viceroy of the Two Kwang Provinces."

[COPY.]

PIRACY ON THE KWANGTUNG WATERWAYS.

REPORT TO MINISTER.

"H.M. CONSULATE,
"CANTON, *November* 7, 1898.

"SIR,—Consul Brenan, in his Trade Report for 1897 (last paragraph), says: 'Probably never since Canton was open to foreign trade has piracy been so rife as in the year under review. The boldness of the pirates is, however, surpassed by the apathy of the provincial Government.' Since Mr. Brenan wrote this, matters have been going from bad to worse. From December last to date no less than *six* cases of piracy have been brought to the notice of this office by the Hong Kong Government, and another case has also come up where an Englishwoman, married to a Chinese, was one of the sufferers. These cases, however, form but a very small proportion of the cases that have actually occurred. I have found no less than *forty-one* cases, accounts of which have been given by the local press. In only one case of those brought to my notice, in spite of continual pressure, has any arrest been made; and matters have now reached such a pass that trade on the inland waters of the province is being very seriously interfered with.

"I have the honor to enclose copy and translation of my despatch to the Viceroy on the subject of the first case, where a launch plying between Hong Kong and Samshui under the British flag was taken possession of and looted by a gang of some forty-five persons.

"Finding that my representations on the subject generally, both verbal and in writing, are of no avail, I find myself obliged to bring the matter to your notice. The persons engaged in piracy and robbery by violence (for the offences are by no means confined to the waterways) must be very numerous, and these being emboldened by impunity, the evil cannot but increase unless some means can be found for dealing effectually with it. In my opinion, the best plan would be the special appointment of a military officer, with an adequate force, who could, in each case reported, be despatched at once to the scene of the piracy and devote all his energies to the discovery and punishment of the offenders. At the same time, to secure for him the energetic support of the District Magistrates, these officers, who are the responsible persons, should be held pecuniarily liable for the property robbed in their districts. In the present state of things, no less radical measures would be effective to put a stop to these outrages, which are having a most serious effect upon trade in Kwangtung.

"The case reported is a typical one, and represents the mode of procedure in almost every case. Actual bloodshed is rare, and it is believed that the crews of the pirated vessels are frequently in collusion with the pirates.

"I have, etc.,
(Sd.) "R. W. Mansfield,
"H.B.M. Consul.
"Her Majesty's Minister, Peking."

PIRACY AT PINGHAI, N.E. OF HONG KONG. HONG KONG LICENSED JUNK No. 5669.

Copy of Statement made by Lo Tak-fat, relative to a Piracy committed on the Hong Kong Licensed Junk No. 5669.

Lo Tak-fat states:

"I am master and one-third owner of the licensed fishing-junk No. 5669; my two partners are also on board. On December 9, 1898, we sailed from Hunghom, bound to Kit Shek Chun; on December 10th, while sailing near Ping Hoi, Kwai Sin district, about fifty miles from Hong Kong, we were attacked by two unlicensed fishing-boats, one about eighty piculs capacity, with a crew of ten to twelve men, and the other of about sixty piculs capacity, with a crew of about eight men. They started firing with muskets at us from a distance of about eighty yards off, on our starboard side, four or five men in each boat firing, and the others rowing. As they neared us we got a quantity of ballast-stones up from the hold to repel them with, having no arms or ammunition of any kind on the junk; when close alongside they threw a number of powder-bags, that exploded on board, then came on board themselves, shooting and cutting with choppers and spears all who opposed them. Two of my folks were killed by musket-balls, three were cut down with choppers and tumbled overboard, and four were wounded, one by a musket-ball in his arm, and the other three with cuts and stabs with choppers and spears. The rest of us hid under the hatches, where we were not further molested. The pirates ransacked the junk, broke open all the clothes-boxes, and took away all clothing of value, one small clock, some jewelry, two clothes-boxes, and over 100 dollars in money that was in the several boxes; clothing, money, and everything will amount to over 200 dollars. I had a good sight of their faces as they came up, and would be able to identify many of them; two or three are men of about fifty years of age, the other men from twenty to forty years old; one man has a very thin yellow face, and no teeth in front; he is about twenty-seven years of age. Most of them are opium-smokers. I saw no fishing-gear in their boats; the boats are fishing-boats. I think by their build they are craft from the village of Ngau Tau, near Ping Hoi. After they left I turned my junk, and looked for my folks who were thrown into the water. I saw no trace of them, and I think that, if not killed outright before being knocked overboard, they sank and were drowned.

"I then sailed back to Hong Kong, arriving at Hunghom about 8 P.M. on that date, where I made this report to the police, December 10, 1898."

[Copy.]

"Hunghom Police Station,
"*December* 12, 1898.

"Sir,—I have the honor to report for your information, with reference to the attached report of piracy:

"That on the 10th inst., at 9.20 P.M., Lo Tak-fat, master of fishing-junk No. 5669 H, reported to me, at this station, that his junk had been pirated in Chinese waters, and several of his crew killed and wounded. I at once telegraphed to Tsim Sha Tsui Police Station for a launch to remove the wounded to hospital. I then went on board the junk, where I found things generally as he had reported.

"No 3 Police Launch (with Inspector Kemp and Sergeant Gourlay on board) arrived soon after, and removed the dead bodies to the public mortuary and the wounded men to the Government Civil Hospital.

"I inspected the junk on the morning of the 11th inst. I found eight bullet-holes in the woodwork. These bullets had all been fired in from the starboard and stern. I also saw four or five blackened spots on the deck where powder had been exploded, and marks of scorching round the rudder-post, where some matting had caught fire. On the stern and stern-rails I found spots of blood, as if some one had been cut down and fallen over the rail. Other blood-stains that I saw on the deck on the 10th inst. had been then washed off.

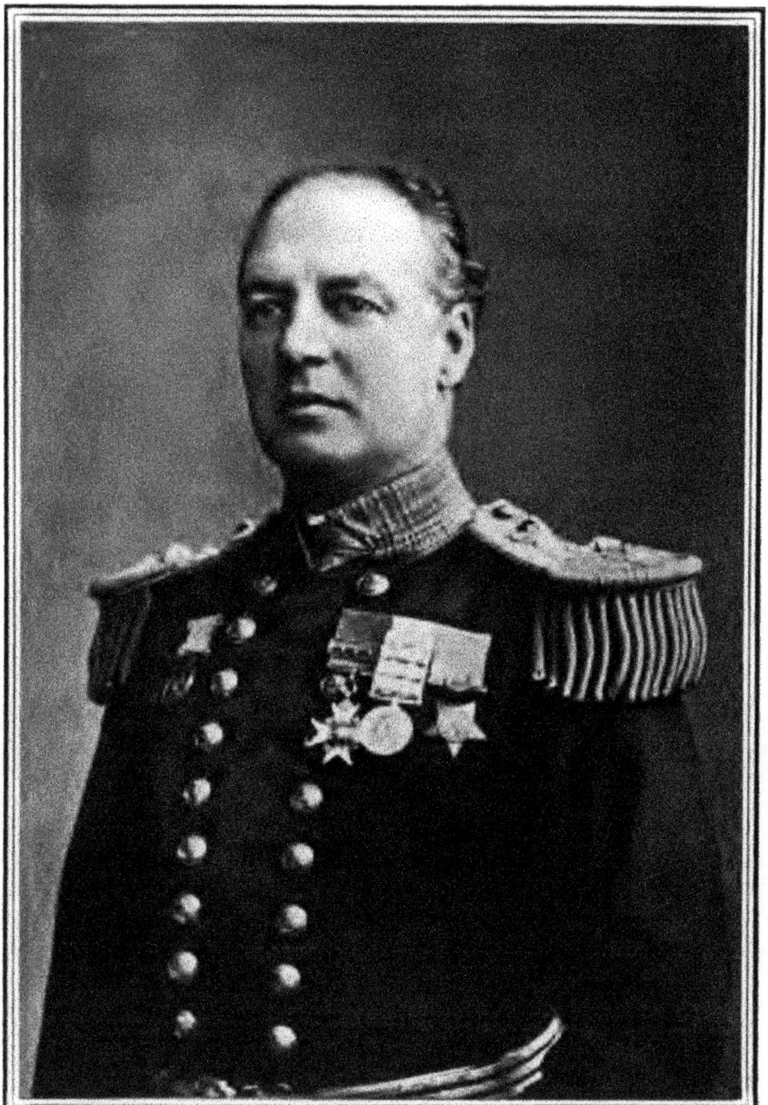

"On the deck and in the stern cabins I found five empty clothes-boxes, all of which had been forced open. When I boarded the junk on the 10th inst. I found two loaded rifles lying on the deck. These, I was informed, were left by the pirates. They are old muzzle-loaders, almost unserviceable, but appear to have been fired, probably by applying a lighted joss-stick to the powder in the nipples. I saw no other arms or any ammunition on board the junk, and there is none entered on the license. I think there is little doubt but that this is a genuine case of piracy.

"I will furnish a list of all the articles stolen, that can be described, as soon as possible.

"I have, etc.,
(Sd.) "J. GAULD, P.S. 59.
"The Honorable E. H. May, C.M.G.,
"Capt. Supt. of Police."

PIRACY ON WEST RIVER BETWEEN CANTON AND WUCHOW.

"*December* 28, 1898.

"The *Chung On* is a small Chinese steamer of about seventy tons burden, running between Canton and Wuchow. On the 28th December, 1898, she left Wuchow for Canton with passengers for various ports between there and Canton. It appears that ten pirates boarded her at Wuchow, as passengers, and at Do Sing several more came on board with some large earthen-ware jars, which they said contained food. All went well until after the pirates commenced business at Chat Par-lin. They broke the jars, and in one there were revolvers and in the other ammunition.

"The Chinese captain got hold of a pistol, and was holding it out of one of the wheel-house windows ready to shoot any one who came along, but one of the pirates crept softly round the house and grabbed the pistol before the captain was able to make use of it. The pirates then shot and mortally wounded him, and while he was lying helpless on the deck they opened his jacket and emptied all the chambers of a revolver into his stomach. After he was dead they cut off two fingers and two toes. One sailor was wounded in the shoulder by a bullet, and another man in the thigh. The pirates then took all the valuables, money, and clothes from the passengers, and left the vessel at Do Kee, a place about a mile below Yuet Sing. The passengers refused to go on to Canton, and the steamer was headed for Tak-hing. As the officials there seemed to be unable to do anything, the vessel was steered to Wuchow, where the affair was reported to the officials. That was about eleven o'clock on the night of the 29th December."

The above instances illustrate very clearly the want of security for commercial enterprises and development. There is no real security for commerce throughout the whole of China. Attention

CANTON

is called to this fact in chapter on "Chinese Armies and Navies."

The merchants were unanimous and emphatic in their protests against any such line of policy being pursued as is embodied in the expression, "Sphere of Influence." They brought to my notice the great predominance of British goods, which form the Export Trade from the provinces of Kwangsi and Kwangtung.

These tables convey much interesting instruction on this point.

RAW SILK

Season ending May 31, 1898.—1897 to 1898.

The Total Export, value Mexican Dollars, 19,417,450. Piculs 29,873 at $650 per picul was bales 37,341.

Exported	Piculs	Value Dollars	Bales	Per Cent.
English firms	18,056	11,736,400	22,570	60.45
German firms	6,182	4,018,300	7,727	20.69
French firms	5,635	3,662,750	7,044	18.86
	29,873			

English Firms does not include 1674 Piculs shipped by Parsees.

WASTE SILK

Exported English firms	...	Piculs	20,627*	77.23
" German firms	...	"	6,084	22.77
" French firms	...	"	nil	—

TEA.—Entirely in British hands.

* Not including 6775 Piculs shipped by Parsees.

THE BREAK-UP OF CHINA

Exports from Canton for 1897, to Europe and America, but not including Shipments by Parsees, which Shipments are very large.

Approximate Value Dollars	English and German	French
500,000 Pigs' Bristles	5,654 piculs	nil
400,000 Preserves	35,000 "	nil
250,000 Canes	30,000 bales	a few hundreds
650,000 Cassia	34,000 piculs	nil
50,000 Cassia Buds	875 "	nil
2,500,000 Matting	452,000 rolls	nil
900,000 Ess. Oil	2,775 piculs	unknown (from Tonquin)
400,000 Duck Feathers	26,000 "	nil
1,000,000 Fire Crackers	190,000 "	nil
6,650,000		

SILK PIECE-GOODS

British	480 cases
German	950 "
French	nil

The British merchants pointed out how detrimental a French "Sphere of Influence" over these two provinces would be to a trade which is almost entirely in their hands. They called my attention to the result of a French sphere of influence on British trade in Madagascar and Tonquin, and conjectured that a similar result would surely follow the admission of a French "Sphere of Influence" over Kwangsi and Kwangtung.

The merchants begged me to assure the Associated Chambers of Commerce that the policy of the "Open Door" and equal opportunity for the trade of all nations was absolutely essential for the continuance of British trade in the South of China. The merchants asked my opinion as to the native authorities according preferential rights to native bottoms as against British-owned steamers. I informed them that I would represent the case to the Associated Chambers.

While I was at Canton his Excellency the Viceroy Tan Chung Lin was seriously ill. His Excellency is of a great age, being over eighty-two. He paid me the honor of sending his deputy, his Excellency Kwei Yun, to call upon me and to explain how sorry he was not to be able to receive me, owing to his ill-health. The Viceroy also sent me a message by his deputy, hoping that I would let him know if there was anything that he could do to oblige me, as he knew I had come to China in the interest of Anglo-Saxon trade and commerce.

I asked the Deputy if I could see the forts, the arsenal, and the powder factory. I received in reply a message from his Excellency to say that he would be delighted, and a request that I should write him a letter, giving him my opinions concerning them. He also said he would place a man-of-war at my disposal in order that I might visit the fort in comfort and conveniently.

I had a long interview with his Excellency Kwei Yun and some other high officials as to the question of the future security and development of Anglo-Saxon trade and commerce. His Excellency Kwei Yun told me that he was not afraid of disturbances.

When I pointed out to him the extent of the damage caused to trade by the continual piracies, he said that the Viceroy intended that they should be stopped, but that it was very difficult to get hold of the real offenders, owing to the innumerable canals and waterways where they were able to conceal themselves.

I remarked that we had an adage in England, " Where there is a will there is a way." I informed his Excellency that, as these piracies were disturbing British trading interests, I should have to refer to them in my Report to the Associated Chambers of Commerce. He said he would be careful to inform the Viceroy that British traders were much concerned in the matter.

I asked his Excellency about the mineral resources of the province. His Excellency said that the province was very rich in minerals, and that the Chinese themselves were just about to open up a coal-mine near Pakhoi. On my asking him if the finances of the province were in a sounder and more satisfactory condition than other provinces which I had visited, he answered that they were sufficiently well off to meet ordinary circumstances.

In my second interview with his Excellency Kwei Yun I called attention to the continual disturbances throughout China, so fatal to the well-being of trade, and pointed out that these disturbances were common in the province of Kwangtung. I also pointed out the necessity for reorganizing the Chinese Army under foreign officers, in order to give that police security which countries trading with China have a right to expect.

I also said, if disturbances continued, and the Chinese Government were unequal to quelling them, China was certain to be broken up, as foreign Governments, in defence of their trading interests, would be compelled to take over Spheres of Influence.

His Excellency saw the point, and said he would convey my remarks to the Viceroy. I could get no opinion from his Excellency as to the necessity of reorganizing the Chinese Army. To any pointed question I asked him he invariably replied that he would speak to the Viceroy on the matter. For this reason the meeting was unsatisfactory, as his Excellency naturally could not express his opinions, the constituted authority being the Viceroy.

He declared that there were 20,000 soldiers in the province, armed with Mauser rifles, but admitted that they had never been drilled or disciplined.

XX

WUCHOW

The estimated population is 50,000

TRADE STATISTICS

The total value of trade in 1897 was Hk. Taels 1,912,711 (over £270,000).

The total tonnage of shipping entered and cleared in 1897 was 52,188, of which 41,402 was British.

WUCHOW was first opened to foreign trade by a special article of the Burmese Frontier Convention, 1897.

I had not time to visit Wuchow, but Mr. Hosie, the British Consul, kindly came down to Canton to meet me, and gave me much valuable information.

Mr. Hosie informed me that the populace are rapidly arming all round Wuchow, and that a rising might break out at any moment. He thought that if it did break out it would be a purely local rising against the Chinese authorities themselves. I asked him if such a rising would not affect trade adversely, and also if he could give me some detailed fact to report to the Associated Chambers in order to substantiate his statement. He re-

WUCHOW

plied that a rising at Wuchow broke out in 1898. There was great loss of property, and trade was stopped for two months. The southeastern part of Kwangsi, the richest part of the province, was most seriously affected, and to a great extent depopulated. This part of the province is a great rice country, and it also grows tea and cassia. There are large paper industries here. Silk and sugar are also exported. The Wuchow trade shows great promise, although the port was opened so recently as 1897, and if it were not for the constant disturbances in the neighborhood trade would be considerably developed. Since the new navigation laws came into force, in June, 1898, only one steamer of very small tonnage has started. She is used for towing; under the restrictions she is only allowed to tow between Wuchow and a spot within a few hundred yards of Samshui, which is the limit of the area of the port where she is registered—Wuchow. She is under the British flag.

Wuchow is an open port, but there is no Anglo-Saxon settlement or concession. The area exempt from likin is far larger than at Canton, where there are foreign concessions.

Mr. Hosie suggested that if a railway was constructed between Wuchow and Chungking by way of Kweiking and Kweiyang, the capitals of Kwangsi and Kweichow, respectively, goods which now take three months or more getting to Hong Kong could be delivered in four days. It would certainly avoid the gorges between Chungking and Ichang. The route proposed has not been surveyed, but I am told it presents no very great difficulties. At a time when so many concessions are being given for railways in China in order to develop trade, I think it right to bring this suggestion to the notice of the Associated Chambers of Commerce.

Mr. Hosie gave me an instance to prove that security was wanting in this part of China. He told me that on June 30, 1898, at the commencement of the trouble near Wuchow, the Chinese authorities had sent four guards for his protection at the Consulate against the rebels. On the afternoon of that date these guards ran to Mr. Hosie and said: "The rebels are coming; will you lend us your rifle?" On making inquiries, he discovered that the four guards had only one rifle between them. Mr. Hosie did not lend them his rifle.

XXI

CHINESE ARMIES AND NAVIES

In the reference I received from the President of the Associated Chambers of Commerce I was particularly asked to report " whether the organization of the Chinese civil and military administration is sufficiently complete to insure adequate protection to commercial ventures." I therefore lost no opportunity of ascertaining for the information of the Chambers of Commerce the strength, efficiency, and organization of the different forces, both naval and military. I also went to all the forts which form the coast and river defences of the Chinese Empire, and in order to find out how the forces were equipped and maintained I visited all the arsenals.

The various Viceroys gave me every facility to see all that was possible. They asked me if I would send them memoranda giving my frank opinion as to the efficiency of all I saw. As the Viceroys allowed me to see everything with a view to eliciting my opinion, it would not be proper for me to make public all that I became acquainted with, but enough will be found in the following Reports to show that no security whatever exists

THE BREAK-UP OF CHINA

for development of British trade and commerce within the Chinese Empire; and, further, that no security exists now for British trade outside the Treaty ports. I refer to that security which only can be given by effective military and police organization. It may have been observed in previous parts of this Report that the Viceroys themselves clearly gave me to understand that in the event of serious disturbances occurring they had not the means to cope with them.

No one knows the real strength of the Chinese armies, not even the Chinese Government itself.

The military forces are divided; some are Manchu, and some are Chinese. The Manchu forces are quite exclusive, no Chinese serving in their ranks; but the Chinese forces have some Manchus among them.

The armies in the North and about Peking are nearly all commanded by Manchu princes. The Manchu armies are supposed to be 170,000 strong; but there is no Manchu army efficient either in drill, discipline, or organization throughout the Empire. The Manchu force is divided and quartered in most of the big towns throughout China —such as Nanking, Hangchow, Foochow, Canton, and other places. All the Manchu armies are under the command of Manchu or Tartar generals. They have considerable privileges over and above those allowed to the Chinese. Every Manchu, whether in the army or not, is supposed to be given his rice and 3 taels a month by the

Government. If not belonging to the army, he is liable to be enrolled if required. Nobody knows the amount of Imperial taxation that is devoted to pay the Manchus. It is variously computed as from one to three millions sterling. Like other sums in the hands of the Government, most of the money finds its way into the pockets of officials and is not expended as intended. The Viceroys of the provinces have no command or authority over Manchu armies commanded by Manchu generals. The Manchu generals have considerable rights in the provinces where they are quartered over the Manchu subjects.

All the armies in the provinces are maintained at the expense of the Viceroys, with the exception of the Manchu garrisons. In the province of Chihli, General Yuan Shi Kai's army and the Imperial armies at and around Peking are maintained by the Board of Revenue out of Imperial taxes. These State-paid Imperial armies are not supposed to be sent away from the vicinity of Peking. Every soldier throughout the Empire is supposed to receive 3 taels (9s.) a month. There are different systems in every province and in every army as to pay, food, and clothing. In some armies the men are paid to feed and clothe themselves. In other armies they are fed and clothed. This matter is left entirely in the hands of the general commanding. As the generals, like all authorities in China, only have a nominal salary, they make large profits or squeezes during their command. In order to report an instance, I questioned one of those in command when in Peking. He informed me that he commanded 10,000 men. I ascertained that all he actually commanded was 800. His method is common to China. He receives the money to pay and feed and clothe 10,000 men. If his army was to be inspected, he hires coolies at 200 cash (5½*d*.) a day to appear on parade. This is well known to the inspecting officer, but he receives a *douceur* to report that he has inspected the army and has found it in perfect order.

The army is entirely a voluntary service, but when once a man has joined it, it is difficult, if not impossible, to leave it.

VISIT TO THE ARMY UNDER THE COMMAND OF GENERAL YUAN SHI KAI

On October 27, 1898, I went to Hsiao Chan to visit General Yuan Shi Kai, and to attend a review of his troops. I stayed two days and one night with the General, and during that time I not only saw all his troops paraded and manœuvred, but had ample opportunity to examine the equipment of all their arms. I also visited the stores, clothing, and provisions, made myself acquainted with the complement of each regiment, and went carefully through the monthly pay-sheets of the whole army. I have every detail connected with the establishment and maintenance of this force.

CHINESE ARMIES AND NAVIES

The strength of the army was 7400 men—mostly Shantung men. These and the Hunanese are reported to make the best soldiers in China. General Yuan Shi Kai is a Chinaman, and his army is composed of Chinese. The infantry were armed with Mauser rifles—German made. He had ten 6-gun batteries of artillery of different calibers, throwing from 1-lb. to 6-lb. projectiles. The cavalry were armed with lances and a Mauser infantry rifle. On parade the whole force appeared an exceptionally smart body of men of extremely fine physique. They were evidently well fed, and their uniforms were very serviceable and well kept. Most other armies are clothed in an ordinary Chinese dress, with a large badge sewn on in front and rear. At my request the General put them through various parade movements, and then carried out manœuvres in the surrounding country which proved to me that both officers and men were thoroughly conversant with their duties. Their discipline was excellent. With the exception of the artillery and the Maxims, all equipment was serviceable and efficient. I suggested to the General to practically test the equipment of the artillery and Maxims by galloping them over some rough ground. The result was to prove conclusively that the equipment was useless.

I found the General most energetic and intelligent, and a well-informed and well-educated man. He is also a thoroughly patriotic Chinaman, and most loyal to the dynasty. He expressed genuine anxiety as to the future of his country, and was quite of opinion that unless she undertook some measures for her own preservation nothing could save her falling to pieces. He said, now that China was weak, all Europe, while professing the most sincere good-will towards her, was seizing portions of the Empire under cover of naval and military demonstrations. I asked the General if he could make any suggestion that would be for the benefit of China, and at the same time one which European countries would assent to. The General answered that no proposal that the Chinese could make would receive the consent of the European Powers; that a Chinese would naturally make a proposition for the maintenance of the Empire, while European countries showed by their actions that they wished to split up the Empire and divide it among themselves.

The General was very sympathetic with regard to the question of reorganizing the Chinese Army as one Imperial Army, but thought that the command and the finance should be entirely in the hands of the Chinese, even if foreign officers were employed.

If all the Chinese generals were like General Yuan Shi Kai the armies and their financial arrangements would not be in the condition they are now. General Yuan Shi Kai spends the money he receives for his army as intended. He personally superintends the payment of his men's wages and the distribution of rations and clothing.

This army is the only army complete in all detail, according to European ideas, that I found in China; and for this reason I have entered thoroughly into its equipment and efficiency.

When I was at Peking there were the following armies in the neighborhood:

GENERAL SUNG'S ARMY

General Sung, who is reputed to be a very able man, but is now eighty years old, has an army supposed to be 20,000 strong scattered all along the coast about Kinchow. As a matter of fact, I could not make out that there were more than 10,000 men—5000 at Kinchow, 3000 at Chung-ho-so, and 2000 at Shanhaikwan.

They are well armed with Mauser rifles and have Krupp artillery and Maxims. Some of these men have been well drilled by German officers.

GENERAL SOON CHING'S ARMY

At Lutai there were thirty camps under General Soon Ching. A camp is a square fort supposed to accommodate 500 men. They, however, rarely contain more than 250 men, owing to the system that I have described. Of the 15,000 men said to be there, there are only between 7000 and 8000. Colonel Warranoff, belonging to the Hussars of the Russian Guard, and some Russian officers were there. They had superseded five German

THE BREAK-UP OF CHINA

officers in March, 1898, who had been instructing the men. There is no drill and very little discipline among these men.

I met one of these German officers, whose name was Schaller. I also met Colonel Warranoff.

GENERAL TUNG FU CHAN'S ARMY

There were about 10,000 Kansuh troops under General Tung Fu Chan—mostly Mohammedans—encamped a short distance from Peking. They were a most disorderly and undisciplined rabble, badly armed and undrilled, but good fighters. They had been ordered from the West, where they had been subduing a rebellion, to Peking. While I was there they assaulted and nearly killed two British engineers who were working on the line at Fungtai. They also broke the windows of the railway station and damaged some boilers and stores. Their presence was deemed so dangerous to the foreigners that the foreign Ministers demanded their withdrawal.

GENERAL NIEH'S ARMY

Between Hsiao Chan and Tientsin General Nieh had some thirty camps, containing about 13,000 men. Some of these men had been well drilled by German officers. They are well armed with Mauser rifles, artillery of mixed caliber, and Maxims, but their discipline is very lax. There were

CHINESE ARMIES AND NAVIES

five Russian instructors there. I asked for permission to visit these camps, but the Chinese officials threw every obstacle in my way.

THE PEKING FIELD FORCE

There is also a Peking field force, commanded from the Palace, of especially picked men—10,000 strong. They are quartered in the Hunting Park in Peking. They are well armed but indifferently drilled.

CAVALRY CAMP AT KAIPING

There was a cavalry camp at Kaiping, the supposed strength of which was 1500 men. Three Russian officers have superseded the German officer who was drilling these men. They are extremely short of horses.

GENERAL YI-KE-TONG'S ARMY

It is reported that there is a large army scattered about in Manchuria. Though fairly armed, they are undrilled and undisciplined. The number of this army is variously estimated at between 8000 and 15,000 men. The name of the general commanding is Yi-Ke-Tong.

MONGOLIAN CAVALRY

Besides the armies that I have enumerated, there are in Mongolia about 100,000 Mongolian cavalry.

They are excellent men, and ruled by their own princes under a system of feudal tenure. They are not paid. I was informed that they are devoted to the present dynasty.

With the exception of Yuan Shi Kai's army, all the armies above referred to have little or no firing practice, and none of them have any organization whatever for transport. It seems incredible, but some of the soldiers are still practised in shooting with bows and arrows at a target. When at Peking, I saw them practising in an open space near the Observatory. Hitting the target is a detail of minor importance; the real merit consists in the position or attitude of the bowman when discharging his shaft.

HIS EXCELLENCY THE VICEROY CHUNG CHI TUNG'S ARMY

I witnessed a review of the garrison of Wuchang. There were about 450 men and a battery of six guns. About 200 of these men were very well drilled, smart, and well dressed. They were well armed with the newest German pattern Mauser rifle. The others had not been drilled, and I was told had only lately been enlisted. The guns were drawn by men and not horses. These were 5.3 centimetre Krupp guns. The ammunition was carried by the gun's crew. The cavalry are quite inefficient in their present condition. The Viceroy has about 6000 troops scattered over his provinces, but these are the same character as the ordinary Chinese soldier—undisciplined, but fairly armed. Besides this, there are supposed to be 10,000 Manchu troops about 300 miles away, between the Tung Ting Lake and Ichang. They are under the command of a general named Ching Heng. They are undisciplined and very badly armed.

HIS EXCELLENCY THE VICEROY LIU KWEN YI'S ARMY

His Excellency the Viceroy Liu Kwen Yi is supposed to have 20,000 troops under his command. I saw about 8000 of them. They were a fine body of men; many of them of splendid physique. The majority of them were Hunan men. The infantry were armed with three different kinds of rifles, this being observable even in companies. Of the 20,000 men 10,000 would be required to garrison the forts on the river. The men were well clothed and apparently well fed, but not well drilled or disciplined.

At Kiangzin there is a garrison of 3000 men under General Li, which comprises two six-gun batteries of artillery and two squadrons of cavalry. I saw these men on parade as well as manœuvring over a country. They were a very fine lot of men, well turned out and well drilled. They had been drilled by German officers, who had left.

THE BREAK-UP OF CHINA

HIS EXCELLENCY THE VICEROY HSU YING KWEI'S ARMY

His Excellency the Viceroy Hsu Ying Kwei is supposed to have an army of some 8000 men; but these men cannot be called soldiers at all. They are mostly coolies wearing the military badge before and behind. His Excellency is commencing, however, to drill some troops, and has enlisted some fine men. I saw some 250 of them. They were in the early stages of learning their drill.

There is a small Manchu garrison at Hangchow.

HIS EXCELLENCY THE VICEROY TAU CHUNG LIN'S ARMY

His Excellency the Viceroy of Canton is supposed to have 20,000 men under his command.

Most of these are undrilled and undisciplined, and many of them unarmed. Those that I saw were the ordinary Chinese coolies.

There are some men in the forts very well turned out, disciplined, and drilled.

There is also a Manchu garrison at Canton of about 5000 men. They live in their private houses, and are entirely undrilled and undisciplined. All these troops were very badly armed, and had, apparently, no system of organization whatever. As an instance, I observed that the guard at the arsenal were armed with the old muzzle-loading Tower muskets.

CHINESE ARMIES AND NAVIES

The town of Wuchow, in this province, is garrisoned by a force of 300, totally unarmed.

HIS EXCELLENCY THE VICEROY KWEI'S ARMY

In Hunan and Szechuan the Viceroy Kwei is said to have an army of 20,000 men. They are totally undisciplined, and worthless as police, as has been evinced by their inability to put down Yu Man Tsu's rebellion, which has lasted ten years.

At Cheng-tu there is a garrison of 5000 Manchu troops, but they are like the others—undisciplined, undrilled, badly armed, and totally ineffective.

During my visit to the different armies I counted in the ranks fourteen different descriptions of rifles.

1. ⎫
2. ⎬ Different patterns of Mauser rifles.
3. ⎭
4. Martini-Henry.
5. Winchester Repeating.
6. Mannlicker.
7. Remington.
8. Peabody-Henry.
9. Sneider.
10. Enfield.
11. Tower Muskets (smooth-bore).
12. Berdan.
13. Muzzle-loading Gingal.
14. Breech-loading Gingal.

A gingal is a weapon between 9 ft. and 10 ft. long. They are different lengths in different armies; some of them are breech-loading, others muzzle-loading. Their weights vary from 40 lbs. to 60 lbs. Three men are required to handle them. When in action, the gingal is laid along the shoulders of two men, while the third man fires it.

I also saw bows and arrows.

As proof of the inefficiency of these armies to protect life and property, and to give security to trade and commerce, the following list of disturbances is appended, showing what has occurred since the beginning of 1898:

AT SHASHI

SPRING, 1898.—A serious riot in which the Customs House and the houses of Messrs. Jardine & Matheson were burned to the ground, and all the buildings and boats of foreigners set on fire. A British man-of-war had to be sent there.

AT WAICHOW

SPRING, 1898.— A general disturbance, which the Imperial troops were in no way capable of quelling. A British man-of-war had to be sent to Kiungchow.

AT CANTON

SPRING, 1898. — Disturbances occurred in the city; incendiarism and looting. Also great in-

CHINESE ARMIES AND NAVIES

crease of piracy on the West River, and its innumerable tributaries.

NEAR WUCHOW, IN KWANGSI

SUMMER, 1898.— Serious rebellion, in which many Chinese authorities lost their lives. Two cities were sacked, and 5000 troops were unable to quell it.

AT YANGCHOW

SUMMER, 1898.—A serious riot, in which launches were attacked and looted. A British man-of-war had to be sent to Chinkiang.

IN SZECHUAN

SINCE 1888.— Rebellion of Yu Man Tsu, in which many lives have been lost and property to the value of 6,000,000 taels (nearly £1,000,000 sterling) destroyed. (*See* chapter on " Hankow.")

AT HANKOW

AUTUMN, 1898.—Serious incendiary fires, in one alone of which 1000 lives were lost and £1,300,000 worth of property destroyed.

AT PEKING

AUTUMN, 1898.—A disturbance in which foreigners and members of the British and American Legations were assaulted.

THE BREAK-UP OF CHINA

AT LUKOUCHIAO (12 MILES FROM PEKING)

AUTUMN, 1898.—A serious attack was made on a party of four Englishmen by soldiers of the Kansuh Army.

NEAR TUYAN, IN KWEI-CHOW

END OF 1898.—The murder of a British missionary, Mr. Fleming. This murder was undoubtedly committed with the connivance of the authorities.

Besides these there is an open rebellion in Anhui, and disturbances reported from Shantung and Kansuh.

China, throughout her history, has been one long scene of rebellion and stern repression, but never before has authority been in so weak or so helpless a condition, the financial position of the Empire hindering the Government from maintaining a force adequate, in either numbers or efficiency, to prevent disturbances and rebellions.

I have already mentioned that some of the troops at Peking still practise shooting with bows and arrows. Many other points were brought to my notice which would be ludicrous if they were not so pitiful. The Consul at Wuchow told me that during the late riots soldiers were armed with every sort of weapon—guns, rifles, and blunderbusses. They also carried long brass horns and gongs and other instruments to make discordant noises. They patrolled the streets and the outside of the town. Many were totally unarmed, and carried only a bird-cage and a fan, being known as soldiers by their military badge.

It must not be imagined from the foregoing remarks that the Chinese would make bad soldiers. From all that I have heard and seen I believe they would make splendid soldiers if properly trained, and if fed, paid, and clothed according to their contract with the authorities. They have all the characteristics necessary to make a good soldier. They are sober, obedient, easily managed, and very quick at learning. There were many instances of heroic bravery during the Chino-Japanese War. General Ysu was found, after the battle of Yalu, surrounded with the bodies of hundreds of his own soldiers, who had died around him.

General Tso was so beloved and respected by his men that, before the battle near Newchwang, the wounded refused to remain in the hospital, and some were actually carried by their comrades to the scene of action to fight for their general. The courage and bravery of the coolies from Hong Kong who worked the scaling-ladders at the forts of Taku in 1860 will never be forgotten by the British engaged in that campaign. No just opinion of the fighting capabilities of the Chinese can be founded upon their late war with Japan. When their troops were fairly armed they had grossly incompetent leaders. When they had gallant leaders the soldiers were either badly armed or

THE BREAK-UP OF CHINA

had no ammunition. Almost every known rifle was to be found in their ranks, and before an action ammunition was served out in handfuls, with no regard to the weapon the soldier carried. These handfuls included all classes of rifle and pistol ammunition. The men are good enough, but they need capable leaders and honest administration.

THE NAVY

The Chinese Navy is divided into two squadrons—the Peyang Squadron in the North, and the Nanyang Squadron in the South.

The Peyang Squadron consists of three cruisers of 3400 tons, German built;
One torpedo cruiser, German built;
One torpedo gun-boat.
I visited these vessels.
Two armored cruisers of 4800 tons have been built and paid for.
They are still lying at Armstrong's, owing to the Chinese Government being short of money and men, and all their dockyards, except one—Foochow, which is useless—being taken by foreign Powers.
There are also four torpedo destroyers lying at Stettin under similar conditions.
The Nanyang Squadron is composed of:

Six cruisers of 3500 tons, German built;
One cruiser of 1800 tons, built in England;

CHINESE ARMIES AND NAVIES

Four old-fashioned gun-boats of 400 tons, built in England;

Four torpedo-boats, 130 feet, built in Germany—modern, and in excellent order.

I visited these vessels, and spent a week on board one of the cruisers, which was placed at my disposal by the kindness of the Viceroy of the Kiang Liang provinces, in order that I might visit the forts on the Yangtse.

The Chinese Fleet as a whole is undermanned, but there are on board many men well trained by English instructors.

Many Chinese authorities asked my advice as to the fleet. I recommended them to put what ships they had left in order for police purposes, pointing out that such vessels should be able to stop the piracies at and about Canton. I strongly recommended them not to expend any more money for naval armaments, since the work of protection which devolved upon them demanded rather a military than a naval development. In my opinion, the first thing they ought to do is to provide that security for trade and commerce which only military and police can give.

I called their attention to many cases of wasteful expenditure, and, in particular, to the fact that they had about the coast and in the river hundreds of men-of-war junks, entailing an absolutely useless outlay of money.

THE BREAK-UP OF CHINA

The Chinese have only one dock-yard left, which is at Foochow.

I ascertained the budget and visited the yard. The waste of money is appalling. There is one dry-dock capable of docking a cruiser of about 3000 tons. The wings of the dock are cracked, and I was told that the dock-yard authorities were anxious about the foundations.

Some torpedo-boats are at and about Hong Kong and Canton, but are employed under the Imperial Maritime Customs.

I recommended the Chinese to sell the cruisers at Armstrong's and the torpedo destroyers at Stettin.

REPORTED POSITION OF RUSSIAN TROOPS IN EASTERN SIBERIA AND MANCHURIA

While at Newchwang I endeavored to obtain the numbers of Russian troops in Eastern Siberia and Manchuria, as well as the localities in which they were quartered. The authorities I consulted were reliable, and had been both in Eastern Siberia and Manchuria. The appended list is a copy of the information given to me:

RUSSIAN FORCES IN EASTERN SIBERIA

HABAROVAK.
    Staff 1st Brigade Eastern Siberian Infantry of the Line;
    2 Batteries (III. and X.) Eastern Siberian Infantry of the Line;

CHINESE ARMIES AND NAVIES

2 Batteries (III. and IV.) 2d Eastern Siberian Regiment Artillery;
Staff Eastern Siberian Engineer Battalion;
2 Companies of Engineers;
2 " 1st Battalion Ussuri Railway Corps.

IMAN.
1 Company 1st Battalion Ussuri Railway Corps.

GRAP KAYA.
1 Battalion (VIII.) 1st Brigade Eastern Siberian Infantry of the line.

KAMSA RUIBOLOFF.
2 Squadrons (one only in time of peace) of Cavalry;
Battalion of Ussuri Cossacks.

ATAMANOVSKAYA.
1 Squadron 1st Battalion Prunivosk Cavalry.

AVATINO.
1 Battalion (II.) Infantry 1st Brigade Eastern Siberian Rifles;
1 Squadron (V.) 1st Regiment Cavalry Trans-Baikal Cossacks.

NIKOLSKI.
Staff of the Commander-in-Chief of the troops of Southern Ussuri;
Staff 1st Brigade Eastern Siberian Rifles;
3d Battalion (III., IV., and V.) Eastern Siberian Rifles;
Staff Ussuri Cavalry Brigade;
Staff 1st Regiment Cavalry Trans-Baikal Cossacks;
3 Squadrons (I., II., and III.) 1st Regiment Cavalry Trans-Baikal Cossacks;
Staff 1st Regiment Eastern Siberian Artillery;
4 Batteries (I., II., V., and 1st Mortar Battery);
1 Company 1st Battalion Ussuri Railway Corps.

OLLAFKA.

1 Squadron (VI.) 1st Regiment Cavalry Trans-Baikal Cossacks.

ASTRININ.

1 Battalion (1st) Infantry Brigade Eastern Siberian Fusiliers;
Staff Prunivosk Cavalry Battalion.

LADIVOSTOCK.

2 Battalions (I. and VII.) 1st Brigade Eastern Siberian Infantry of the Line;
Staff 1st Battalion Ussuri Railway Corps;

Garrison
- Staff Vladivostock Fortress;
- 5 Battalions (20 companies) Fortress Infantry;
- 6 Companies of Garrison Artillery;
- 1 Company of Garrison Engineers;
- 1 Torpedo Corps.

ARABISKE.

1 Battalion (VIII.) 2d Brigade Eastern Siberian Rifles;
1 Squadron (IV.) 1st Regiment Cavalry Trans-Baikal Cossacks.

TAVANSKAYA.

1 Battalion (V.) 1st Brigade Eastern Siberian Infantry of the Line.

OSSIET.

Staff 2d Brigade Eastern Siberian Infantry of the Line;
2 Battalions (IX. and XI.) Eastern Siberian Infantry of the Line.

OVOKIROSIK.

Staff 2d Brigade Eastern Siberian Rifles;
4 Battalions (VI., VII., IX., and X.) Eastern Siberian Rifles;

4 Batteries (III., IV., VI., and 2d Mortar Battery) 1st Regiment Eastern Siberian Artillery.

FUNTIN.
1 Squadron 2d Prunivosk Cavalry Battalion.

The ten battalions of Rifles are being reorganized. In April, 1896, their effective strength was increased by one-third, and this was again done in 1897.

I was told that a reorganization of the Cavalry has lately been effected, having for its object an increase in the number of squadrons forming each regiment. Thus to the above list five squadrons of 1st Regiment of Ussuri Cossacks have been added. They are stationed at Novokirosik.

Briefly there are some

    28,000 men at Vladivostock.
    20,000 " Nikolski, where there are 6 Generals.
    8,000 " Blagovensk.
    40,000 " Haborosk and neighborhood, with Commander-in-Chief and Headquarters and 12 Generals.
    7,000 or 8,000 men at Kirin.

About 120,000 men in Eastern Siberia and Manchuria altogether. At Newchwang there were 200 men when I was there, and I was informed that there were 40 men at a place called Liao Yang, where there is a coal-mine.

The Russians are now building three docks at Vladivostock, each big enough to take the *Rossia*, and each at a cost of nineteen to twenty millions of roubles. Also a wharf $2\frac{1}{2}$ miles long, and barracks to hold 8000 to 10,000 men.

XXII

FORTS AND ARSENALS

FORTS

By permission of the Viceroys I visited over forty of the forts and batteries which form the coast and river defence of the Chinese Empire. At all these forts I asked that the guns' crews might man the guns in order that their state of efficiency should be tested. The guns were laid and trained, and some of them were fired. Some of the forts are immensely powerful, and a few guns' crews knew how to handle the guns. Physically, the garrison artillery throughout the Empire are a splendid body of men.

The forts are armed with every conceivable sort of gun; most of the batteries with muzzle-loading guns; the modern forts with heavy modern breech-loading artillery of the best description. Many of these guns are made in the Chinese arsenals from British and German patterns.

The Viceroys asked me to write and say what I thought of their forts. This I did.

In one of these forts there was a heavy battery of 60-ton muzzle-loading guns, which were loaded by depressing the muzzle into the magazine. I

FORTS AND ARSENALS

ventured to point out to the General the danger of this proceeding, and the likelihood, through careless sponging, of the magazine being blown up.

The General congratulated me on my acumen, and immediately showed me where a magazine had exploded the year before from the same cause, and had been rebuilt for a probable repetition of this accident, which cost no less than forty-two lives.

At another fort I asked to see the powder used in the heavy guns, and was shown some powder of Chinese manufacture. I suggested that such powder was not suitable, and might burst the gun. The General in command replied, " Yes, it does; we have lately blown the breech off two 12-inch 50-ton Krupp guns, and killed and wounded thirty men." Before this conversation I had observed in a fort, some distance off, two 12-inch Krupp guns fitted with Armstrong breech mechanism, and on inquiring the reason had been informed that the breech had been blown off, owing to the use of Chinese powder at exercise. These guns had been beautifully converted at the Shanghai Arsenal.

I spent much time in viewing these forts in different parts of the Empire, and obtaining all details concerning them. I have not entered into minute particulars, as I have in regard to the armies, since the forts can have very little to do with the security of British trade and commerce in the interior of the Empire. Nor would it be courteous to those who asked me to give an opinion upon them.

ARSENALS

There are seven arsenals in the Empire of China. They are at Tientsin, Shanghai, Nanking, Hanyang (Hankow), Foochow, Canton, and Ching-tu.

I visited all these arsenals except the one at Ching-tu in Szechuan.

I made myself thoroughly acquainted with the budget allowed for each arsenal, what they were manufacturing, the number of men employed, the European countries from which they had procured their machinery and tools—in fact everything which concerned the management, equipment, and work done in these arsenals. The Viceroys, when giving me permission to visit them, asked me to write to them and say what I thought as to their management and efficiency. I did this and received very courteous letters in reply.

TIENTSIN

This arsenal is under the provincial Government of the Viceroy of Chihli. Considerable expense must have been incurred in fitting it up. The shops and sheds are excellent. There is an hydraulic press of 1200 tons, 4 cupolas which could cast up to 20 tons, and a good supply of furnaces, Siemens' process. There is also a 12-ton traveller, and a driving engine of 40-horse power, which were built at the arsenal. While I was there another driving engine of 130-horse

FORTS AND ARSENALS

power was in course of construction. The tools are very good, modern, and of British or German manufacture, and include everything necessary for the repair and maintenance of a squadron and also for the construction of small guns. I saw them making four 160-lb. pressure circular boilers. There is enough spare room in this arsenal to put up plant to supply the whole Chinese Army. There is deep water right up to the arsenal.

Mr. Stewart, a Scotsman, is in charge of this arsenal. It is wonderful what he has achieved under the difficulties of Chinese management. The arsenal is under the administration of a Chinese official, who receives 150 taels (about £21) a month. A man at home in a similar position would receive between £2000 and £3000 a year.

I have already referred to the results attending the under-payment of officials in the Chinese Empire.

With proper European management this arsenal could turn out three times the amount of work they do now for the same budget.

In this arsenal there is a mint, with two modern machines. They can, if necessary, turn out 30,000 dollars a day; when I was there they were making 15,000 dollars a day.

Close to the arsenal is a Government powder factory. It has good machinery, and is well and carefully organized by a German.

I visited the Naval School which is located here. It is in excellent order, and apparently very well managed. There were sixty students, the sons of gentlemen, between the ages of sixteen and twenty. They remain at the school for five years, and then proceed to a training-ship. As the Chinese Navy is reduced to such very small dimensions, it is difficult to say what will become of them when they have served their time in the training-ship. All these students are taught English. The Peking Government finds the budget (which is a very liberal one) for this college. The school is under Chinese management.

Next door to the Naval College there is a school for thirty Chinese students under Russian supervision. They are learning to become Russian interpreters. The Peking Government finds the money to maintain this school.

SHANGHAI

This arsenal is under the provincial Government of the Viceroy of Nanking. It is full of modern tools and machinery, stores and material of every description. Everything is extremely well found, and the arsenal is in perfect order. If properly organized under entirely European control, and with some extra expenditure, it alone could supply war material for the whole of the Naval and Military forces of the Chinese Empire. There are two Englishmen at this arsenal who act

FORTS AND ARSENALS

as advisers to the Chinese Authorities, under whose administration the arsenal is placed. Mr. Bunt is in charge of the whole of the engineering works, and Mr. Cornish is in charge of the gun-making and gun-mounting. If these gentlemen's advice was always followed, a great economy would result, and the output would be enormously increased. The Chinese Authorities informed me that they quite appreciated the invaluable services these two Englishmen have rendered to them. There is water transport to the arsenal, a small dock, and a steam purchase 60-ton shears. The whole arsenal is tram-lined. The tools and machinery are of British manufacture, supplied by a German firm. I found that this practice was common in China, and have seen the names of foreign agents stamped on British machinery. As the agent would probably make from 10 per cent. upward, I asked several of the Chinese authorities why they did not buy direct from the British firms. They explained that if anything proved unsatisfactory with the machinery they could easily obtain compensation from the agent who was in China, whereas if machinery were purchased direct from England, if anything went wrong, compensation could only be obtained after great trouble and expensive lawsuits.

There are facilities for casting up to thirty tons. To show the Associated Chambers of Commerce what this arsenal is capable of, I append the work going on when I happened to be there.

THE BREAK-UP OF CHINA

There were in hand:

Two 9.2 guns to be mounted on hydro-pneumatic disappearing carriages.
Two 9.2 guns for garrison batteries.
Eight 6" guns, Q.F.
Twelve 4.7 guns, Q.F.
Twenty 12-pounders, Q.F.
Twenty 6-pounders, Q.F.
Fifty 3-pounders, Q.F.

These guns were of the latest Armstrong pattern.

All the steel for these guns is made in the arsenal, chiefly from native ore. The gun factory does not accept this steel until it has passed through the same tests as the British Government use, and each gun is proved by the tests the British use before it leaves the arsenal.

I saw machinery for making guns of every calibre up to the 12" 50-ton gun.

Several of these last-named guns have been manufactured in the arsenal, and I saw some of them mounted in the forts I visited.

The rifle factory of this arsenal is turning out a large number of first-rate magazine rifles, latest Mauser pattern.

The cartridge factory could turn out millions of cartridges a year, and there is excellent machinery for making all the cylinders for cartridges for the heavy guns. There is also plant for casting and turning projectiles of all calibres. Many hundreds

FORTS AND ARSENALS

of thousands could be made in the course of the year.

The powder factory is making three kinds of powder—smokeless, black, and brown.

All the coal used comes from Tongshan, near Tientsin.

There is a machine designed and made here by Mr. Bunt, of a most serviceable and economic character. By means of a system of clutches the same engine can drive an hydraulic press 2000 tons pressure, or a rolling-mill which can roll a ten-inch plate.

The arsenal can manufacture steel guns of all calibres both for naval and military purposes, rifles, powder, and all classes of ammunition. Amid all this splendid work I saw the steel barrels for the useless gingals being made, incredible though it seems. Great economy could be effected in the administration. All leather equipment for the armies of the Chinese Empire is bought in Europe. If machinery were put up in the Shanghai arsenal, leather equipment could be made there easily.

In a conversation with the director of the arsenal (a Chinese mandarin), he expressed much anxiety as to what was going to become of China in the near future. He said that he hoped Great Britain would assist China to keep her integrity. I informed him that I did not think the British people would feel inclined to assist China unless China showed some signs of assisting herself.

I also pointed out to him the large and useless expenditure of money incurred by the manufacture of heavy artillery, which could have nothing to do with the maintenance of the integrity of China under present conditions; whereas if the same money was devoted to equipping a serviceable army, it would provide that security for trade and commerce which foreign nations perceived did not at present exist.

He seemed to think there was some force in these remarks.

NANKING

This arsenal is under the provincial government of the Viceroy of the Liang-kiang provinces. It is well found in machinery and tools, principally of British manufacture, but some German and some Swiss. There is no European adviser or foreman. The Chinese manager and officials did not appear to know what they were making, or why they were making it. The machinery, which is modern, and of first-class make, is entirely devoted to making obsolete and useless war material. A large number of small guns are being made throwing about a 1-lb. shell. There are, too, some 5 pr. guns being made on the Krupp pattern, but without limbers, the guns' crews being supposed to carry the ammunition. I asked the official in charge to show me how. He attempted to do this with the aid of some coolies, but soon saw its impracticability. He had never tried it before. Some of

FORTS AND ARSENALS

the machinery here was making one-inch four-barrel Nordenfeldts—an obsolete arm. The greater portion of the machinery was directed to making gingals. The Chinese authorities showed me with great delight that they have fitted a Mauser breech-loading action to some of these weapons. One of these mandarins informed me that the bullet would go through four inches of wood, and observed with some pride and satisfaction that no nation had a similar weapon. It was heart-breaking to see both officials and workmen taking pleasure and using diligence in the manufacture of costly but absolutely useless war material. They bought all their steel from Shanghai arsenal.

HANYANG (Hankow)

This arsenal is under the provincial government of the Viceroy of Hupeh and Hunan. It has a first-rate modern plant, all by German makers. I noticed a large number of modern milling machines. There is a very good rifle factory, which turned out about 8000 rifles a year, modern Mauser pattern. There is also a large gun factory which at present turns out about 200 of the small 1 pr. shell guns I have referred to on previous occasions. The work turned out in this arsenal was another instance of the terrible waste of money in manufacturing war material of no possible value. I saw heavy and expensive machinery lying about all over the yard, intended for the manufacture of 12" 50-ton guns of Krupp pattern. None of this machinery had been set up. I also saw a large quantity of machinery for a powder-mill, but this had not been set up either, and the powder required for making cartridges at this arsenal came either from Germany or the Shanghai arsenal. There was a modern rifle cartridge factory, with an excellent machine, which could turn out 10,000 cartridges a day. There was a large plant for making coke, but all the coke required for the arsenal was brought from the Tongshan colliery in the north. Besides the machinery lying about on the ground, not set up, there were plenty of machines idle.

There seemed to be no organization, and no responsible foreman. There were some Germans employed in this arsenal, and the condition of the machines and work turned out showed foreign assistance. As at other arsenals, if these foreigners were allowed control and management, the waste of money would be stopped, and the machines would be turning out war material of some utility.

FOOCHOW

This arsenal and dockyard are under the sole responsibility of the Manchu General, Tseng Chee. They have some small cupolas of about two tons, three tons, and five tons capability. There is a fair lot of machinery in this arsenal for making engines; some of it is British, but most of it is

French. There is a good boiler-shop with modern fittings, but all the boilers required were bought in France. The casting-shop was employed in casting projectiles for heavy Armstrong guns, M.L.R. From the budget allowed for this arsenal the waste appeared even greater than that in other arsenals which I visited.

CANTON

This arsenal is under the provincial Government of the Viceroy of Kwangtung and Kwangsi. An enormous mass of obsolete war material and old tools was lying about in this yard, and thousands of cast-iron spherical shot of all sizes. There were some very good modern tools of British and German make, but they were, as in other yards, employed in making 1-pr. guns and gingals.

While at this arsenal I was shown an old powder-factory, and observed it had open grating windows. On remarking to the mandarin that such want of precaution was dangerous, and it was liable to cause an explosion, he replied: "Yes, that is true; it blew up two years ago, and killed and wounded twenty men. We have rebuilt it, but do not intend to use it again."

There was a rifle-factory here turning out good rifles, Mauser pattern, but the arsenal was turning out two gingals for every rifle made. The gingals manufactured here were the longest I have seen, being 9 feet 8 inches in length. They made their own tool steel at this arsenal.

There are two small cupolas for casting. Though the machinery in this arsenal is old, it is in very good order. In the moulding shop they were making moulds for ornamental railings.

On the opposite side of the river there is a powder-factory, which had commenced work three days before I arrived. The factory is complete, and built under the most modern conditions. The boilers, engines, and shafting were made in the arsenal, and looked first rate. The factory was employed in making German smokeless powder. They hoped to turn out 90,000 lbs. in the year.

There is a cartridge factory about four miles from this powder-factory. The machinery is very good and all German. It was employed in making cartridges, Mauser rifles, and gingals.

CHING-TU

I was unable to visit the only other arsenal, that of Ching-tu, as it is far away to the west, in the province of Szechuan; but I was informed that this arsenal is under the administration of the Manchu General, and that the machinery is of German and British make, and is employed turning out rifles and cartridges, Mauser pattern.

I found in those arsenals, under entirely Chinese management, that in many cases neither the foremen nor the workmen understood the feed and speed gearing of their tools, and often the tool itself was not set to take full advantage of its cutting edge. They appeared much interested when shown how to set and gear their tools correctly.

My visits to the arsenals showed me that enormous sums of money are being expended on war material that in most cases is absolutely useless. Even the Shanghai arsenal, which turns out work second to none in Europe, is making heavy guns for men-of-war, or forts, which can be of no possible utility to the Chinese Empire under present conditions. I ventured to point this out to the Viceroys with whom I communicated.

If all the arsenals but Shanghai were closed as manufactories, and only used as depots, a very large sum of money, which is now wasted, would be saved. This sum of money would be more than ample to make Shanghai a manufacturing arsenal capable of equipping an army of 200,000 men in an efficient manner.

XXIII

RAILWAYS

The railways of China should be divided under three heads:
- I. Built.
- II. Building.
- III. Projected.

There is a very wide difference between railways built and building, and those which are only projected, as in the latter case some of the ground over which the railways are supposed to pass has not even been surveyed.

Those British lines not surveyed can scarcely be counted as commercial assets in favor of Anglo-Saxon trade, against foreign lines already in course of construction.

RAILWAYS BUILT

The only railways actually built at present are Imperial Chinese railways.

I. Peking to Tientsin, and from Tientsin to Shanhaikwan—300 miles—under the control of his Excellency Hu at the time of my visit.

RAILWAYS

II. The other from Shanghai to Woosung —about 17 miles—under control of his Excellency Shêng.

The Peking-Shanhaikwan line is a double-track line, well built and maintained, and all details connected with it are to be found in the chapter under Tongshan, as all materials, with the exception of wheels and axles, are manufactured in that place.

The Shanghai-Woosung Railway is a double track, but is not well built or maintained, although there is a daily service of trains. I have travelled by, and examined, both these lines.

The summary of the railways in the Chinese Empire is as follows:

Built: All Chinese	317 miles.
Building: Chinese	170 miles.
Belgian	700 "
Russian	1,400 "
Total	2,270
Projected (Surveyed, or being surveyed):	
Chinese	97
German	430
British	730
Anglo-American	700
Russo-Chinese	130
French	420
Total	2,507
Projected (Unsurveyed):	
Anglo-German	600
British	470
Total	1,070
Total projected	3,577 "

THE BREAK-UP OF CHINA

RAILWAYS BUILDING

The only railways building are:

    I. The Lu-Han or Peking-Hankow Railway, a trunk line of about 700 miles.

    II. The Shanhaikwan-Newchwang Railway—170 miles.

    III. The Stretensk-Vladivostock line, of which 1000 miles is in Chinese territory.

    IV. The Russian-Manchurian line, a branch from the Stretensk-Vladivostock line, to Talienwan and Port Arthur—about 400 miles.

The *Lu-Han Railway* is to run from Peking to Hankow, passing north and south through the provinces of Chihli, Honan, and Hupeh. A syndicate, capitalized by Belgian and French financiers—of whom the French subscribed £3,000,000 and the Belgian £2,000,000—have secured the concession. This railway is supposed to have great prospects, but it is a matter of opinion as to whether those of the rival (projected) Tientsin-Chinkiang line may not be better.

I visited the Lu-Han line, both in the North, where it is to join the Imperial Chinese Railway, and in the South, where it had been commenced at Hankow.

In the North there was fair activity; but in the South work had been suspended altogether, although there were about twelve miles of embankment ready for the metals.

RAILWAYS

As the Yangtse River is continually encroaching on the north bank, it appeared to me that the railway embankment was far too close to the river, and probably a large extra expense for bunding will have to be undertaken by-and-by.

This line is under the control of his Excellency Shêng, and quite distinct from the Imperial railways of North China.

The Government engineers of the Imperial railways were borrowed by his Excellency Shêng to prevent starting his line with raw hands, as he did at the southern end—*i.e.*, from Hankow.

The section under the Imperial Railway Authority is from the big bridge over the Hun Ho at Lu Kao Chiao to the city of Pao Ting Fu—eighty miles in length.

The line is being constructed for double track, but only one will be laid until another is required.

Works have been carried on very slowly, due to his Excellency Shêng using rails, etc., made at his works at Hanyang, causing great expense and delay.

At date of my visit forty-five miles of track had been laid on main line, and the ten-mile branch to the collieries and quarries west of Liu Li Ho; the remainder awaits arrival of 4000 tons of rails from England, which eventually had to be ordered to complete track to Pao Ting Fu.

I was told that traffic on the line will be inconsiderable until it extends much farther south. There has been great delay in making surveys, and the Belgian engineers for this purpose had only just arrived when I was there.

Delay was said to be due to hitch in Belgian Loan. The Americans had the reversion of this concession in the event of the Belgian Syndicate not being able to raise the money.

Traffic to Pao Ting Fu will probably be open in May, 1899, but one or two large bridges will not be completed, as girders for them may not arrive before that date

The *Shanhaikwan-Newchwang Railway* is an extension of the present Imperial Chinese Railway, and is to run from Shanhaikwan to Yingkau (the port of Newchwang), *via* Kinchow and a junction with the projected line to Sin Min Thun.

The line is in course of active construction as far as Kinchow, and will probably be open to this point in May, 1899. A British corporation financed this railway. There was some misunderstanding between the British and Russian Governments as to the security for the loan. This is fully referred to in the chapter on Newchwang.

This railway is a very valuable one, owing to it passing the new Treaty port of Ching Wang Too, which, with some expenditure of money, can be made into a mercantile port.

Further, this railway passes the extensive coalfields of Nan-Paian, and when it is extended to Sin Min Thun it will pass close to the Kwang Ning coal and iron field.

RAILWAYS

This railway is also valuable for the fact that it will, when the junction is made with Yingkau (or Newchwang), be able to carry the trade from Manchuria in the winter, which is now stopped for four or five months in the year, owing to the port of Newchwang being blocked with ice. It is generally supposed that this is a British railway, and a counterpoise to the Russian railway to the North. As a matter of fact, it is a Chinese railway, under Chinese control, protection, and administration, but a British corporation advanced the money to build it, being secured by a lien on the existing railway as far as Shanhaikwan and a guarantee from the Chinese Government.

The *Stretensk-Vladivostock Railway* is a continuation of the Russian Trans-Siberian line, and is a concession to the Russian Government by the Chinese, and built with Russian money.

This is an admittedly strategic line. I was told there was great activity being displayed in the completion of it. It is expected to be finished in from three to four years. Some considerable difficulties are being encountered with regard to the tunnels and bridges, but the line is to be in working order before these are finished. I was informed that it was to be a single-track line.

The *Russian-Manchurian Railway* is a branch of the Stretensk-Vladivostock line, coming south to Talienwan and Port Arthur.

This is a concession to the Russian Government, and is also of Russian gauge, finance, administration, construction, and protection.

It is admittedly a strategic railway, but will also be a valuable commercial line, and if the "equal-opportunity-for-all-nations" policy remains in force in the North, it will be a valuable line for the development of British trade and commerce, as it will open up a very rich country where the line of communication is bad.

When I was at Newchwang, the Russians had about 150 miles of the main line from Talienwan to the North ready for the metals, etc. The branch line to Newchwang to the main line was nearly finished. I rode along it for some considerable distance. The whole of this railway is patrolled by Cossacks. I was informed that this was to prevent the Chinese stealing the rails.

RAILWAYS PROJECTED

The railways projected are thirteen in number, and are as follows:

I. The Taiyuan Fu-Chengting Railway—130 miles.

II. The Kiao-chow-Yichow-Tsinan Railway, a triangular line joining these three places—about 430 miles.

III. The Tientsin-Chinkiang Railway—about 600 miles.

IV. The Hankow-Canton-Kowloon Railway—about 700 miles.

V. The Pekin Syndicate Railway—250 miles (not including branch lines).

VI. The Tonquin-Nanning Fu—200 miles in Chinese territory.

VII. The Langson-Nanning—100 miles.

VIII. The Pakhoi-Nanning line—120 miles.

IX. The Shanghai-Nanking Railway—180 miles.

X. The Pu-kon-Hsin-Yang Railway—270 miles.

XI. The Soochow-Hangchow-Ningpo Railway—200 miles.

XII. The Burmah Extension to Yunnan—about 300 miles.

XIII. The extension of the Shanhaikwan Railway from Kinchow to Sin Min Thun—97 miles.

The Taiyuan-Fu-Chengting Railway is a branch line from Chengting, on the Lu-Han trunk, to Taiyuan-Fu, and this concession has been granted to the Russo-Chinese bank, who have signed a contract for its construction. I was informed that there was some difficulty as to finding the money, but I should think this unlikely, as the Vicomte Breteuil, with some engineers, was surveying the proposed route while I was in China, and I believe he represents the Credit Lyonnais in France. There should be no difficulty about the money if the survey is satisfactory, as this railway, when

THE BREAK-UP OF CHINA

completed, will be one of the finest properties in China.

The Kiao-Chow-Yichow-Tsinan Railway is a triangular railway in the province of Shantung, and is a concession to the Germans. This railway is being surveyed now. A noteworthy point about it is that the Germans have determined that they shall have preferential rights, as far as railway enterprise goes, in the province of Shantung, and that both Great Britain and China have agreed to this demand.

The Tientsin Chinkiang Railway runs north to south to the east of the Lu-Han, and commercially is expected to pay better, as it runs nearer the coast. It is an Anglo-German line, and the contract has been signed, but no survey has yet been made.

The Hankow-Canton Railway runs from the Yangtse to Canton, where it is to join the *Kowloon-Canton* railway. It is an Anglo-American concession, and an extremely valuable one, as it passes through some very rich provinces, particularly the province of Hunan, which as yet is entirely closed to the foreigner.

This is supposed to be the second richest province in the whole of China. The signing of this contract was eminently satisfactory, as it brought an American and British syndicate together. The whole line is 700 miles in length, but of this 600 miles originally belonged to the American syndicate.

RAILWAYS

The Pekin Syndicate Railway is a railway to give an outlet for the enormous deposits of coal, iron, and petroleum which this British syndicate has the right of working. From all I could gather in China, the coal and iron field, if not the largest, is one of the largest mineral fields in the world. It is in the province of Shansi. This syndicate has a most valuable concession, as it also has the right to construct branch railways to connect with main lines, or with water navigation, to facilitate the transport of the Shansi coal. The nearest head of navigation giving access to the Yangtse is Siangyang, on the Han river, about 250 miles from the coal-field. The railway route is unsurveyed at present, but quite lately a large number of the best engineers procurable have gone out to report fully, not only on the railway route, but upon the coal area also.

The Tonquin-Nanning-Fu, the *Langson-Nanning*, and *Pakhoi-Nanning* railways are all intimately connected. The French contracts for these railways have been signed, and some of the routes surveyed. I heard that the French engineers had made themselves and their Annamite escort most unpopular by their rigorous treatment of the natives.

Among the mercantile communities in the south, the idea was freely expressed that none of these lines would be built, anyhow with French capital, as the French commercial communities have declared that such lines would not divert trade for

French benefit, but if built would develop British trade immensely.

The Shanghai-Nanking Railway is a British railway projected to connect Nanking with the coast. If this railway is constructed it will be a most valuable property. The contract has been signed, and part of the route has been surveyed.

The Pu-kon-Hsin-Yang Railway is a projected branch from the Shanghai-Nanking Railway from Pukon to Hsin-Yang in Honan, a distance of 270 miles. The right has merely been conceded to a British firm, but the contract has not been signed, nor has there been any survey.

The Soochow-Hanchow-Ningpo Railway.—The same British firm have the right to construct this railway. It should be a very paying line, if constructed, as it passes through very populous districts. The contract has not been signed, nor has any part of it been surveyed.

The Burmah Extension Railway is a projected British line to connect the Burmese Railway, when it reaches the frontier of China, with the capital of Yunnan. The route is supposed to be quite impracticable, but this theory is unreliable till it has been practically tested by those sent to survey the country through which the line is to pass. From what I could gather, I believe that this line will be found practicable.

The Shanhaikwan Extension is a project on the part of the Imperial Chinese Railway authorities to extend the line at present being built in two

RAILWAYS

directions, one from the proposed junction, 10 miles south of Kwangning, to Sin Min Thun, 67 miles, and from the main line to the Nan Paian collieries, 30 miles. This is a Chinese railway under Chinese control and administration. It is managed by Mr. Kinder, a British subject, and is to be financed by a British Corporation.

The line is a particularly valuable one, as it passes near the rich coal area of Kwan Ning, and has the undoubted advantage of being near the sea. It also, under present conditions, will be able to tap the great trade of Manchuria.

It was brought to my notice while in China that if railways were built connecting the following places a great development of trade might be expected.

It would appear that these routes should be surveyed.

1. A railway between Wuchow and Chungking, *via* Kweiking and Kweiyang, the capitals of Kwangsi and Kweichow respectively. If this railway could be built, goods which now take three months or more getting to Hong Kong could be delivered in four days.

2. A railway between Nanning-Fu and Chang-Sha. It would open up a very rich country if on survey this line was found to be practicable.

3. A railway between Chungking and Ching-tu in Szechuan. I was informed that

this railway would be certain to pay if found to be practicable.

In addition to these a railway has been suggested through the Chekiang and Fukien provinces, along the coast, from Hangchow to Canton. This railway has been applied for by a British syndicate.

The gauge for all railways built in China is to be 4 feet 8½ inches, with the exception of the Russian-Manchurian Railway, which is 5 feet.

It is important that railways built in China should be built to suit the people, the climate, and the country.

The costly methods in use in Europe and the rough light structures on pioneer lines in the United States are both equally inapplicable. The construction needed is somewhere between these two extremes, and more dependence must be placed on the talents and experience of those on the spot than in any account of high-class opinion or data obtainable from elsewhere.

Tariffs must be kept low, or advantage will not be taken of the railways for goods traffic, and if the fares are not low the Chinese will prefer to walk.

From inquiries I made I should think that, unless killed by initial extravagance, most lines in China can be made to pay well. The whole details connected with the expenses of running a railway in China are to be found in the chapter headed " Tongshan."

RAILWAYS

If the "Open Door" policy is maintained throughout China, the more countries who employ their capital and energy in making railways, the better it will be for British trade; but in order to secure the "Open Door" policy, it may be that we shall have to concede to other countries preferential rights, or spheres of interest, as far as railway enterprise is concerned. This we have already done with regard to Germany in Shantung and Russia in Manchuria, and the question arises, What is our position in the Yangtse Valley, where other Powers possess railway concessions? In my humble opinion, it would be better for Anglo-Saxon trade and commerce if we keep clear of "Spheres of Influence" in every shape and form, and adhere firmly to the "Open Door and Equal Opportunity" policy.

XXIV

WATERWAYS

The Waterways of China are the natural lines of communication throughout this great Empire. There are few places of importance which could not be reached by water transport. The country is irrigated by some of the most splendid rivers in the world, and intersected by a system of canals which is six hundred years old. Like everything else in China, however, the wonderfully complete system of water communication is falling into decay. The Grand Canal, one of the finest pieces of engineering in the world, and which connects North China with the Yangtse Valley, is absolutely dry in some places; but while I was at Hankow one of the Pekin Syndicate engineers arrived from the North, having travelled nearly the whole distance by the Grand Canal, and he reported that it is still navigable for many hundreds of miles.

Large sums of money are set apart for the maintenance and repair of the waterways, but very little of it is applied for its legitimate purpose. The banks are falling in through want of

WATERWAYS

bunding and proper care. The general silting up of so many of the important waterways of China causes both delay and inconvenience to trade.

Whatever improvements are made in the direction of increasing the facilities of transport by railways, the waterways should not be neglected. They are not only the principal and natural line of communication, but the cheapest mode of transport, and would materially assist the extension of foreign trade if kept in efficient order.

The principal river in China is the Yangtse River. This magnificent river is second only to one river in the world—the mighty Amazon. Its broad stream, 3000 to 3500 miles in length, taps the heart of the Chinese Empire and passes through its richest provinces, its basin extending over an area of 700,000 to 750,000 square miles. It is navigable in the flood season (the summer) for ocean-going steamers for a distance of 680 miles from the sea—viz., to Hankow, where the Han River flows into it. Beyond Hankow navigation becomes difficult, but not dangerous, and ordinary steamboats can go up to Ichang, in the province of Hupeh, a distance of 370 miles farther. It will thus be seen that this mighty artery is navigable for steamers for 1050 miles from the sea, and for another 440 miles—viz., to Chungking—it is at present navigated by large junks; the rapids above Ichang being impossible for any but shallow-draught steamers to pass. A steam-launch has, however, succeeded in getting up there;

Mr. Archibald Little, a British resident in China, being the pioneer of steam and civilization in the Yangtse gorges. Small junks go as far as Pingshan, 1750 miles from the mouth, and small native boats, I was told, go 200 miles higher still, so that for nearly 2000 miles this magnificent river is a highway of trade.

I ascended the Yangtse from Shanghai as far as Hankow, touching at the various Treaty ports on the way. The shortness of the time at my disposal rendered it impossible for me to proceed beyond Hankow, but I made full inquiries on the subject of navigation and trade above this point. One of the British pilots navigating the river between Hankow and Ichang gave me the following particulars of this part, with the names of all intermediate stations and their distances:

THE YANGTSE RIVER BETWEEN HANKOW AND ICHANG

Distance from Hankow

Hankow.	
Keun Kan	7 miles.
Kwa-ma-Chiu	19 "
Mei-tan-chu	26 "
Paechu	44 "
Han-chu-kwang	57 "
Lung-kau	75 "
Singti	93 "
Moopachin Rocks	110 "
Kinhokow	115 "

WATERWAYS

Just below here Yohchau is situated. Practically it is at the mouth of the Tung Ting Lake. Yohchau has recently been opened.

    Pagoda Village . . . . . . 128 miles.
    Sze-pa-kan . . . . 136 "

A bad place, with shifting sands. Plenty of water in summer — up to 16 feet; in winter lowest water 7 feet to 8 feet.

    Fanchi . . . . 146 miles.
    Low Point . . . . 157 "

A bad place, with shifting sands. The channel is always changing. In winter there is 6 feet to 7 feet of water.

    Shan-chi-wan . . . . 167 miles.

Just below here is Hia-chi-wan, where there is a good anchorage. It would be a good place for a coaling-station.

    Sin-ho-kan . . . . 184 miles.
    Liu-ki-kan . . . . 193 "
    Tian-hien-kan . . . . 205 "

Here is the "Salimis" bar, 6 feet to 7 feet of water; but the channels change sometimes daily.

    Sunday Island . . . . 248 miles.

A very bad place indeed. Sand always shifting; never the same channel.

    Ho-hia . . . . 261 miles.
    Tuh-kechow . . . . 274 "
    Shasze . . . . 303 "

A bad place; ever shifting channel; 6 feet to 8 feet of water.

    Broad Point . . . . 313 miles.
    Tung-Tsze . . . . 332 "

Sometimes bad; shifting sand; 6 feet to 8 feet of water.

    Grand Point . . . . 333 miles.
    Chikiang . . . . 338 "
    E-too . . . . 350 "

Rocks and shingle bottom; buoyed in winter.
Tiger Teeth . . . . 360 miles.
Ichang . . . . 370 "

There are no channel lights at night. The three steamship companies — Messrs. Jardine & Matheson, Messrs. Butterfield & Swire, and the China Merchant Company — keep permanent buoys at E-too; but otherwise each company sound every time their steamers go up or down, and then place buoys. The sand is always shifting, and in many places the bars change daily. Going up the river there may be seven or eight feet of water, coming down there may not be four feet in the same place. In summer any steamer drawing sixteen or even eighteen feet could get to Ichang, but in winter no steamer can pass up drawing more than six feet. There is plenty of water at Ichang for a big ship to lie, if once she gets there.

The famous gorges or rapids of the Yangtse lie between Ichang and Kweichow, a distance of about 146 miles. Although I had no time to visit them personally, I obtained all the information possible about them, not only from foreigners who have constantly passed through them, but also from the Chinese pilots and captains who are always traversing them in junks.

From what I could learn, they are in no way so difficult or so dangerous for steamer traffic as those on the Nile, and before many years are over the

WATERWAYS

energy and enterprise of British merchants should have cargo-steamers proceeding through these rapids. At any rate it ought to be tried.

I could not find that any British company intended to start steamers to run through the gorges, but I was informed that a German company was getting capital together and making preparations for this object. Although the question is one of open competition, both for the sake of Anglo-Saxon trade and prestige it is to be hoped that the first cargo-steamer to navigate these rapids will fly the British flag.

I went on board several of the junks used for the traffic through the gorges; they are beautifully built, of very superior workmanship, and totally unlike any other junks in China. Near the waterline they are cigar-shaped, with very high coamings on the upper deck, and every arrangement made for battening them down securely. These junks carry between fifty and sixty tons of cargo. They are very suitable for the export trade of Szechuan, as they can get down the rapids without much difficulty or danger. But steamers are urgently needed for the import trade, owing to the risk and delay incurred in getting these junks up the stream against the rapids.

The chief difficulties to be contended with are the extraordinary bends that the river takes, the speed of the stream, which, as far as I could make out, was from eight to nine knots, and the slope of the water in some of the reaches sometimes amounting to a fall of from 5 to 6 feet in 800 feet.

I have the daily rise and fall of the river at Ichang for 1897. The greatest rise in twenty-four hours was 132 inches; the greatest fall in twenty-four hours was 59 inches. These were on May 6th and 8th respectively.

I could not discover that these rapids are regarded as dangerous by those who are accustomed to them, provided proper care is taken. Junks are occasionally stove in, but as they are built with water-tight compartments they are seldom lost. The crews occasionally have to swim, but the loss of life is very small, as sanpans are used as life-boats in all the dangerous places. Damage to cargo is the most frequent cause of complaint.

I firmly believe that H.M.S. *Woodcock* could proceed up and down the rapids with perfect safety if carefully handled.

It might be possible to use these gorges for obtaining water power, as at Niagara. Electric plant might be established here, and manufactories for the treatment of tobacco and other products of this district could be started. The water power could also be used for hauling up boats on a system similar to that which I have described as being in use at Lake Biwa in Japan.

In my opinion, with a certain expenditure of money and the assistance of the brain and energy of the civil engineer, these rapids could easily be

WATERWAYS

rendered safe for cargo-steamers with a speed of not less than twelve knots.

So far as I could gather from expert opinion, at no place throughout the whole of the gorges do any great engineering difficulties exist which could not be overcome. A British engineer who quite recently passed through this district informed me that he estimated that the New Rapid could be permanently improved at a cost of £12,000. He also estimated that an expenditure of £50,000 would be more than enough to clear the rapids sufficiently to enable steamers to pass through the gorges at any time of the year. The sum seems ridiculous when compared with the advantages to be obtained by opening up steamer traffic with the rich provinces of the country beyond.

The Chinese authorities are reported to have allocated 150,000 taels (about £21,000) in trying to render the New Rapid safe for navigation.

Up till now they have not succeeded in doing much good, and the general belief is that most of the funds remained in the pockets of one of the local officials.

It was brought to my knowledge that just about the same time as I arrived in Hankow (November, 1898) the French were very active surveying for a railway in Szechuan, and their surveyors have openly declared that if the "Spheres of Influence" policy is adopted they would certainly consider Szechuan (one of the Yangtse provinces) as within their Sphere of Influence. If this claim were admitted, the British "Sphere of Influence" might end at the Tung Ting Lake, but certainly would do so at Ichang.

The French base their claim on the fact that the Chinese themselves declare that the Yangtse River proper flows out of the Tung Ting Lake, and that the Upper Yangtse is only a tributary. As a matter of fact, the Chinese hardly ever call the Yangtse by the name by which the foreigner knows it. Up to the Tung Ting Lake they generally call it the Taking, or Great River; from the Tung Ting Lake to the westward, generally called by the foreigner the Upper Yangtse, is to the Chinese known by the name of the Chingchow River.

This is a very important point: it adds one more to the international complications likely to lead to war if the "Sphere of Influence" policy is ever adopted in China. Accounts of the progress of the French survey party on the Upper Yangtse which reached me were not satisfactory. They appeared to have failed to propitiate the Chinese, and to have caused a good deal of ill-feeling against foreigners by their procedure. I submit to the Associated Chambers that British interests would be well served by keeping this part of China under British observation.

The British Government had just completed putting together a shallow-draught gunboat—H.M.S. *Woodcock*—and it was placed on the Yangtse River while I was in China. This boat was sent

WATERWAYS

out in pieces from England, and is built on the model of the shallow-draught gun-boats used lately with such great success on the Nile, and which draw less than two feet of water.

As will be seen by the account of my interviews with the Viceroys of Nanking and Wuchang, the Chinese authorities would warmly welcome British gun-boats on the waterways in order to assist the provincial Governments in securing respect and security for the foreigner.

The establishment of landing-places and coal-hulks (particularly the former) on the Yangtse and other rivers is very desirable. Hulks for bonding goods at the Treaty Ports on the rivers might assist the trader.

There is a good deal of passenger traffic on the Yangtse as well as cargo. Accommodation is provided for European passengers, but the majority of the passengers are Chinese. Fares are very low, and great numbers of the latter are carried. I inspected the Chinese accommodation on the river steamers on my passage up to Hankow. The steamers carry a large Chinese crew, and, in addition, a number of men under the supercargo. The commander and officers are all Europeans; both a Chinese and European pilot are carried. The pay of the European officers is good, and the life and work not unpleasant in a healthy climate, although malaria is rife on shore during some parts of the year.

It is perfectly possible to get from Shanghai

(which is situated on the Wangpoo, a tributary which enters the Yangtse River near its mouth) to Chinkiang through a creek to Soochow, and from Soochow, *via* the Grand Canal, without touching the Yangtse except for a distance of 5 miles. This was done by a British gentleman in June, 1898, in a steam-launch drawing 3 feet of water. I mention it to show how the whole country is traversed by waterways which only require proper attention to make them valuable and cheap channels for trade into the interior. I had ocular proof of the advisability of placing small tug-boats on the river in this locality in order to hasten the departure of junks with cargo for the canal. They usually have to wait for a fair wind. Sometimes they wait for days.

THE GRAND CANAL

The Grand Canal, the longest artificial waterway in the world, starts from Tientsin and runs south from there to Hangchow, a distance of about 600 miles. It crosses numerous rivers in its course, including the Yellow River and the Yangtse.

While at Chinkiang my attention was drawn to the Grand Canal on the south side of the Yangtse, and I saw that there was no water in it; pigs were disporting themselves in the bed, which was actually dry. It was silted up where it should join the Yangtse, simply from want of care. The canal is in this deplorable state for some eight or

WATERWAYS

nine miles south of the Yangtse for about four months out of the year, during which time it has to be entered some miles southward by means of other branches.

This illustrates one of the many thousand cases where the civil engineer is wanted in China.

If this waterway was dredged and made efficient, it would add largely to the commerce of Chinkiang and improve the lines of communication with the interior of the Empire. This question is referred to in the memorandum of the Chinkiang Chamber of Commerce. Most of the large sums of money given for the preservation of this canal are regularly peculated by the officials. The mandarin who is paid a large sum of money annually to keep the canal clear has never been south of the Yangtse River.

In the north I was informed that the Grand Canal was blocked for miles owing to the periodical floods of the Yellow River.

It would be impossible to over-estimate the importance of this canal to trade and commerce if opened up and rendered navigable.

WEST RIVER

The next most important river to trade in China is the West River, which enters the sea near Canton, and which flows through the fertile provinces of Southern China, where almost every inch of soil is cultivated.

THE BREAK-UP OF CHINA

There is a large and growing British trade between these provinces and Hong Kong, and statistical Tables showing the details of this trade are enclosed under " Hong Kong."

To merely take the figures given without any explanation would be to convey to those unacquainted with the conditions of the carrying trade of the West River an erroneous idea of the proportion which the British possess. As a matter of fact, with the exception of one small steamer of about 100 tons, flying the American flag, the whole of the carrying trade is either British or Chinese. With the inland waters open and equality of treatment accorded to all, a vast increase can be looked for, carrying with it an increase of the proportion of British vessels which will find employment; none of which would be allowed to compete if the French, under a " Spheres of Influence " policy, were allowed to claim the Two Kwang Provinces as within their sphere. The trade itself can be divided into foreign imports; exports to Hong Kong destined to foreign countries; domestic trade—*i.e.*, carriage of Chinese goods from one port in China to another; and exports of Chinese goods to Hong Kong, whence they come back into China, the object of this being to qualify such goods to go inland under transit pass.

A representative of Messrs. Jardine & Matheson had occasion last year to visit Fatshan, and on discussing various questions with the merchants at that place discovered that large quantities of

WATERWAYS

goods manufactured there and destined for Nanning-Fu still followed the old route *via* Pakhoi, into which they had been forced, as it was the line of least resistance as far as likin was concerned. Cargo *via* Pakhoi route costs $3.47 per picul to land at Nanning-Fu—likin, freight, coolie hire overland, etc., all included. To send it to Hong Kong, bring it back into China, and send it up to Nanning-Fu under transit pass, entails the payment to the I.M. Customs of two full duties and a half (that is, one duty on export, one on its return for imports, and half for transit dues), in all $2.44, which leaves a balance quite ample to cover freight, etc., by the West River route. On being asked why, if they were determined to dodge provincial taxation, they did not choose this way of doing it, which would be quicker, more direct, and presenting the additional advantage of gaining the cover of a transit pass to their goods, they quickly grasped the idea; the result has been that increasing quantities of cargo now go *via* Hong Kong. In fact, nearly the whole of the exports, and a corresponding proportion of the imports which appear in the Customs Returns for the Port of Samshui, are due to this cause. The carriers are: First, those engaged in the direct trade to Hong Kong, picking up such domestic trade as they can *en route;* second, those engaged in the domestic trade purely, such as from Canton to Wuchow. The first consist of British steamers, British sailing lorchas, or junks, one small American steamer,

THE BREAK-UP OF CHINA

and a number of junks flying no flag at all; the latter towed by Chinese steam-launches. The second consist of British steamers, one or two Chinese launches, and a large number of specially constructed Chinese junks, towed by Chinese launches; these latter are run by semi-official Chinese companies, in which likin officials are interested.

The junks referred to above as flying no flag at all require some explanation. At the opening of the West River the Customs, foreseeing the necessity of providing for craft of this nature, made the following rule:

SECTION II.—CLAUSE 1.

"Foreign-owned steam-vessels and foreign-owned vessels not being steamers, if not holding national or colonial registers, are permitted to trade on the West River under the West River certificate.

This regulation was promptly taken advantage of by the Hong Kong Chinese, who saw in it a means to avoid both the likin officials under which their craft would properly come under the Chinese flag, and the responsibility and expense which attach to the flying of a foreign flag. The West River certificate costs $100 per annum, paid to I.M. Customs. The system they adopt is as follows:

Chinese capitalists engage some foreigner, hith-

WATERWAYS

erto generally a British subject, to assume nominal ownership of certain junks which they intend to run, and usually of the bulk of the cargo carried by such junks. This foreigner communicates to the Consul and Customs at the port or ports the fact that he is the owner of these vessels; that so-and-so—naming one of the Chinese capitalists—will act as his agent; and he also, as a rule, allows his name to be placed on a sign-board outside the Chinese Hong, where his pretended agent resides. This foreign name is then used by the Chinese to transact all Customs business, take out transit passes, etc., and by assuming nominal ownership of the goods to their destination secures Consular intervention in case of likin interference *en route*. Thus it is that various foreign names figure at Wuchow and appear in the Customs books as the importers of considerable quantities of goods, whereas, in reality, they are Chinese engaged as Customs brokers under a foreign name. One difficulty of the assumed ownership system is that it enables Chinese to practise evasions of likin, necessitating the closest scrutiny on the part of the Consul of any case brought before him. At the best, it is a state of things which does not commend itself to those interested in the legitimate expansion of trade; but it has been brought into existence by the corrupt fiscal administration of Chinese officials, which drives their own nationals to seek protection under cover of a foreign name to secure equality of treatment. No doubt it will

THE BREAK-UP OF CHINA

disappear with the introduction of reform, the first step towards which will be the publication of the likin tariff on inland waters. I have referred to this in the chapter on "Trade."

The reason the British flag is not better represented on the West River, and that the junks flying no flag at all have been permitted to gain the ground they have in the carrying trade, is as follows:

Previous to the opening of the river, the likin exactions were so heavy and vexatious as to cause nearly all trade to be diverted to such routes as the Pakhoi overland to Nanning, Hanoi-Lungchow to Nanning, etc., all of which routes are inferior to the direct route by the West River. The difficulty of estimating the volume of such trade, and how much of it could be relied upon to return to its natural channel under the *régime* of the I.M. Customs, caused the large shipping companies of China to pause before investing capital in a class of boats adapted to river work, and for that work only, nor were they unsupported in their exercise of caution when such an authority as Sir Robert Hart did not anticipate that the staff of the Wuchow Customs would need to be more than a nominal one. The delay has, however, been utilized to gain experience of the needs of the trade and of the class of craft best adapted for carrying it. These are now under construction, and should be included in any estimate of the British capital employed on the West River. With regard to the

WATERWAYS

trade between Treaty ports, etc., at the opening of the river two British steamers were placed on the Canton-Wuchow line, but the differential treatment which is accorded to Chinese goods if carried in foreign steamers from port to port on the river has restricted the earnings of the British steamers above-mentioned, and also those on the direct line to Hong Kong, although in a less degree, to practically passenger traffic only.

Under such restrictions it is not to be wondered at that the shipping companies interested were slow to invest capital in the building of steamers for a trade so little likely to prove remunerative.

The practice at present prevailing at the Treaty ports with regard to the junks towed by steam-launches, is for the junk towed and her cargo to come under the likin authorities, and the launch which tows it, but carries no cargo, comes under the I.M. Customs; a dual system of control, productive of much smuggling and evading of revenue.

The merchants complain very much on the West River of the preferential rights accorded by likin officials to native craft, in which officials are interested, and also to similar rights being extended to native-owned cargo. This practice is opposed to Treaty rights.

I will summarize the points of interest about the West River trade as brought to my notice by the merchants:

1. British merchants do not possess a direct

pecuniary interest in goods to the point of destination in China.

2. That the British ship-owner does possess a direct interest, and can be relied upon, if allowed, to push his vessels to all and any parts of China where navigable waters exist.

3. That with the advent of the British ship comes establishment of genuine British firms in the interior. The reform of taxation will follow, and with it a greater sale of British goods.

4. That the ship-owner at present is under a grave and serious disadvantage, owing to the differential treatment which is accorded to *Chinese cargo* carried in junks. That it is not a matter which concerns the ship-owner only, nor is it a matter solely between the Chinese Government and its subjects; but that it is a direct tax on all steamer-borne British goods.

5. That according to the interpretation put upon the Inland Water Regulations by the I.M. Customs this state of things will not be remedied.

If the foregoing contentions be correct, it is a matter for the earnest consideration of the Associated Chambers. It appears to me that it is necessary to secure an equality of treatment for all goods, no matter how carried, as, in pushing the interests of ship-owners, merchants, and manufacturers who supply China with foreign goods will also benefit. The first step to be taken in this direction is to make the Inland Water Regulations apply to all inland waters without distinc-

WATERWAYS

tion, and to all craft and their cargoes, whether steamers or junks.

Piracy on the West River is another serious hinderance to trade. Under the chapter on Canton I give some instances of the proportions to which it has grown, and the inability of the local officials to cope with it.

The West River, like all the waterways in China, should be surveyed by foreign civil engineers, in order that some economic and effectual proposal should be made to secure the conserving of this cheap and valuable method of transport.

THE YELLOW RIVER

The Ho Han Ho, or Yellow River, is so called from the yellow deposit of mud which it brings down, and which makes even the sea of a yellow tinge for many miles from its mouth. Although less important to trade than either the West River or the Pei Ho, in length and volume it is equalled among the rivers of China only by the Yangtse.

It rises in the plains of Odontala, not far from the source of the Yangtse, and is about 3000 miles in length. After a long course among the mountains, it reaches the great plain of China, which, as a matter of fact, consists of the alluvial deposit brought down by it and other rivers in former ages. It may be said to leave the hills at a place called Kung (hsien), some 80 miles west of Tai Fong Fu, and from this point it has from time to time wandered sometimes to the northwest of Shantung, discharging into the Gulf of Pechili, and sometimes to the south of Shantung, where it was flowing at the time the first authentic map of China (1853) was made. In 1853 another of those changes took place in the course of the Yellow River which have earned for it its terrible reputation, and it then cut out for itself the present channel. The Yellow River has often been called "China's Lament," as, from the earliest history of the Empire, it has periodically broken its banks and flooded the country, causing dreadful devastation and loss of life. In our own times the floods of 1887, when the river broke its banks and caused wide-spread misery, are especially to be remembered, and from the accounts which I received while in China it would appear that the disaster of 1898 was equally terrible in its effect. Large parts of the Province of Shantung and over one-half of the Province of Honan were inundated. Millions of lives were lost and whole towns and villages were swept away. These periodical inundations, which are the scourge of the population of the basin of the Yellow River, are due to a curious fact. The river brings down many millions of tons of yellow mud yearly, and this causes the bed to rise till in some parts it is 60 feet above the level of the surrounding country. The Chinese keep building up the banks, but sooner or later the river bursts its bounds, and, after flooding the

WATERWAYS

country all around, cuts out a fresh channel for itself, which is sometimes hundreds of miles from its old bed. Then in a few years the same process is repeated. Soon after I reached Peking his Excellency Li Hung Chang was sent to investigate the causes of the late floods, and to report how they could be prevented in future. Germany has also sent engineers for the same purpose, and the Pekin Syndicate, a British corporation, has sent engineers to survey this river. I have the honor to submit to the Associated Chambers the importance of this question, as, although some of the accounts point to the impossibility of its navigation, it has yet to be proved that this is so.

From inquiries I made of engineers and others who have navigated part of this river I believe that it offers few facilities for navigation. Above Tsinan, for a distance of 250 miles, there are immense numbers of boats and a large traffic, but boats drawing only 18 inches are often ashore for hours. With care, however, boats drawing 3 feet can navigate the river from the crossing of the Grand Canal up beyond Kung at low water, while below the Grand Canal as far as Lokow, the port of Chinan, large boats can be used. Soundings at low water here vary, I am told, from 7 feet to 14 feet. Below Lokow to the bar, vessels drawing 8 feet can pass, and the bar is passable for vessels of this draught at high water. The irregular freshets, the constantly changing channel, and the swiftness of the current (the river has a fall of $13\frac{1}{2}$ inches in a mile), combined with the low depth of water on the bar, render it improbable that European steamers will ever be able to develop the trade of the surrounding country under present conditions. The alluvial plain through which it passes is the finest crop-growing country in China. It is possible that something might be done to improve this river. The cost of such improvements will be enormous; but when the benefit derived from the time and money spent on the Danube, the Mississippi, and the Irrawaddy are remembered, it would appear that the Yellow River ought not to be abandoned, especially as it is necessary to prevent the inundations which recur so frequently with such terrible effects.

THE WANGPOO

The Wangpoo River is a tributary of the Yangtse, and is chiefly important owing to the fact that the chief Treaty port of China, Shanghai, stands upon it. The great difficulty of this river is the Woosung bar.

As nearly 8,000,000 tons of shipping entered and cleared at Shanghai in 1897, the urgency of something being done to improve this bar is apparent. Passengers and cargo often have to travel some fifty miles up the river to Shanghai in steam-launches and barges. It has been suggested that the nature of the silt would render it possible for a channel to be cut, which the current would probably keep open, although the bar would possibly extend farther than it does now, owing to the silt carried through the channel depositing itself on either side.

The Chamber of Commerce at Shanghai, composed of all nationals, were extremely urgent in their representations that something should be done. As they very justly pointed out, if the large fees collected from foreign shipping were used properly they would allow of conservancy charges being met. The remedy asked for by the merchants is the establishment of a proper Conservancy Board, with European representation upon it.

THE PEI HO RIVER

The Pei Ho River is the most northern river in China proper. On its banks stands the important Treaty port of Tientsin, with a total tonnage of over 1,300,000. Here, again, there is a troublesome bar. Large sums of money have been spent upon its improvement by the Chinese authorities, but without success.

The difficulties are twofold. The river overflows its bank, and also makes a bar by depositing mud. Some years ago a French engineer undertook to remedy the inundations, and constructed canals to take off the surplus water. An unfortunate error was made. The level of the locks was placed below the level of the water at flood. The result was that all the clear water flows away over the top of the locks and only the sediment goes down to the sea to be deposited on the bar. In flood the freshet is of no use for the purpose of cleaning the river.

The Anglo-Saxon and other foreign merchants here took the matter into their own hands and bestirred themselves so well that the Viceroy of Chihli offered 100,000 taels towards the 250,000 which an English engineer estimated would be the cost of deepening the river. This offer was made on condition that the foreign community should contribute the 150,000 taels remaining.

The Municipal Council at Tientsin Foreign Settlement raised a loan for this amount at six per cent., issuing bonds for the money to the Hong Kong and Shanghai Bank who negotiated them. In order to provide the interest on this loan and repay the capital in twelve years, the Municipal Council, with the consent of the Chinese authorities, will levy wharfage on all goods landed at the settlement. It is hoped that the expenditure of this 250,000 taels will permanently improve the river; but if not, there is a proposal to ask the authorities that Tongku, at the mouth of the river, be made a Treaty port.

THE LIAO RIVER

The Liao River flows through Northern Manchuria. Some distance up the river stands the important port of Newchwang, which is generally called Yingkau by the Chinese. At the time of my visit there was probably an increase of shipping, owing to the winter being so close at hand. The change in temperature is very sudden, and the port often closes in twenty-four hours, owing to ice. I counted twenty steamers and 2000 junks while coming down the river. The *E. Sang*, the vessel I was travelling by, touched the bar going out, but did not stick. A vessel coming in was less fortunate, and we left her on the bar waiting for the next tide.

The river has a curious bend above the port, and while it has gradually washed away all but a few hundred yards of the British concessions on the right bank, it deposits mud in the bend on the left bank. The new British and Japanese concessions are on this new land in the bend of the river. The Russian concession is higher up the river, and is situated on the extreme apex of the bend.

THE HAN RIVER

The Han River is a tributary of the Yangtse, which it enters at Hankow. It is navigable for the largest Chinese junks for about ten months in the year as far as Laohoken. There is no steamer traffic on it whatever, owing to the fact that there is no open port upon it. In January and February the water is very low, less than 5 feet. The two most important towns situated on it are Laohoken and Siangyang. The former is a

THE BREAK-UP OF CHINA

very big place. Siangyang is connected by telegraph to Hankow. Between Hankow and Siangyang there is a big " bore " which runs from 4 feet to 12 feet in height. It formerly caused enormous loss of life and property. This " bore " is active between the middle of March and the middle of June. A 12-feet " bore " takes eight hours between Hankow and Siangyang—a distance of about 160 miles. A 4-feet " bore " takes much longer. Now telegraphic communication is sent to Siangyang, and the junks get due warning of the approach of the " bore."

I was only able to go a short distance up the Han River in a steam-launch, as my time was short.

Many of the smaller rivers in China are silting up; and several cities, at one time of great importance, have lost their water communication and are now places of little note. For instance, at Haikwan there was formerly a great cotton trade, but now the growers have had to reduce their crop. Hwangpi is another town that has suffered from a similar reason. The silt in nearly all the rivers is very light, and could be easily dredged with dredges similar to those used on the Mersey. I believe there is also a special dredger used for work where the silt is always in motion. There used to be one of this character used on the Thames. Similar dredges would be very useful on Chinese rivers. Many of the rivers pass through gold districts. I heard that gold was found both up the Yangtse and the Liao rivers. Gold dust is also brought down the Yuen River (which runs into the Tung Ting Lake) in fairly large quantities. Prospectors might direct their attention to these rivers.

TUNG TING LAKE AND SIANG RIVER

In dealing with the waterways of China it is impossible to overlook the Tung Ting Lake and Siang River. Although I was unable to visit either of these, from what I could learn the lake is gradually getting shallower. The position of this lake, and its connection with the Great Yangtse, which flows through it, and with the Siang River, which runs into it from the south, renders it an important inland water. At the opening of the lake is the port of Yohchau, which has lately been open to foreign trade.

The Siang River comes from the south of Changsha, which is an important city in Hunan. It seems very desirable that this town should be opened up to foreign trade.

Between Changsha and Siangtang the Siang River is half a mile wide. Hunan, the province through which it flows, is the most anti-foreign in China, and probably the least known to the foreigner. Its capabilities are said to be enormous. The universal opinion is that it is very rich in minerals. The new inland navigation rules, by opening up the Siang River and the Tung Ting Lake, should add to foreign trade very considerably.

THE POYANG LAKE

The Poyang Lake is of some considerable importance to Chinkiang and other ports on the Yangtse River, with which there is direct communication. Since the new navigation rules, six British-owned steam-launches have been sent from Chinkiang, and there is every likelihood that this venture will be a very successful one.

ROADS

There are said to be 20,000 miles of roads in China, nearly all of which were made in the reign of a former emperor. I visited Peking about thirty years ago. On my return visit last year I found it unchanged, except that it was thirty times dirtier, the smells thirty times more insufferable, and the roads thirty years the worse for wear. A mule was drowned in a hole in the middle of the roadway opposite one of the Foreign Legations a few weeks before my arrival. China has a very good system of roads in spite of their bad condition. All that is required is to make the so-called roads available for locomotion and transport. The caravan and trade routes all require good roads to be made upon them, and among the reforms I have suggested in my concluding observations, a

WATERWAYS

Department for Roads and Waterways will be found included. The roads might be placed under the proposed Conservancy Board of the Waterways. In Egypt the making and maintenance of the roads have been undertaken by the irrigation officers with the greatest success.

Large sums of money are put apart for repair and maintenance of the roads in Peking, but it is only the officials who know where the money goes to. A Mandarin gets a high salary, and a large budget is allowed him for lighting the Peking roads. I was informed there are only six oil-lamps that represent this outlay, but I could not ascertain their locality.

XXV

THE BRITISH CONSUL IN CHINA

THE British Consul in China is, as a rule, hard-working, painstaking, and devoted to the interests of his nationals; but throughout China I was struck by the strong sentiments expressed by the British commercial community on the subject of the Consular Body. In my humble opinion, the British merchant is too harsh in his judgment on this question; but it is only fair to add that nearly all the merchants and Chambers of Commerce with whom I conferred on this subject readily admitted that the faults which existed were due more to the system than to the Consuls themselves. However, the Consular Body, like any other public officials, are accustomed to receive all the blame when things go badly, while their Government appropriates all the credit if affairs go well. They will readily understand that in drawing attention to the facts which were brought to my notice it is not my intention to blame individuals, but to show where improvements in the present system are possible.

The complaints made by the mercantile community may be tabulated as follows:

1. That the Consuls are diplomatic agents more than representatives of trade and commerce.
2. That under the present system they are not, except in a few cases, good business men.
3. That the Consuls of other nations do more for their nationals, particularly in the matter of promoting trade, by introducing commercial men to Chinese officials.
4. That in the matter of transit passes and other facilities for trade, the British national receives less privileges from his Consular officer than any other foreigner in China, and that all fees charged by the British Government are higher than by other countries.

Although the Consuls deserve every support and consideration in their difficult duties, it is well to remember how very important it is, in the interests of trade and commerce, that everything should be done to secure to the British merchant in China that assistance and support to which he is justly entitled. I talked over these complaints both with the Consuls themselves and with the Imperial Chinese Customs authorities, who naturally have a good deal to do with the Consular Body, and I am bound to state that the Consuls admitted there were defects in the present system, and that the Customs authorities appeared to support the views of the British merchants.

The first complaint, that the duties of the Consuls are more diplomatic than commercial, is quite true; but is easily explained. In countries like China extra-territorial rights are conceded by the native Government to all foreigners. In other words, no foreign subject can be tried and punished by the native tribunals, but is subject to the law as administered by his own authorities. The result is that the British Consul in China is not only a representative of the British Government, to protect British trade, but he is also a member of the Diplomatic Corps, and is the representative of his Government (acting through the British Minister) in all political questions in his district. The ordinary Consul in an European port is merely a British trade agent; but in China he is something more than this. He may be the representative of the British Government in an area as large as France or Germany, and the native population in his district may be as widely separated in language from the rest of China as the inhabitants of one European country are from the inhabitants of another country.

The duties of the British Consul in China do not end here. He exercises all the authority of a judge in both civil and criminal cases, and is expected to have some knowledge of English and Chinese law, although he is never given any facilities for acquiring such knowledge. He also exercises a general supervision over the British community and possesses considerable power over them. He is bound to register every British subject in his area of jurisdiction once a year. He registers all sales and purchases of land by his nationals, and no marriage is legal without his aid.

It is quite impossible under the present system to avoid making the work of the Consular Body diplomatic as well as commercial, and the consequence is that the commercial duties are bound to suffer. The merchants have, therefore, a legitimate ground of complaint on this head.

A COMMERCIAL ATTACHÉ WANTED

The remedy which I would suggest to the Associated Chambers of Commerce is that a commercial attaché, with a proper Intelligence Department, should be appointed for China, and that assistant judges, police magistrates, etc., should be appointed, so as to relieve the Consular Body of part of their work. These latter should have a legal training. Very few Consuls possess a legal training, and when they do it is only because they are energetic, brilliant men, who have studied law at their own expense while on leave at home.

With regard to the commercial attaché, this is a point which has long been pressed by the China Association and British merchants in China. It is more needed, perhaps, than in any other country. It may be said that a commercial attaché has been appointed, but the so-called appointment has been only a farce.

What the merchants asked for was the creation of a distinct office; to be filled by a qualified man, with a sound business training and of sufficient position and ability to make the Chinese authorities treat him with respect, and his representations with prompt attention and consideration.

In order to meet their wishes, the appointment was offered to one of our best Consuls in China, but at a lower salary and allowances than he is already receiving. Very naturally he declined this generous offer; and to make matters more ludicrous, the title of "commercial attaché" was added to the office of Consul-General at Shanghai, with a salary of one hundred pounds a year. This was merely adding an impossible task to the already over-burdened work of the Consul-General, and making him a present of a hundred pounds a year for work which he could not perform. The merchants generally made one special point as to the appointment, and that was that they would prefer not to have a Consul appointed unless a man of high standing, whom they could have confidence in, of which there are several in China. They were of opinion that he should have a special business training.

The second complaint, that the Consuls—with few exceptions—are not good business men, is perfectly true. This again, however, is the fault of the system rather than of the men themselves. There are some notable exceptions. The Consu-

THE BRITISH CONSUL IN CHINA

lar Body is selected by open competitive examinations among mere lads. The examinations are usually held twice a year. The young gentlemen who succeed are sent straight out to China and go up to Peking, where they are shut up for two years grinding at the official Chinese dialect. They are then sent direct to one of the smaller ports of China as assistants in the Consul's office for another three years, doing despatch work, etc., and very often are Vice-Consuls before they have any knowledge or experience of the world, or have moved about among English commercial men. The consequence is that the system makes men narrow and pro-Chinese in their sympathies, and when this is not the case it is only due to superior ability and energy on the part of the men themselves.

The remedy suggested is that after the two years in Peking, and a year in a port, the young Consuls should be sent home for a couple of years to study law and gain a wider experience of men and matters than a small Chinese port can teach them.

The third complaint—viz., that other foreign nations in China give better Consular assistance to their commercial men than Great Britain—seems to have some foundation. The Consuls, on the other hand, present a very good case in reply. They say: "We have 64 per cent. of the whole foreign trade of China, and that trade has been built up under the British system of allowing the merchant to know his own business better than any Government can know it for him. The system also works well with the Chinese, as they appreciate the fact that we are not always bullying them on behalf of our nationals as the Consuls of other Powers often do."

There is a good deal to be said on both sides; but there seems to be no doubt that we have arrived at a time when the British Government will seriously have to consider whether the system of non-intervention hitherto pursued should not be modified. Up till now private enterprise has brought Great Britain to her present superior commercial position, and, therefore, the existing system has been a success. Conditions change, however, and policies should change with them. The British merchant does not ask for grandmotherly interference with his business. He is quite capable of attending to it himself, but in these days of fierce competition what he does want is an equal opportunity with the merchants of other nations in dealing with the Chinese officials.

In matters such as obtaining concessions, mining rights, etc., tenders for Government work, or the introduction of goods specially adapted to the requirements of the provincial officials' needs, or the needs of their departments, the merchant—no matter how enterprising—has no status which will enable him to obtain a hearing. British merchants complain that their Consuls have been known to refuse to afford them the introductions and facilities which other Consuls give to their nationals.

In every case where this complaint was made I asked for evidence, and here are a few examples which were quoted to me. All the cases occurred in 1898:

A British mining engineer wanted an introduction to a Viceroy with the idea of applying for the post of surveyor under the Chinese Government to prospect for minerals in Western China. Apart from the personal advantage to be gained, he claimed that it was to the advantage of any country that its nationals should make such surveys, as they would become acquainted with the mineral wealth of the country, and have a voice in the employment and nationality of the engineers who come out, and would advise where the necessary machinery should be bought. The Consul to whom he applied flatly refused to give him such an introduction, giving as a reason that if he gave him an official letter and he was refused an interview, it would be an insult to Great Britain, and the Consul would be put to a great deal of trouble.

In another case application was made for a letter of introduction to a Mandarin in high authority. A very curt letter was given. As the British subject in question was specially recommended to the American Consul, he went to him and asked for a letter of introduction to his Excellency, receiving at once a very warm letter, which procured him an interview. At this interview his Excellency inquired, " How is it that you, a British subject, have a better recommendation from the American than from your own Consul?" His Excellency also stated that on the English letter he should not have taken him, but as it was he gave him employment.

At another place the British Consul refused to give a letter of introduction to the Arsenal, and said that privately he would do all he could, but that officially he could not do anything.

Without pronouncing any opinion on these cases, I think they are matters for the consideration of the Associated Chambers of Commerce. Reference to the complaints of the British communities will be found in other chapters, notably under Chinkiang, where there had been twelve changes of Consuls in three years.

The last grievance, with regard to fees, was this. That the fees charged all round were much too high; but the fee for transit passes, even when only two and a half dollars a pass, was exceptionally obnoxious, because American transit passes were issued free of charge by many American Consuls. One large firm calculated that they used 1000 to 1500 passes in the year, and their American rivals the same number. This meant that the British firm had to pay between 3000 and 4000 dollars a year more for the privilege of being British traders.

The scale in force appears to be as follows:
- Japan . . . . 2 dollars
- France . . . . 2.40 "
- Russia . . . . 1.50 "
- U.S.A., nil
- Germany, often nil

The British charge has lately been reduced to 2.50—it used to be 4.50. It certainly seems desirable that the Associated Chambers of Commerce should take up this point in order to secure equal opportunity for all merchants. It would appear that endeavors should be made to arrive at an understanding with other Powers for a uniform scale of fees to be charged. The difference seems a trifle, but in the aggregate it amounts to a sum equal to the rent of many firms.

A most serious complaint against the Consular system appears to be that contained in a letter from the Chinese subjects of Great Britain in Hong Kong. This I have already referred to at length under the chapter on " Hong Kong."

The consensus of opinion in China is that there is great room for improvement in the Consular Body. The men do not obtain the experience or training so necessary to fit them for their responsible work. They get worn out under the present retirement system; the service has been starved, overworked, and underpaid. The men must deteriorate mentally and physically during the last few years of their service.

The remedies suggested are more men, better pay, and earlier retirement. There should be a few very well-paid men, and the others should get better paid than at present. The pension should be £500 a year after twenty-five years' service. To reduce the cost of these improvements, there should be more Vice-Consuls instead of Consuls at the smaller ports.

The merchants are very anxious that additional Consuls should be appointed at one or two places where there is no British Consul now; one of these places is Changsha, in the province of Hunan, and another is Kirin, in Manchuria.

XXVI

FINANCE AND CURRENCY

I AM fully aware how incompetent I am to deal with such an intricate subject as the Finance and Currency of China, and for the opinions and facts in the following chapter I am indebted to the various authorities whom I consulted during my Mission, and to recognized experts on Chinese finance, including various bank managers at the ports throughout China and in London, and especially to Mr. T. Jackson, chief manager of the Hong Kong and Shanghai Bank, Hong Kong, and to Mr. C. S. Addis, of the same bank's Shanghai branch, from whose letter to the London Chamber of Commerce I quote fully.

Recognizing the difficulties of this subject, not only to myself, but to the ordinary public, I made a very complete collection of the coinage in use in China in the various provinces, for the benefit of the Associated Chambers, and I hope to place this on view in some public place where it will be accessible to all who are interested in the matter. It illustrates effectively the diversity of the coinage, and the consequent difficulties of the trader,

THE BREAK-UP OF CHINA

owing to the variations as well as the fluctuations in the rate of exchange.

The collection consists of the following:

SYCEE

Province	Town	Tls.	Value	£	s.	d.
Province Hunan	Town Changsha	Tls.	5·⁰⁰ Value		15	10
" Shansi	" Taiyuanfu	"	5·²⁵ "		14	6
" Hupeh	" Hankow	"	4·⁹⁰ "		13	5
" Chihli	" Tientsin	"	10·⁰⁵ "	1	9	5
" Yunnan	" Talifu	"	1·⁸⁰ "		4	10½
" Szechuan	" Chingtu	"	10·³⁵ "	1	8	1
" Chekiang	" Hangchow	"	5·²⁵ "		14	6
" Shantung	" Chefoo	"	10·⁰⁰ "	1	9	8
" Fengtien (Manchuria) Town Newchwang		"	56·⁵⁵ "	7	13	2
" Kiangsi	" Kiukiang	"	7·⁰⁵ "	1	1	6
" Kiangsu	" Soochow	"	55·²⁰ "	7	9	6
" Shanghai Sycee . .		"	53·⁰⁰ "	7	5	5

Central Szechuan 1150 cash per tael.
Chungking   1080   "   "
Wuhu   1320   "   "
Shantung   1210   "   "
Shanghai   1170   "   "
Peking   550 large cash per Kung Fa tael.

Subsidiary Coin

Ten-cent and twenty-cent pieces:

Minted at Kiangnan,   approximate value 2¼d. and 5d.
   "   in Kwangtung Province   "   "   "
   "   " Fookien   "   "   "   "
   "   " Hupeh   "
   "   " Anhui   "

FINANCE AND CURRENCY

Chinese Dollars

Minted at Tientsin Arsenal, approximate value 2s. 8¼d.
" " Kiangnan " " "
" " Kwangtung Province " " "
" " Anhui " '
" " Hupeh "

Also current in China:

Mexican Republic scale dollar.
Spanish Carolus dollar.
Japanese yen.
Indo-China dollar (French Republic).
British dollar.

The want of military organization in China has much to do with the financial weakness of that country. Bad security means a high rate of interest, or curtailment of borrowing powers. The credit of this great Empire is now far from good. Her only honest available asset — the I.M. Customs — is pledged to the hilt, and under present conditions she has neither good security to offer for future loans, nor revenue to meet her growing obligations.

As is shown by the remarks of several of the Viceroys (quoted in other chapters), even the funds allocated to the provincial Governments are being encroached upon to provide security for present indebtedness, and there is a growing anxiety among the people as to whether the authorities will find it necessary to impose increased taxation to make up for the loss of provincial revenue.

It needs no expert knowledge of finance to see that the whole system of Chinese financial administration is utterly rotten. China is in a state of great financial embarrassment, not because her assets are small, but because her revenue is wasted and badly administered, and her capital resources undeveloped or squandered. China is not so much overtaxed as badly taxed, and all that she requires is advice and assistance in reorganizing her finances, which, provided her military and police administration were perfected, would place her in the forefront of national credit on the Western money markets.

The present revenue of China is estimated to amount to 85,000,000 taels, but this only represents about one-fifth of what is actually collected. In other words, the machinery of collection is so bad that it absorbs 80 per cent. of the amount collected. Under proper supervision and administration the revenue of China would go up by leaps and bounds, and taxation could actually be reduced.

The case of Egypt is a splendid example of what sound and honest financial administration can effect. If China were assisted by the European Powers to effect the reforms necessary, her position would be infinitely superior to that of Egypt. Her resources are unbounded, and if the present system of peculation and waste were stopped, she would soon be in a sound financial position.

The Chinese Empire at present owes between

FINANCE AND CURRENCY

£50,000,000 and £60,000,000, for which the revenue of the Imperial Maritime Customs is pledged.

The loans are as follows:

1. The 7% silver loan of 1894 (English) for Tls. 10,000,000, to be paid off in 20 years.
2. The 6% gold loan of 1895 (English) for £3,000,000, to be paid off in 20 years.
3. The 4% gold loan of 1895 (Russo-French) for £16,000,000, to be paid off in 36 years.
4. The 5% gold loan of 1896 (Anglo-German) for £16,000,000, to be paid off in 36 years.
5. The 4½% gold loan of 1898 (Anglo-German) for £16,000,000, to be paid off in 45 years.

In addition to these there are two loans of £1,000,000 each, raised on other revenue, but with a provision that if other revenue fails the Customs shall pay them. There are also one or two old silver loans for small amounts still running, but as far as ability to meet responsibility is concerned, the five loans above enumerated are the only ones worth taking into consideration in connection with the duties collected by the Imperial Maritime Customs and the seven likin collectorates pledged as collateral security for the last loan. That it was necessary to supplement the Customs guarantee by seven of the likin collectorates for the last 4½% Anglo-German loan, points to the fact that no part of the Customs revenue can be available for additional loans.

In addition to this, China has in the last year guaranteed the interest on foreign loans negotiated for railway purposes to the amount of £4,000,000 for the Lu-Han Railway, and £2,300,000 for the Newchwang Railway. Under the most-favored-nation clause this will have to be continued for all railways employing foreign capital, and in the present financial position of the country these Government guarantees are certain to hamper China very materially.

The immense natural resources of China render reform very easy. At present the system is fatal to honest finance. The provincial officers of all grades receive bare pittances for salary. They often have to pay very large sums before they take office, borrowing the amount of the "squeeze" from Chinese banks, or among their own friends. The consequence is that the officials make as much as they can during their term of employment, in order to repay themselves for the amount it cost them to obtain office. In addition to this, they expect to pay for the expenses of keeping up the necessary state of their position, and to make a good sum over as a sort of retiring allowance when their period of office is completed. As a matter of fact, unless they get into disgrace, they usually succeed in doing all this, and it is therefore perfectly easy to understand the enormous leakage in the revenue collected before it is remitted to Peking. One of the first necessities of financial reform in China is a system of public accounts and proper salaries to all officials. China has ample funds for all purposes, including the provision of an efficient military and police, but she must be assisted from without if the present corruption is to be replaced by honest and capable financial administration. In her mineral rights she has a source of revenue scarcely touched. The whole of the mineral rights are the property of the Government, which exacts a rent for working them.

The day for loans guaranteed by revenue is past and gone, to pledge more revenue can only result in serious embarrassment; no more money ought to be lent except for productive enterprise, and then only on proper conditions—that is, such conditions as shall give lenders security on the one hand, and, on the other, enable China to see her way not only to meet her obligations, but also to derive sure and certain additional benefit from the enterprise the borrowed money is wanted for and expended upon. With the question of loans is mixed up the matter of railway and mining concessions. Do people really understand what these amount to? Are they merely to put some money into the pockets of promoters, or are they to do good work for both China and bondholders? Concessions may look most enticing on paper; can they really be given effect to? and, if so, will they at once, or ever, show the profits that the people say they promise? The public cannot act too warily in these matters, and if they wish to avoid loss they would do well to consult firms of good repute in China all about any concession; where is the region, what are its contents, how are the inhabitants inclined, how were the officials induced to support the scheme, what local difficulties are there to be encountered, what kind of carriage is provided for, and what demand is the new supply to find, meet, or make. All these are points deserving of attention.

The appointment of a foreign financial adviser to direct the administration and collection of internal revenue, the reform of currency, the establishment and centralization of mints, the establishment of a Government Bank, and the remittance of provincial revenues and tribute-rice by open public tender instead of the present extravagant close system, might, under proper administration, quadruple the present revenue of China without increasing taxation by a single cash.

Great Britain's enormously preponderating trade and her financial stability, coupled with the success of her reforms elsewhere, would entitle her to offer China assistance in reforms of this character. A proper department of finance would have to be inaugurated, and while the head of it might be an Anglo-Saxon, its foreign employés should be of a cosmopolitan character, similar to the *personnel* of the Customs Department. The policy of the Open Door should be maintained in this as in other matters.

Nothing would be more materially affected by

FINANCE AND CURRENCY

a Spheres of Influence policy than this question of the finances of China. Splitting up the Chinese Empire means loss to bondholders and the disappearance of the security mortgaged to them. As an instance of this, the first Anglo-German loan was partly secured on Formosa. Formosa is no longer part of the Chinese Empire.

If Spheres of Influence are marked out in China, and the resultant downfall of the Chinese Government is brought about, who will pay the bondholders, and what security have they for their loans? What becomes of China's guarantees in the matter of the railway loans? And even if these matters were amicably settled between the Powers grabbing at Chinese territory, how can there be any security for interest being paid on loans by a country plunged into anarchy and rebellion, which must seriously disturb trade and diminish the Customs receipts?

The question of China providing adequate security against disorder and trouble, which may lead to the intervention of Foreign Powers and the partition of the Empire, is, as I have endeavored to show throughout this Report, entirely a question of the reorganization of her army. Without this there can be no security and no public confidence, and therefore she is bound to provide such adequate military and police protection. The present position of China disturbs confidence and causes loss to foreign bondholders. A drop of even 1 per cent. in the price of Chinese loans

THE BREAK-UP OF CHINA

means a loss of half a million sterling to foreign investors.

The last Anglo-German loan, floated in March, 1898, at 90, fell to 85¼ in October, 1898, at the time I reached China, and is now standing at 85 in April, 1899.

The 5 per cent. loan of 1896 dropped from 98¾ to 97¼, the price at the time of my visit. It now stands at 99—April, 1899. The prices of other loans I have mentioned are as follows:

7th April, 1899.

1894. Tls. 10,000,000 7 % Silver, issued in London @ 98 %, quoted £105
1895. £3,000,000 6 % Gold, issued in London @ 96¼ %, quoted £106
1895. £1,000,000 6 % Gold (Cassel), issued in London @ 106 %, quoted £109
1895. £1,000,000 6 % Gold, issued in Berlin @ 104¼ %, quoted £106
1895. £15,820,000 4 % Gold, issued in Paris @ 99 % (guaranteed by Russia), quoted £103¼

The currency of China is as confusing and as hopelessly involved as her finances. The general standard of value throughout the Empire is the tael, which is not a coin but a weight of silver, averaging about 1⅓ ounce. This, again, varies in the different provinces. The commercial standard of tael is the Haikwan (or Customs) tael, which in 1897 averaged in value:

2s. 11¾d., English;
$0.72 gold, American;
3.73 francs, France;

FINANCE AND CURRENCY

3.03 marks, German;
2.34 rupees, Indian;
1.50 dollars, Mexican;

at the sight exchange on London, New York, Paris, Berlin, Calcutta, and Hong Kong respectively. There are various other taels in use, the most notable being Kuping (or Treasury tael), the Kuaiping (or Shanghai) tael, and the Hankow tael. The latter may be said to be exactly 3 per cent. in value above the Shanghai tael. There is 10 per cent. difference between the highest and lowest of the other three taels. Not only is the tael not a coin, but I believe no weight of silver exactly corresponding to a tael is ever used. The smallest piece of silver in my collection, unminted, is 1.80 taels in value. The silver coin used all over China is the dollar, and there are no less than nine different sorts of dollars current in China, five of which are minted in the country. The dollar which is most commonly used, and which has the highest value, is the Republican scale dollar minted in Mexico. The other foreign dollars in use are:

1. The Japanese yen;
2. The Spanish Carolus dollar;
3. The French Republic dollar (Indo-Chinese piastra).

But none of these are so extensively used as the Mexican dollar. The Chinese dollars are those minted at

1. Tientsin Arsenal;
2. Kwangtung Province;
3. Kiangnan;
4. Hupeh Province;
5. Anhui Province.

The subsidiary coins are five cents, ten cents, twenty cents, and fifty cents, which are minted in

1. Kwangtung Province;
2. Kiangnan;
3. Fookien Province;
4. Hupeh Province;
5. Anhui Province.

The coins most commonly used by the Chinese themselves, however, are copper *cash*, the nominal value of which is, on an average, 1000 to the dollar. The relation between the copper cash and silver is so important that I can best explain the question by quoting the following three questions from the London Chamber of Commerce to the Hong Kong and Shanghai Bank, and the replies of Mr. C. S. Addis, of the branch at Shanghai, to these questions:

"Question 1.—Whether copper cash is issued from the Mints in China at higher rates since the closing of the Indian Mints, or if the increase in value (alleged to have taken place) occurs after issue?

"It is difficult to answer this question in the terms in which it is put. Mints in China are not 'open' in our sense of the word. They are Government institutions which purchase copper, cast

FINANCE AND CURRENCY

it in coins of a fixed weight and composition, and finally place them in circulation through the pay of soldiers and Government officials. They cannot be said, therefore, to issue cash at either higher or lower rates, because, while the standard of weight and fineness of the coins is fixed, there is no fixed ratio between copper cash and silver.

"The exchange between the two—*i.e.*, copper cash and silver—is determined by the quantity of copper cash in circulation.

"The question may be asked, however, if any reduction has been made since the closing of the Indian Mints in the weight and fineness of the coins issued by the Mints in China? The answer is that no such change appears to have taken place. How well the standard has been maintained will be seen from the accompanying memorandum by Dr. Stuhlmann, Professor of Chemistry at the Peking College, containing a tabulated analysis of coins issued by the Pao Ch'uan and Pao Yuan Mints during the present reign.

"A tael (Kung Fa weight) of silver at present prices would purchase sufficient copper to produce 388 Peking large cash, or say 7¾ tiao (1 tiao=50 large or 1000 nominal cash). At the capital, where soldiers and Government officials receive their pay at an old commuted rate of 14 tiao to the Government tael, copper cash may still be minted to a small extent, the loss being borne by the Imperial Treasury. Some recent memorials to the Throne, advocating a reduction in the weight of the coins, met with an unfavorable reception from the Empress-Dowager, who feared to excite discontent among her soldiery.

"As regards the provinces, there is reason to believe that the production of copper cash during the past five years has been almost entirely superseded by the minting of a subsidiary silver coinage. In 1897 the number of these subsidiary coins issued by the mints at Tientsin, Wuchang, Foochow, and Canton was as follows:

50 cent pieces	214,796
20 "	31,852,571
10 "	17,892,931
5	66,921

"On the basis of, say, 920 cash to the dollar, those subsidiary coins represent a substitute for 7,608,907,242 copper cash of the aggregate value of over $8,000,000.

"Question 2.—What the exact increase in value amounts to, and the extent of any fluctuations that may have taken place?

"The increase in the value of copper cash as compared with silver since the closing of the Indian Mints varies in different parts of China. Speaking broadly, it may be said to amount to about 25 per cent., as the following Tables will show:

"The number of cash which a dollar would purchase has fallen since 1892.

Wenchow from	1,140	to	950
Shanghai "	1,050	"	920
Tungchow "	1,075	"	925

FINANCE AND CURRENCY

"The number of cash which a tael would purchase has fallen since 1892.

                Central Szechuan from 1,600 to 1,150
                Chungking   "   1,700 " 1,080
                Wuhu   "   1,600 " 1,320
                Shantung   "   1,450 " 1,210

"The variations observed in the above figures may be ascribed partly to the percentage of spurious cash in circulation and partly to the variety of the taels in use at the different centres.

"The following Table shows the fluctuations from year to year in the value of the Peking large cash (1 tiao = 50 large cash).

"Number of Peking large cash (1 large = 20 small cash) obtainable for one Kung Fa tael during

                1892 Tiao 14.200 = 710 large cash
                1893 "   14   = 700   "
                1894 "   13.500 = 675   "
                1895 "   13.600 = 680   "
                1896 "   12.800 = 640   "
                1897 "   12   = 600   "
                1898 "   11.500 = 550   "

"Number of cash obtainable in Shanghai during

                1892 Tls. 1 = 1,400 cash = $1,050 cash
                1893 "   = 1,370 "   = 1,030 "
                1894 "   = 1,300 "   =   970 "
                1895 "   = 1,270 "   =   950 "
                1896 "   = 1,210 "   =   880 "
                1897 "   = 1,170 "   =   910 "
                1898 "   = 1,170 "   =   920 "

373

"It will be observed from the above Table that copper cash, probably on account of the large number of spurious coins in circulation, command a market price considerably below their intrinsic value in silver. A tael of silver, as has already been stated, would purchase sufficient copper at present prices to produce, if minted, 388 Peking large cash, while 550 of these cash would be required in exchange for a tael in the open market. There is still, however, a substantial rise in value of about 25 per cent. to be accounted for.

"The cause may be sought: first, in the scarcity of cash due to the cessation of coinage during the past five or six years; second, in the large quantities believed to have been illicitly melted down for the purpose of making domestic utensils instead of using copper; and third, to the growing demands made upon an already restricted currency by the steady increase of population.

"Question 3.—Whether any fall in the value of (*a*) food grains, or (*b*) wages, has followed the rise in the value of copper cash.

"Copper cash having appreciated in terms of silver might naturally be expected to show a similar increase as regards food and wages. In other words, we should have expected to find a corresponding fall in the price of commodities. As a fact, the exact reverse of this has taken place. While cash will purchase more silver than formerly, they will purchase less of other articles. The purchasing power of cash has risen in terms of

FINANCE AND CURRENCY

silver and fallen in terms of commodities. The following Tables show the fluctuations year by year of the two staple articles of diet in China:

AVERAGE PRICE OF FLOUR (NATIVE PRODUCTION) IN PEKING

1892 per 133⅓ lbs. Tls. 2.40 or, large cash 1,704
1893 "   "   "   2.60 "   "   "   1,820
1894 "   "   "   2.70 "   "   "   1,822
1895 "   "   "   3   "   "   "   2,040
1896 "   "   "   3   "   "   "   1,920
1897 "   "   "   3.40 "   "   "   2,040
1898 "   "   "   4.20 "   "   "   2,310

AVERAGE PRICE OF RICE IN SHANGHAI

1892 per 213⅛ lbs. $3.37 or cash, 3,538
1893 "   "   3.41 "   "   3,512
1894 "   "   3.52 "   "   3,414
1895 "   "   3.65 "   "   3,467
1896 "   "   4.76 "   "   4,189
1897 "   "   5.18 "   "   4,714
1898 "   "   6.33 "   "   5,823

" The foregoing figures, though drawn from two cities only, may be taken as typical of a widely spread movement. There is no reason to doubt the correctness of the statement made by Mr. Grosvenor in his Report on the trade of China in 1896, that the general increase in prices is universally applicable throughout the whole Empire.

" The question remains, How are we to reconcile this upward movement of prices with the admitted appreciation of copper cash—why do cash cost more and buy less?

THE BREAK-UP OF CHINA

"This question, or something like it, was addressed last year by the Royal Asiatic Society to members residing in different parts of China. Some thirteen replies were received, covering a great extent of the Empire from north to south, and from east to west. In a Report on these papers, prepared by Mr. F. E. Taylor, Statistical Secretary to the Imperial Chinese Maritime Customs, a variety of explanations have been adduced, of which the following is a brief summary:

"Increased population is reported everywhere, making a greater demand upon products of all kinds, while the fall in the gold value of silver has stimulated exports and thereby reduced the supply circulable for the natives. The enormous quantities of debased cash in circulation have also contributed to send up prices. In some districts short crops, and in some the extended cultivation of the poppy, are held to be largely responsible for the dearness of food. In Shangtung it is said that the cost of agricultural labor has been increased by the immigration of laborers to Western Siberia; Szechuan complains of short crops, poppy cultivation, and export of foodstuffs. From Foochow we learn that the province is poorer, owing to the falling off in the tea trade, while taxation is heavier. These attempts to explain obscure and complicated phenomena are interesting as far as they go, but can scarcely be considered conclusive. Perhaps the only really logical hypothesis of the appreciation of cash in terms of

FINANCE AND CURRENCY

silver and the depreciation of cash in terms of commodities is that suggested by Mr. Taylor, viz:

> "'That silver has fallen in value as a commodity still deeper than debasement of the coinage has forced down the purchasing power of cash.'

"This still leaves open the question of which much might be written as to what has lowered the value of silver in China.

"In conclusion, apology must be made for the generally tentative character of the information presented in the foregoing pages. The statistics cited have no pretension to more than approximate accuracy. In a country like China, where there is nothing approaching a Bureau of Statistics, such scraps of information as are available must be taken for what they are worth. It is hoped that they may be found not without value as a means of comparison."

The memorandum on Chinese copper cash, by Dr. Stuhlmann, of the "Tuan Wan Kwan," Peking, to which Mr. Addis refers, is as follows:

"Not only has the price of silver in comparison with gold constantly fallen of late years, but at the same time, and to a certain extent in connection with this, a depreciation of the former metal as compared to Chinese copper coin has taken place. In other words, one receives to-day considerably fewer cash for the tael than a few years ago. Thus, for instance, the rate of exchange for the Peking tael, which in 1893 was still 13½ to 14 tiao, has gradually fallen to 10 tiao. In spite of this, the value of copper coin has otherwise remained the same, so that the quantity of foodstuff, etc., procurable for a tiao is not greater than formerly. To what extent, then, a further fall in the tael exchange is to be expected, should no new factor come in, may possibly be arrived at with the help of the analysis of locally current cash comprised in the following Table. I premise that the first and the second columns of the Table refer to the so-called large Peking cash, and moreover to such as have been cast during the reign of Kuang Hsu. These are marked in Manchu characters with the words " Pao Ch'uan " or " Pao Yuan," according to whichever of the two mints established here they come from, and they form the greater portion of the copper coin at present circulating in Peking. The third and fourth columns of the Table show the composition of the so-called small cash which have been struck here during the same period, and which, almost without exception, are only current in the province. In the latter class of coin there appears to be a much greater proportion of old-time coins than is the case here in Peking.

" Nevertheless, the weight and composition of all these coins are, generally speaking, pretty much the same. Finally, the fifth column refers to the analysis of a cash coined during the reign of Chien Lung, and this analysis was made in con-

FINANCE AND CURRENCY

sequence of the view widely held by the Chinese that coins of that period contain a considerable quantity of gold. It will be seen from the Table how far this has been confirmed; at any rate, in so far as concerns the pieces analyzed by me. I have added these figures in order to show to what extent coins of that period differ from those of the present day.

"Naturally a great number of cash were employed for each analysis, and the figures quoted are the average results of several tests:

	Kuang Hsu	Large Peking Cash		Small Peking Cash		Chien Lung
		Pao Ch'uan	Pao Yuan	Pao Ch'uan	Pao Yuan	Small Cash
Weight per Cash		8,961	8,242	3,726	3,511	4,021
		Gramm.	Gramm.	Gramm.	Gramm.	Gramm.
Tin		1.20%	0.63%	1.09%	0.52%	3.11%
Gold*		Strong Trace	A trace	Slight Trace	—	—
Silver		0.02%	0.02%	0.04%	0.03%	0.04%
Lead		2.52%	4.17%	4.43%	2.38%	5.64%
Copper		53.25%	51.93%	56.11%	56.86%	50.10%
Zinc		38.19%	38.91%	36.50%	39.40%	39.88%
Iron		4.70%	4.14%	1.61%	0.66%	0.98%
Sand, etc.		0.12%	0.20%	0.22%	0.15%	0.25%
Total		100.00%	100.00%	100.00%	100.00%	100.00%

"As may be seen from this Table, the cash from the two mints show small differences in both

* In no case did the gold contained amount to as much as ½ oz. to the English ton.

weight and composition. If we take the mean of the two, then we get for 50 large cash = 1 tiao, a weight of 430.08 gramme = 11.526 Kuping Liang (1 Kuping Liang, or tael = 37.31256 gramme = 575.82 grains), containing 52.59 per cent., or 6.062 Kuping Liang of copper, and 38.55 per cent., or 4.443 Kuping Liang of zinc. If we then calculate the value of the copper at 28 taels per picul (= 1600 Liang), and that of the zinc at 8¼ taels per picul (the prices lately ruling here in Peking) we have, omitting the other component parts, the value of the metals contained in 50 cash as equal to 0.1289 taels. A tael is, therefore, only sufficient to provide the necessary copper and zinc for 388 large cash, or 7⅘ tiao. Actually, however, as already mentioned, the present rate of the tael is 10¼ tiao, and consequently, in spite of the fall in the past few years, still considerably higher than one could expect, for the copper money purchasable for a tael costs the Government, as shown above, in copper and zinc, not less than 1.354 taels, exclusive of the cost of minting. One obtains similar, though not quite such startling, results from a calculation on the above lines of the value of the small cash, which amounts to 0.115 taels per 100 pieces. Consequently, a tael is only sufficient to provide the material for 870 small cash, and at the present rate of 1000 cash to the tael the purchaser receives an amount of copper and zinc which actually represent a metal value of 1150 taels. The interesting fact may be submitted that

FINANCE AND CURRENCY

at present in Peking—and as far as I know, elsewhere in China—the tael, as compared to the copper coinage, still possesses a more or less imaginary value. This shows itself on the one side by the rapid depreciation of silver in relation to gold that has lately taken place, and on the other side by the steady rise in copper prices, which two movements of the foreign metal markets the value of the cash has not to the full extent followed. Nevertheless, during the last few years the raw material, so far as the local coins are concerned, has been principally drawn from Europe and Japan.

"It is therefore to be expected that a further fluctuation in exchange in favor of cash will take place, and, indeed, the limit of that fluctuation, other considerations excluded, may be determined by the cost of production of the coins. A fall of the tael to 350–400 large (7–8 tiao) and 850–900 small cash is, therefore, within the bounds of possibility. That in such a complicated question many other factors are involved is evident from the already alluded to relatively high rates of exchange of the small cash as compared to the large ones, and this is explained by the increased demand created by the Tientsin Peking Railway."

Upon the general question of currency and exchange I asked two questions, and obtained the following expert opinion. The whole question is so difficult that I will offer no opinion upon the replies, interesting as they are. The questions I asked were:

THE BREAK-UP OF CHINA

> 1. Is a gold standard possible?
> 2. How has the varying rate of exchange affected the price of commodities?

The answers I received may be shortly summarized thus:

> 1. No; because the balance of trade being against China, it is improbable that gold would remain in the country.
>
> 2. The answer is, out of six of the principal commodities imported, prices have gone up from 30 per cent. to 40 per cent. in five instances, and declined 42 per cent. in one instance, between January, 1890, and October, 1898 (the date at which I arrived in China). The exchange in 1890 was 4s. 6d., and in 1898 2s. 8d. It has also tended to make the Chinese merchant more of a commission agent than a *bona fide* trader.

To those who are interested in the questions, the detailed replies I received are more fully given below:

1. "The currency of China is based on silver and copper cash; the former at its intrinsic value, the latter approximately so. As silver has during recent years declined relatively to copper, exchange between silver taels and copper cash has more or less adjusted itself to their relative values. This has been probably brought about by two causes:

FINANCE AND CURRENCY

"(a) The curtailment of coinage of copper cash, as the operation could only be carried on at a loss.

"(b) The melting of cash, as the metal they contained was worth more than their nominal value as money.

"The Chinese having been accustomed to a standard of value based upon silver at its intrinsic value, they would probably look with distrust upon any coinage which had a fictitious value; as gold and silver are constantly fluctuating in value in relation to each other, it is impossible to have a gold currency with subsidiary silver coinage which is not a fictitious value; it is probable that such subsidiary coinage would depreciate or appreciate in accordance with its intrinsic value, unless it were exchangeable for gold in all important centres.

The balance of trade, as far as the foreign Customs statistics show, is against China; there is no data to show how far the balance may be redressed by the trade in native vessels from Chinese ports to foreign countries—such as Corea, Japan, Siam, and the Straits, and by native overland trade to Thibet, Central Asia, and Siberia; the loans recently floated by China will virtually augment the balance of trade against her, and therefore it is improbable that gold would remain in the country, even if it could be introduced with the object of starting a gold currency, at any rate until Chinese exports increased to such an extent that the balance of trade were turned in her favor.

"The question as to the prices of commodities in relation to exchange naturally divides itself into two headings—namely:

"(*a*) Commodities imported from gold countries, and

"(*b*) Commodities produced in the country itself.

"As regards imported commodities, prices here must naturally conform to the varying gold exchange, and in the process of adjustment much risk attaches to those engaged in the trade; the reason is plain, because, seeing that goods have to be bought at home for arrival here months ahead, there is the terribly uncertain factor of the fluctuations in exchange during the interval. The following few figures will show how the declining gold exchange has affected the prices of imported commodities:

	Jan., 1890. Ex. 4*s.* 6*d.* Tls.	Oct., 1898. Ex. 2*s.* 8*d.* Tls.	Per cent. Fall 42
Gray shirtings	1.73	2.24	Rise 30
White shirtings	2	2.65	" 32
Woollen camlets	10.20	14.20	" 40
Nail-rod iron	2.80	3.60	" 30
Lead	4.80	7.10	" 48

"Of course, exchange is not the only factor influencing prices; a very important factor is the price at which goods can be purchased at home, which, in turn, is dependent upon the price of raw material. For instance, first-cost prices at home of cotton and woollen goods, in 1890, were some 20 per cent. higher than they are to-day.

"In connection with the general question of the effect of a varying exchange upon trade as a whole, there can be no doubt that it has largely influenced foreign traders towards endeavors to eliminate from their business, as far as may be, the speculative exchange factor. Much has been written about the disappearance of the *bona fide* British *merchant* in China—that is, a trader who buys and sells on his own account—it being alleged that the trader in China has degenerated into a mere commission agent. The answer is that the *bona fide* merchant's business has, in consequence of varying exchange, become so largely speculative that the careful trader naturally endeavors to minimize his risk by getting a *third* party to assume the risk of exchange; consequently his object is to sell his goods *before* he buys them, whether in imports or exports. Commission business is naturally the result. As, however, the volume of business constantly continues to increase, it may be taken for granted that, so far as imports are concerned, our manufacturers at home care little whether we conduct our business on 'merchant' or 'commission' lines, and it is difficult to see where the cry of the degeneracy of the British merchant in China comes in.

"Another point is that, business being now

largely conducted on commission or 'indent' lines, we are at least certain of supplying Chinese with what they actually want, and not with what we may think they want; our manufacturers consequently are obliged, if they accept our indents, to arrange their machinery according to the wants of the market they are supplying; this consideration has an important bearing on the oft-repeated cry of the want of adaptability of the British manufacturer, our method of business at least compels him to subordinate his conservative ideas to our actual wants.

"As to the second point—viz., *Commodities produced in the Country*, there is no doubt that, concurrently with the fall in silver, there has been a general rise in China's home products; the fall in silver has something to do with this, at any rate, so far as the prices of exported produce is concerned, the Chinaman being smart enough to take advantage of the fact that the depreciated silver enables the foreigner to pay more silver than formerly for his produce, but undoubtedly the main reason for the rise in Chinese commodities, including necessaries of life, and hence wages and general cost of living, is the appreciation of copper cash in terms of silver. The actual worker in China, whether in field or factory, looks for his wages in cash, and whereas in 1890 a tael ($1\frac{1}{3}$ oz. of silver) purchased 1400 cash, it now purchases less than 1200. Wages and prices have therefore, as expressed in silver, advanced accordingly."

FINANCE AND CURRENCY

With regard to the statement, in the opinion I have quoted above, that the Customs returns show a balance of trade against China, this is perfectly true; but other expert opinion I have obtained states that if the overland trade is taken into consideration, and the movements of bullion are included with trade returns, it will be found that in 1898 there was a balance of six millions in favor of China. Experts have been known to differ on other occasions.

It is beyond my power to do more than lay these statements before the Associated Chambers of Commerce, and to leave them to draw their own deductions from them. I trust, however, that this chapter will be found useful to all interested in the subject, and that the object-lesson of the collection I have brought to England may be equally instructive to the ordinary business man.

There is room for very great improvement in Chinese finance and currency. This is beyond doubt. The currency hinders trade, and is troublesome to every one. As an instance of this, there are no less than five different currencies between Tientsin and Peking, a distance of 80 miles. As an example, the railway fare between Peking and Tientsin was 1 dollar 40 cents, but from Tientsin to Peking it was 1 dollar 30 cents. The remedies which I would suggest for this state of affairs, for the consideration of the Associated Chambers of Commerce, are these:

    1. A Bureau of Finance to be established

THE BREAK-UP OF CHINA

with a foreigner at the head of it, as financial adviser to the Chinese Government.

2. The establishment of a system of public accounts and audits, and reform in the collection of internal taxation of all kinds.

3. The establishment of a Government bank (or official status to be given to one of the existing banking corporations in China).

4. The establishment of a national mint, and a uniformity in the coinage minted and allowed as legal tender throughout the Chinese Empire.

5. The establishment of a commission of experts by China to investigate these questions, and to report how reforms should be initiated.

I feel confident that if the Associated Chambers of Commerce can do anything to secure these points being attended to, that trade and commerce will be beneficially affected thereby.

The Banks of China at the date of my visit were the following:

Hong Kong and Shanghai Banking Corporation	English.
Chartered Bank of India, China, etc.	"
Mercantile Bank of India	"
Bank of China and Japan	"
National Bank of China	Chinese.
Imperial Bank of China	"
Yokohama Specie Bank	Japanese.
Deutsch Asiatische Bank	German.
Russo-Chinese Bank	Russian.
Banque de l'Indo Chine	French.

XXVII

TRADE, TREATIES, AND TARIFFS

UP till now foreign trade in China has been checked and hindered less by political changes than by the failure of the foreign merchant to secure all he expected or was entitled to under his Treaty rights, and by the tariffs illegally imposed on goods which have already paid customs and other duties at the port of entry.

British commercial interests in China have been fostered by the treaties and tariffs she dictated, by the energy of her merchants, and by the possession of the lead among native competitors as well as foreign rivals. But competition is telling adversely, the energy of the British merchant is being equalled by other nationals, the failure of China to keep strictly to the letter of her treaties, and the fact that the dictated treaties have not sufficiently considered both sides of the case, are all beginning to have an effect. The competition of the Chinese and the introduction of steam into the country are also combining to produce changed conditions in China, bearing in an important degree on British commerce. The diligence, frugality, and skill of the Chinese make them formidable trade rivals, and in order to keep the preponderance of trade in British hands it will be necessary for both our merchants and the authorities at home to recognize these changes.

New markets must also be sought. If the merchant finds that the native workman is seriously cutting into one branch of his business, it is advisable that he should try and turn the activity of his opponent into a profitable channel for himself and Anglo-Saxon trade generally. New industries must be opened up, and I would especially direct the attention of the Chambers of Commerce to the openings for glass factories, among others, of which there at present seems only one in China, and to the fact that the more the native competes with the British manufacturer in certain classes of trade the more machinery he will require, and the orders for such machinery will come to this country if our machinery manufacturers are enterprising enough. Special attention should also be directed to the variations in the buying and selling of goods, as there is a great difference between certain classes of goods in which the trade is ephemeral instead of permanent. For instance, dealings in cotton goods and teas will probably go on as long as China lasts, but purchases of arms and railway material are only to supply temporary wants, and may cease altogether when once China is in a position to produce her own plant. At the present moment, however, there is a great opening for railway material. Some of the orders have

TRADE, TREATIES, AND TARIFFS

come to this country, but at this moment the greater proportion are going to America. It appears to me that the first necessity of the British manufacturer is to study the special requirements of the China market, and of these I have given some indication in the chapter on "Tongshan."

Political occurrences, due to the action of Foreign Powers, have affected trade much less than has been supposed. The steady growth in the foreign trade of China has, on the whole, been maintained. The Customs Returns for 1898 are not yet public, but from good authority I learn that the figures will be as follows:

Imports in Hk. taels	209,000,000
Exports " "	153,000,000
Total	362,000,000

This shows an increase of 7,000,000 taels in imports, and a decrease in exports of about 10,000,000 on 1897. This bears out what I have continually drawn attention to in the course of my Report—viz., that trade has suffered by the want of security and the lack of confidence. The action of Russia in the North, Germany at Kiao-chow, or France along the Tongking frontier has had no effect, because *no markets have yet been closed to trade which were open before.*

On the contrary, trade with all these districts has never been really open, and has only reached them through the hands of the Chinese. The action of these Powers has, therefore, had no effect on the import trade unless to increase it, by improving the line of communication, and the facilities for transport. The danger in this direction is a prospective one, and lies in the fact that paper guarantees are not sufficient to assure the British merchant against regulations and preferential tariffs, which will hinder the present steady development of his trade in the near future. The case with regard to exports is far different. The foreign export trade is almost entirely in the hands of British merchants, and the feeling of unrest throughout China, the disturbances and riots, and the anxiety of the people, have arrested the natural growth of the export trade. Goods have been unable to come down from the interior, and instead of the increase we might reasonably have expected to find, there is a decrease of 10,000,000 taels on the returns of 1897, although still an increase on previous years. The wealth of China, and the proof that I am not wrong in dwelling so much in this Report on the prospective trade possible, is very clearly demonstrated by the fact that the total foreign trade has actually doubled itself since 1888. In my opinion, it will more than double even the present figures in the next decade if China is loyally assisted by Foreign Powers from without, and if she is also prepared to undertake reforms within.

It is not always wise to confound political with commercial questions, but in China the two cannot be separated. Strong political influence at

Peking must have a beneficial effect on commercial relations, and a strong and friendly China is the best guarantee for whatever extension and development are necessary for trade.

We cannot, however, afford to overlook two positive and important facts *if the " Open Door" policy is maintained.* The most-favored-nation clause of all the treaties makes it impossible for any country to obtain anything by negotiation for her own exclusive benefit, which will not either be shared by all other Powers, or enable them to force a *quid pro quo* from China. Secret understandings with China are impossible, and any attempt to monopolize control in any direction will be opposed and neutralized, if not completely foiled, by the threats which others will hold out over China's head.

Thus, if Manchuria remains Chinese, preferential railway rates cannot be introduced, the Russian railway will offer increased trading facilities to all nations, and profit to Russia herself. This is exactly a case in point where the political question is inseparable from the commercial. All that we know at present is that Russia has been in negotiation with the Imperial Chinese Customs for the establishment of Chinese Customs Houses all along the line of her railway. Germany, also, at Kiao-chow, has consented to allow a Chinese Customs House to be established at that place.

The object of all treaties made between Great Britain and China has been to promote trade; but the Chinese provincial authorities, owing to their more or less independent position, have, in many cases, succeeded in nullifying the effect of these treaties, and by illegal and vexatious tariffs on goods *en route* to the interior have caused both delay and loss to British trade.

The Imperial Chinese Maritime Customs, under the able control of Sir Robert Hart, levies an *ad valorem* duty on all foreign goods landed in China. This duty amounts to only 5 per cent., and as China's Treaty with Great Britain regarding the Customs Tariff is about to expire, China has announced her intention of asking for an increase of duty.

The British merchants in China do not object to an increase in the *ad valorem* duty, because it gives them an opportunity of raising the whole question of taxation on foreign trade, and an opportunity of getting the present abuses remedied. As they justly observe, a slight increase in taxation, levied at the port of entry, will be less injurious to trade than the uncertainty of the taxation levied on goods and the delay caused in transit by provincial authorities.

The principal treaties under which British trade with China is conducted are as follows:

  I. Treaty of Nanking 1842
  II. Tientsin Treaty 1858
  III. Chefoo Convention . . . 1876

In addition to this there is the Customs Tariff

itself, to which China and Great Britain are contracting parties. The rights and privileges theoretically conceded under these treaties have, in many instances, been withheld for thirty years.

These privileges are as follows:

NANKING TREATY OF 1842

The Nanking Treaty of 1842 provided that " When British merchandise shall have once paid at any of the said ports (Treaty Ports) the regulated customs and dues, agreeable of the tariff to be hereafter fixed, such merchandise may be conveyed *by Chinese* merchants to any province or city in the interior of the Empire of China on paying a further amount as transit duties, which shall not exceed .... per cent. on the tariff value of such goods." ARTICLE X.—*Treaty of Nanking*.

This Treaty is perfectly clear. It provides that British merchandise may be admitted to Treaty Ports on payment of the tariff, and to the interior, in the hands of Chinese merchants, by an additional tax as transit duty, the percentage for transit duty being apparently left open for several years.

The original intention of the framers of this Treaty was to secure free entry of British goods to the ports opened to trade under ARTICLE II. of the same Treaty, and to allow them to be imported into the country not open to foreign trade by a further payment. In course of time, however, the Chinese began to take advantage of the fact that duties other than these two were not expressly forbidden, and in 1858 the whole question was thoroughly gone into and a new Treaty was signed, which may be said to be the *Magna Charta* of the British merchant in China. This was the

TIENTSIN TREATY OF 1858

This Treaty covers a very wide field connected with the rights and privileges of foreign trade, but the clause with which we are most concerned is that known as ARTICLE XXVIII.

This commences that "Whereas it was agreed under ARTICLE X. of the Treaty of Nanking that British imports having paid the tariff duties should be conveyed into the interior *free of all further charges*, except a transit duty." And then goes on to describe how British merchants had complained that the duty not having been stated, charges were suddenly and arbitrarily imposed by local officials, and therefore—

"It shall be at the option of a British subject desiring to convey *produce purchased inland to a port*, or to convey imports from a port to an inland market, *to clear his goods of all transit duties* by payment of a *single charge*."

The Article goes on to state that this charge is to be levied at the first barrier passed by exports proceeding to the sea, or on imports going

TRADE, TREATIES, AND TARIFFS

inland at the port where they are landed. It also provides that this duty or "single payment" shall not exceed 2½ per cent. on the value of the goods, and provides that:

"On payment thereof a certificate shall be issued *which shall exempt the goods from all further inland charges whatsoever.*"

There could be no possible misunderstanding in this plain language. It was clear that two duties only need be legally incurred by foreign traders.

1. The ordinary Customs duty.
2. The transit-pass fee, which was to cover all goods whether going to or from a port.

To set the point beyond cavil, however, the following extract from a despatch of Lord Elgin (the framer of this Treaty) to the Foreign Office in November, 1858, may be quoted:

"Henceforth, on payment of a sum in name of transit duty, goods, whether of export or import, will be free to pass between the port of shipment or entry to or from any part of China without further charge of toll, octroi, or tax of any description whatsoever. I confess that I consider this a most important point gained in the future interest of foreign trade with China. I have always thought that the remedy (against the grievance pressed upon me by mercantile bodies or individuals since I came to China) was to be sought in the substitution of one fixed payment for the present irregular and multiplied levies, ... although it was obviously difficult to devise a scheme for the commutation of transit (*i.e.*, inland) duties which, without creating great financial disturbance, should prove an effectual protection to the importing and exporting merchants."

In spite of this, as years went on, the Chinese officials, with undiminished perseverance, continued to try and impose various additional taxes under specious pretexts and different names, the principal of these being a tax known as likin, and which was not only illegal but was a great source of hindrance to trade, as the merchant never knew what the amount of the likin might be. The great difficulty also was that, as goods were entirely in the hands of Chinese compradors in transit, the Chinese were naturally less able to resist the squeeze. than if the goods had been under the control of a foreigner when the tax was charged.

In 1868 Sir Rutherford Alcock, the British Minister at Peking, took the matter in hand, and in a despatch which he wrote to the Foreign Office he said:

"China has, by her treaties, foregone all further right of taxation on whatever can be shown to constitute the foreign trade, import or export. The likin continues a violation of

TRADE, TREATIES, AND TARIFFS

treaty rights. . . . This question of the assumed right of the Chinese Government to tax foreign trade *ad libitum* is one of principle, and of such vital moment to the interests of commerce that a British Minister can have no discretionary power in protesting against it as a violation of treaty."

Sir Rutherford also drew up a Convention, in 1868, which was intended to clear up the whole question; for while the Tientsin Treaty, as quoted above, very clearly stated that it was "*at the option*" of a British merchant to clear his goods by one payment of transit duty, the weak point in the clause was that which ordered that, upon the application of the Consul, the duty between the port and any place in the interior should be published in Chinese and English for the benefit of the merchants at large. In other words, it permitted the provincial authorities to still levy duties on goods *en route* as long as the duties were notified to the British Consul, and it only gave the merchant "an option" to clear his goods from such duties by paying for a transit pass or certificate.

Sir Rutherford Alcock's Convention was intended to clear up this point, and to make it imperative that there should be a simultaneous payment of duty and all dues on imports at the time of landing, and their subsequent exemption from all further taxation, in the Treaty Port provinces. Unfortunately, this Convention was never ratified, but it undoubtedly was the solution of the difficulty, as while provincial officials are allowed to levy likin at all, they will do so as they do now, whether the goods have paid transit-pass dues or not. If those in charge of the goods covered by a transit pass refuse to pay this illegal exaction, they have to submit to detention and delay, which is, in the long run, as costly to the merchant as if he paid the illegal squeeze imposed by the officials. The present Inspector-General, Sir Robert Hart, talked the matter over with me, and he was of opinion that the provision I have quoted in the unratified Alcock Convention was a good one, and "that it will only be by an understanding of a similar nature that any transit system will ever be made to work well."

The efforts of Sir Rutherford Alcock having proved abortive, the abuses continued to flourish and increase. Trade was hampered, and the merchants continually complained. The most common complaint was that, ignoring the terms of Treaties, the provincial officials steadfastly refused to recognize the rights of Chinese merchants to carry goods under the transit-pass system. The result of this was to restrict the expansion of trade with all parts other than Treaty Ports. Another Convention was drawn up to settle this point, and by

TRADE, TREATIES, AND TARIFFS

THE CHEFOO CONVENTION OF 1876

Section 3 of ARTICLE IV. enacted that:

"The Chinese Government agree that Transit Duty Certificates shall be framed under one rule at all ports, no difference being made in the conditions set forth therein; and that, so far as imports are concerned, *the nationality of the person possessing and carrying these is immaterial.* Native produce carried from an inland centre to a port of shipment, if *bona fide* intended for shipment to a foreign port, may be, by treaty, certified by the British subject interested, and *exempted by payment of the half duty from all charges demanded upon it en route.* If produce be not the property of a British subject, or is being carried to a port not for exportation, it is not entitled to the exemption that would be secured it by the exhibition of a transit duty certificate. The British Minister is prepared to agree with the Tsung-li Yamen upon rules that will secure the Chinese Government against abuse of privilege as affecting produce. The words *nei-ti* (inland) in the clause of Article VII. of the Rules appended to the tariff, regarding carriage of imports inland and of native produce purchased inland, apply as much to places on the sea coasts and river shores as to places in the interior not open to foreign trade; the Chinese Government having the right to make arrangements for the prevention of abuses thereat."

Article VII., appended to the Customs Tariff, is equally plain. As to imports it says, on the transit certificate being issued "no further duty will be leviable upon imports so certificated, no matter how distant their place of destination." The regulations of this Article as to exports, however, are a direct contravention of the Treaty of Tientsin, for, instead of providing for the payment of transit dues at the first barrier which the goods pass, it provides that they shall only be examined there, and the transit duty be paid at the last barrier before arrival at the port of destination. This rather left the door open to the provincial authorities to "squeeze" the goods *en route*, as they could say that no duty had been paid. Another harassing condition in this same rule is that "unauthorized sale *in transitu* of goods that have been entered as above, or a part, will render them liable to confiscation."

The effect of this regulation was to prevent the merchant taking advantage of any opportunity of selling his goods *en route*, and any accident or loss of part of the cargo *in transitu* gave the local officials an unequalled opportunity of inflicting heavy penalties on the merchant. For instance, about a year ago an American merchant at Wuchow shipped 2000 cases of kerosene oil to Kweilin under transit pass, but on arrival at a barrier near

TRADE, TREATIES, AND TARIFFS

Kweilin it was discovered that the cargo was short of twenty cases mentioned on the pass. It is more than probable that the local likin officials, who are up to all sorts of tricks, had arranged to have these twenty casks stolen, for on arrival at the barrier near Kweilin they seized the cargo and imprisoned the Chinese supercargo, on the ground that, these twenty casks being missing, the whole cargo would be confiscated for violation of Rule 7. Months passed before a settlement was arrived at, the merchant losing a contract for 120,000 cases of oil owing to the delay, besides having to pay a heavy sum as demurrage to the owners of the native junks he had employed.

The consequence of this and similar cases was that in 1898, not long before my visit, a new set of Transit Pass Rules had been promulgated by arrangement between the Tsung-li Yamen, the Inspector-General of Customs, and the foreign Ministers. I append a copy of these Rules for the information of the Associated Chambers, and for the benefit of merchants who are contemplating catering for the China market:

RULES

1. Certificated imported goods going from a Treaty port to any inland place duly specified shall be free, after payment of a half duty for transit pass, from further taxation of any kind.

2. On arrival of the goods at the place of destination the certificate shall be cancelled.

3. If the entire quantity of goods duly certificated are sold while *en route* to a stated destination, then the certificate must be cancelled at the barrier where the goods are sold.

4. Should the entire quantity of certificated goods not be sold, but only a portion be sold, on the remainder reaching the next barrier the quantity and description of the goods sold and the place where the sale took place must be reported by the merchant to the Likin Office, whereupon the official in charge of the Likin Office will make an endorsement on the certificate under his seal of office, and the balance of the goods will be allowed to pass without delay.

5. Clear and strict instructions must be issued to the officials in charge of the barriers nearest the port whence goods are despatched inland that they must not allow certificates duly stamped by them to pass goods a second time.

6. If on examination it be found that certificates are being used a second time, the goods specified by them will be confiscated.

I am well aware that none of this information is new to the Associated Chambers nor to the China Merchants, but, in view of the forthcoming revision of the Tariff, I have thought it wise to shortly summarize the whole question of our Treaty rights from 1842 down to the present day, and so to place the exact position of affairs before business men who have not time to turn up treaties and regulations to verify important points.

With regard to the new rules, excellent as they are, I agree with the Inspector-General that no satisfactory settlement of this much-vexed question will ever be arrived at till it is made a necessary condition of foreign trade with China that all taxes on goods imported or exported on behalf of foreigners shall be levied at one place, the port of arrival in the case of imports, and the port of departure in the case of exports, and to secure this China must make it illegal for any duties to be collected *en route* under any pretext whatever.

ILLEGAL TAXES

The principal illegal taxes at present collected on goods *in transitu* are Likin (a sòrt of provincial Customs due levied in every province, and sometimes in nearly every district of a province), Chingfui (or Defence tax), the Haikow, and the Loti-Shui (or Destination tax).

The likin tax is said to have originated owing to the necessity to raise money after the Taiping rebellion. The whole object of it appears to be to squeeze the poor, the weak, and the enterprising. It is an effectual bar to the extension of trade.

No sooner is a new trade route opened than likin exactions are imposed, and in every province it is merely an excuse for tyranny and extortion. Illegal as it is, when levied on foreign goods under transit pass, it is curious to find both the British and German Governments giving the tax a legal status by accepting seven Likin Collectorates as collateral security for the last Anglo-German loan.

The seven collectorates are as follows:

Salt Collectorates.
    Tchang ⎫
    Hankow ⎭ . . . . . . Province of Hupeh.
    Tatung (Wuhu) . . . .   " " Anhui.

General Cargo.
    Kiukiang . . . . . .   " " Kiangsi.
    Suchow . . . .   " " "
    Sung-Hu (Shanghai) . . " " "
    Eastern part of province, Chihkiang.

Collection is estimated at five million taels per annum.

The likin is not only a hinderance to trade, but also causes most wasteful expenditure of men and money. Only about one-fifth of the amount collected ever reaches the authorities, and to avoid the tax coolies are employed to carry goods miles round a likin barrier, which delays traffic.

The Native Customs House working alongside the Imperial Maritime Customs is a great anomaly. It hinders trade by enabling heavy charges to be levied on Chinese merchants who have

TRADE, TREATIES, AND TARIFFS

bought goods from the foreigner which have already paid all legitimate dues. It is from beginning to end a bad system, and foreign trade suffers less by the amount levied upon it in going up or coming down country than it does by the intolerable delays and difficulties which this system entails.

The British merchants drew my attention to the fact that these duties, illegally levied, checked the import trade, and often caused serious loss in the export trade. A merchant in China undertakes to deliver in London a certain quantity of goods by a certain date. The merchant is compelled to deliver or to pay. The fact of the rate of exchange being against him, when the time comes for him to deliver, is one unavoidable cause of loss, but when there is added to this the heavy sums he has to pay to the Likin Collectorates to get his goods in time to deliver, it will be seen how serious a matter it is.

At several places the merchants pointed out to me that the officials know very well that the merchant must have his goods delivered by a certain time, and so they ignore the transit pass, and the supercargo has either to pay the squeeze demanded or suffer months of delay. News is a long time reaching the coast. The Consul protests, and orders are sent to release cargoes. Total detention runs into months. Next time the Chinese in charge of goods pay, to avoid delay. British merchants pay it either in increased freight, if price of goods is already settled, or, if not, in increased price. If contract has been made for forward delivery at a fixed price, this seriously affects the margin of profit. The merchants intend to press for indemnity if the present system continues. They claim that the present way of getting an apology from the Taotai is of no use. The only way to deal with the Chinese authorities in such cases is to attack their pockets. It is of no use for the merchant to take the case before his Consul, because there is great difficulty in getting the Chinese compradors and supercargoes to give evidence before the Taotai. If they give such evidence, the Likin Offices pass the word along the line, and the Chinese comprador finds himself boycotted when he next goes up country for goods. The remedy the British merchants suggest is that when a cargo has been delayed for weeks at likin barriers, despite the transit pass which covers it, the Consul should be authorized to fine the local official, and remit the fine to the Imperial Maritime Customs. The merchants claim that if this system was inaugurated the present squeezes would soon be stopped, as the Peking authorities would take care the local mandarin paid the fine, which would go to swell the receipts of the Imperial Chinese Customs; on the other hand, the local Taotai would be less supine, having an interest in finding and punishing the offenders, in order to recover the sum by which he was out of pocket.

TRADE, TREATIES, AND TARIFFS

Sometimes the officials refuse to issue transit passes for frivolous reasons. A Mr. Morrison applied to Mr. Brenan, Consul-General at Shanghai, some six weeks before I left China, for a transit pass for sheepskins. The Taotai refused to grant this, giving no better reason than that such business was a novelty. Mr. Brenan sent in a bill to the Taotai for actual damages for delay and loss of time. To give the Taotai a lesson, Mr. Morrison should be allowed to claim moral and indirect damages as well, which should amount to 1000 taels rather than 100 taels. This sort of thing puts enterprising merchants off, whereas if Mr. Morrison received encouragement and succeeded, it would benefit and stimulate trade and commerce.

The transit-pass system cannot be said to be an "utter failure," as the facts reported in the chapter on "Chinkiang" will show. The new rules have, no doubt, done a good deal towards stimulating this system, but much still remains to be done. We have only ourselves to blame for the troubles which have arisen. The text of the treaties was clear, but the British Board of Trade gave away our case by admitting the destination tax to be legal 30 years ago; while Sir Thomas Wade, when Minister at Peking, actually laid down the extraordinary dictum as to likin that "it was *not* legal within foreign settlements," implying that it *was* legal outside. The whole wording of the treaties as to transit-pass dues contravenes this, giving an exactly opposite decision.

The French have made a much better stand, and their action has benefited British trade in the South. Of late years, however, the British Legation at Peking have directed their efforts to protecting British interests on this question, and the good effect of their action is now being felt.

Of the other taxes, the " Loti Shui " is probably the most obnoxious. It is generally farmed out to some official whose interest it is, therefore, to get as much as he can. Although described as a destination tax, it is also very often imposed as a growers' tax.

The taxes levied on exports are the greatest possible evils to Chinese products. The tea trade has been nearly crushed out, and taxation, combined with the deterioration which necessarily follows in cultivation, is destroying it. If foreign capital came to its assistance and better methods of cultivation were introduced, it might still stand a chance. Russia is now attempting to cultivate Chinese tea in the southern parts of her Empire, and some thousands of coolies have been deported to Russia to assist in starting the cultivation. Most of them, I was told, went from the district around Hankow, which is the great tea centre. Silk has also suffered from taxation, and Japan is now actively competing with China in this branch; while the taxation placed upon the cotton grower is slowly but surely killing that industry also.

Although these taxes are paid by the Chinese,

TRADE, TREATIES, AND TARIFFS

they are all subjects for the Associated Chambers' attention, as taxation which injures and reduces the productive capabilities of a country affects not only the natives of that country, but all foreign merchants trading with it.

One of the harassing taxes in China which prevents and retards the expansion of trade is the tax imposed on their own domestic trade—viz., a duty of 2½% *ad valorem* on all goods passing from one port in China to another port.

The salt monopoly is another of the taxes which requires to be reformed if China is to prosper. At present it presses very hardly on the poorer classes, and is a drag on the natural resources of the country. In other parts of the Report I have given instances where the inhabitants of fishing towns actually imported salted fish as an article of diet, as it was cheaper than salting the fish they caught themselves. Salt is a necessity of life, particularly in Eastern countries, and while it may legitimately be made a source of revenue if so desired, no one can doubt that its taxation, if improperly administered, is a great hardship to the people. The reform in Egypt in this department might be well imitated in China.

The land tax is constantly complained of by both foreigners and Chinese. In any revision of the tariff the reform of this tax will be asked for by the foreign communities.

There are two sides to every question, and before entering into the question of tariff revision I should like to say a few words upon the Chinese side of this question.

The difficulties in the way of reform lie chiefly in the fact that the provincial Governments must have revenue from some source or other, and you cannot hope to suddenly suspend indirect taxation which the people are accustomed to, and replace it by direct taxation, as would appear to be necessary if likin and other octroi are abandoned. The provincial Governments rely chiefly upon likin for their revenue, and although the Chefoo Convention authorizes Chinese purchasers to take out transit passes to cover goods, the authorities, who see their revenue disappearing, look upon the Chinese, not as making use of a treaty right, but as abusing it to evade the payment of Chinese taxes. This is one of the matters in which a proper appreciation of Chinese official needs must be shown before the arrangements can be expected to work smoothly and without friction.

Another point is that, at present, Canton sugar goes to Hong Kong in native junks, and is thence sent in foreign bottoms to treaty ports, claiming transit privileges as having acquired a foreign character. This is regarded as an abuse of transit rights, and native officials proceed to make difficulties for the whole transit system. Revision and fuller definitions, coupled with consideration for China's financial necessities, may put the transit pass system on a proper and workable basis.

TRADE, TREATIES, AND TARIFFS

REVISION OF TARIFFS

The request of China for a revision of the tariff is complicated by the fact that all the treaties do not expire together. To protect the British merchant, it may be necessary for the Associated Chambers to see that whatever is done in this direction is done by all the Powers together.

Neither the Anglo-Saxon nor other foreign merchants appear to object to any increase in the tariffs, provided greater facilities for trade are granted, and necessary reforms in the fiscal system are given as a *quid pro quo*. The merchants and Chamber of Commerce with whom I discussed this question expressed themselves in different ports in China to be willing to consent to an increase of the present duty from 5 per cent. to 10 per cent., 12 per cent., or even 15 per cent. all round, but if increased to this extent they hold that the transit-pass dues should be done away with, and that all merchandise, having paid duty on entering the country, should be free of all further taxation whatsoever.

The Associated Chambers of Commerce will notice that the present duties amount to 7½ per cent. (5 per cent. customs and 2½ per cent. transit), but that even after this 7½ per cent. the merchandise is liable to be illegally taxed. It would appear, therefore, that even an increase of the present duties to 15 per cent. would in the long run pay the foreign trader, provided that this 15 per cent. was a full, final, and inclusive charge, and no other taxation of any kind was imposed. It would also pay the Chinese Government, as even if they returned a percentage of this increase to the Provincial authorities, in order to reimburse them for their loss of likin, etc., they would still have a considerable surplus over the present receipts. More than this, both the Imperial and Provincial revenue would soon feel the effect of increased trade which greater privileges and a certain fixed duty would undoubtedly produce.

The foreign merchants without exception agree that tariff revision which grants China any increase of revenue must include the following as a *quid pro quo*:

1. Extended rights of residence and trade to foreigners.
2. Removal of all restrictions on navigation on inland waters, and opening up of internal communication by railways.
3. Guarantees for the immunity of foreign merchandise from further taxation, after it has paid the duties fixed by treaty.

They also considered that other necessary reforms, not directly connected with the question of tariffs, should be undertaken. These reforms I have fully mentioned in my " Observations " at the end of this Report, and I would submit to the Associated Chambers of Commerce that, if

TRADE, TREATIES, AND TARIFFS

treaty revision is undertaken, it would be an excellent opportunity to bring that moral pressure on the Chinese Government which would ensure all of these reforms being carried out. The Chinese authorities must have money to carry on administration, and the commercial classes must have some return for the concessions they will be asked to make.

One important point in tariff revision should not be overlooked by the commercial classes of this country. *Ad valorem* duty is based upon a fixed scale of values in certain commodities. The fall in prices in some of these has made the 5 per cent. *ad valorem* really much more than 5 per cent. In some cases the increase has been so great as to wipe out almost any margin of profit.

On the Chinese side one important matter should be considered when treaty revision takes place. The Chinese authorities complain that some merchants have been known to declare the value of their goods at much below the real sum. This dishonesty not only affects customs receipts, but also injuriously affects their more honest trade rivals. Some method should be devised of giving the customs authorities a check upon the value of the cargoes.

The next question is, How is treaty revision to be carried out in fairness to both sides, and to secure that all these just demands of the merchants receive proper attention? The difficulty about some of the treaties having several years yet to run before they expire will not be dealt with easily. The French treaty and our own are conterminous, but the Japanese has eight years and the German four years to run. I submit that the proper thing for China to do would be to try and induce these countries to allow their treaties to lapse, and join Great Britain and France in a new general commercial treaty. Failing this, the only way will be for China to give a continuation of the British and French treaties till the date the others fall in. Unless this is done, Great Britain and France will be binding themselves to pay specially high rates of duty, while the most-favored-nation clause would allow other Powers to share in the privileges and concessions which they obtained from China in return for such duties.

The Marquis Ito, in one of the interviews I had with him, suggested that the only way to settle treaty revision in a satisfactory and speedy manner was to have a conference of Ministers in China. He pointed out that to refer the questions involved to the various home Governments would involve needless delay and confusion. Those on the spot, who knew the subject thoroughly, should be intrusted by the Governments with the work of discussing and agreeing upon the points to be determined, and the result of their deliberations could then be forwarded in the form of a draft treaty to their respective Governments. It appears to me that this suggestion of the Marquis Ito is one worthy of consideration.

TRADE, TREATIES, AND TARIFFS

The merchants suggested that, in order to arrive at a proper understanding and to assist the Ministers, there should first of all be a committee of consuls sent round to the various ports to obtain the views of the mercantile communities upon certain definite questions, and to formulate their demands. Such a commission should consist, they thought, of Chinese officials, British consuls, European (not British) consuls, and a British merchant. Due care should be taken that the interests of all nations were fairly represented, but that it was in proportion to their trade.

What the future of foreign trade in China might be is well illustrated by a comparison between the foreign trade of that country and Japan at the present moment. Japan is a country without a tittle of the natural resources of China. Japan has only a population of 42,000,000; China has a population of over 400,000,000. Japan's foreign trade last year was $444,000,000; China's foreign trade last year was $495,000,000.

In conclusion, I cannot avoid noticing here the very hearty, sound, business ideas of British merchants in China as expressed to me in the interviews I had with them. I found no petty feeling of commercial rivalry animating them. On the contrary, they were most anxious to impress upon me how successful their methods were, and how little they feared the competition of other nationals, if a fair field was assured them. There is more danger of their undervaluing the effect of commercial rivalry

THE BREAK-UP OF CHINA

than of complaints or ill-feeling because of such rivalry.

To summarize this weighty subject, the points are as follows:

 1. There are many fresh openings for trade, to which the attention of British manufacturers should be directed. The commodities I would specially note are—glass, tool-steel, steel wire rope, electric plant, railway material, mining machinery, high explosives for mining purposes, and machinery of all kinds.

 2. Treaty rights must be enforced, and illegal impositions on trade be prevented.

 3. In return for tariff revision the whole question of fiscal and other reforms ought to be raised as a *quid pro quo*.

 4. This *quid pro quo* must include all and every facility for trade and commerce to penetrate into the interior.

 5. Help the Chinese to reorganize their forces, to police the country, or trade cannot be secure.

The situation in China to-day bristles with international, commercial, and financial difficulties. British commerce, once the only occupant of the field, has now to face competition and adverse political influences, and if the 64 per cent. of British trade is to be maintained and increased, our commercial classes will have to use all their energies and abilities to keep the flag of Great Britain in the front of commercial enterprise in China.

XXVIII

JAPAN

As I received several invitations from Chambers of Commerce and prominent personages interested in Chinese trade to visit both Japan and America, I came home through those two countries, hoping that I might be able to gather some useful information for the Associated Chambers of Commerce.

On arriving at Nagasaki, January 11, 1899, I visited the large mercantile docks and works of the Mitsu Bishi Company.

Perhaps the following facts may be interesting to the ship-building community of this country:

There are two yards, a short distance apart, both under the direction of the same company. They employ 4000 men. I found on the stocks a steamer building for the Japanese mercantile fleet —6000 tons, 430 feet long, and 45 feet beam. She had a double bottom right fore and aft, 11 watertight bulkheads, *without doors*, twin-screws to run 12 knots with 7200 tons dead-weight. I was much struck by the safety and capabilities of this vessel. She had a sister ship already launched and carrying freight. I was told that both of these ships will be built at a loss, owing to the steel they use, which comes from Scotland, costing £10 a ton on delivery. This loss is borne by Baron Yonoski Iwasaki and Baron Hisaya, two rich Japanese gentlemen, in support of the patriotic idea of starting shipbuilding in Japan. With the exception of the loss on these two ships, the yards are doing a thriving business. I saw two good docks, one 520 feet long, and the other 360 feet long. I also found an excellent example of the art of competition. The Americans are trying to introduce both tool steel and pig-iron at such a low price as must entail a loss. All the tool steel and pig-iron at present comes from Great Britain, as does all the coke that is used, and the boiler tubes and ingot steel—the latter from Glasgow. All the boilers and engines and ordinary shafting are made at the works, but very heavy shafting comes from abroad.

The shops were in first-rate order, well found, well built and cared for.

The Japanese are making strenuous efforts to convey all their water-borne commerce in Japanese vessels. From what I saw in Japan I should be inclined to think that the trade most likely to be developed with Great Britain is machinery. A large amount of machinery in Japan is of British manufacture, and it will be satisfactory to the Associated Chambers to know that the last order for twenty engines for the Government railway has been given to Great Britain.

JAPAN

In the near future Nagasaki is certain to be a point of departure, being such a good harbor, and right in the route between America and China. The energy and enterprise of the Mitsu Bishi Dock Company is sure to find its reward.

I arrived at Kobé on the 13th of January. I found the minds of the British merchants here much occupied over the new jurisdiction which is to come into force in Japan 1st of July, 1899. After receiving several addresses I was asked to give an opinion on this matter. In answer, I remarked that it would be well to see how this new treaty acted before criticising it adversely, and that it would further the interests of British trade if the British merchants allowed it to be understood that as far as they were concerned they would do their best to help the Japanese Government to carry out the tenor of the treaty, and so endeavor to make it a success.

At Osaka I visited the Military Arsenal. It was principally employed making a new quick-firing gun—12-pounder—for horse and field artillery, Japanese patent. The principle was certainly second to none. They were also making a magazine rifle, Japanese patent, and quite perfect in design and construction. Most of the machinery in this arsenal is British.

I visited one of the factories of the Japan Sugar Refining Company. This enterprise pays well. The sugar comes from Java and is refined for use in Japan. The machinery here was made in Great Britain.

I also visited the largest of the 17 cotton mills at Osaka. All the machinery I saw was British, and I was told this was the case throughout all the mills. This mill employed 5000 men, women, and children. I saw some weaving mills also. There were some 54,000 spindles and 600 looms at work. In Japan there are 70 cotton mills altogether.

There are 30 match factories at Osaka, but most of them are on a very small scale. I visited one, the Osaka Sei Sui Company. A great part of the work is done by hand, but what machinery they have is German. They employ 1500 men, women, and children. I made particular inquiries as to whether any of the diseases generated by match-making were common in these factories. I was informed they had no experience of such diseases whatever.

I went over some very busy iron and steel works, which belonged to an Englishman but were registered as a Japanese Company. The works are extensive and show great enterprising energy. Twelve hundred men are employed. I saw a very good small dry-dock and three steamers on the slips, the biggest of which was 600 tons. Several steam-pinnaces were building.

I have called attention to these facts in the Report, for although they are not connected with Anglo-Saxon trade proper, they are industries developing in Japan, and increasing the volume of Japanese trade. This increase in volume must create a demand for goods of Anglo-Saxon manufacture.

I was invited to attend a meeting at which the Mayor, the General Commanding, the Members of the Chambers of Commerce, and all representative citizens were present. The Mayor spoke of the importance of the Mission sent by the Associated Chambers to China, and declared that it was imperative for the future of Japanese trade that the "Open Door" policy be adhered to.

On the 15th of January, at Kioto, I went over the great electric plant worked by water-power, produced with a fall of 120 feet. This power supplies Kioto with two-thirds of the electric light, works the electric trams, the pumping for the water-works, and no less than sixty different industries in or near the town. All the machinery, which is excellent, is American. The entire plant cost £50,000. This sum was found by the municipal council, who are solely responsible for the scheme and its successful carrying out. This system of electric batteries is, I think, one of the most remarkable examples of municipal progress, energy, and enterprise to be seen in Japan, or perhaps in any country.

Another further interesting example of municipal enterprise is illustrated by the following:

There is a great trade and passenger traffic from Kioto to Lake Biwa, and through the lake to the surrounding country. Boats used to come up the river from the sea to Kioto and there discharge their passengers or cargo. A mile had then to be traversed to reach the lake, where passengers and cargo again embarked for distribution. This interruption has been done away with by the following ingenious device. On arrival at Kioto the boats are now floated into a cradle and hauled up the mile, the incline of which is 120 feet, by a steel wire hawser worked by an electric motor. By this means the same boats perform the whole distance of sixty miles from the sea to the farther end of the lake. This electric tramway for boats is most extensively used, there being always boats waiting to take their turn. The municipality only charge a small carriage of thirty cents on each boat hauled up the incline. The invention and the whole plant is American.

There is no country which I have visited where electricity as a motive power has been taken advantage of to the same extent as in Japan, for the furtherance and development of trade and commerce. Telephones and telegraphs abound in every street in nearly every town throughout the empire, and a very large and increasing number of manufactures are worked by electric power. I made many inquiries as to the original outlay and working expenses, comparing electricity with steam-power, and, taking all circumstances into consideration, the former is unquestionably the cheaper.

Before leaving Kioto I was invited to a meeting

JAPAN

at the Mayoralty, which was attended by all the leading Japanese officials and merchants. His Excellency the Governor, Wutsumi Tadakatsu, formally welcomed me, as representing British trade and commerce, to Kioto. He spoke of the future of China, and maintained that it was necessary for Japan to keep the Open Door for her trade in that country. I met J. Naiki, the Mayor of Kioto, K. Hamaoka, President of the Chamber of Commerce, K. Amenomori, Chairman of the City Assembly, and many others. All these gentlemen were very earnest in their hopes that the "Open Door" policy would be strongly supported and guaranteed by those countries who have trade in China. They made frequent allusions to the friendly feeling existing between Japan and Great Britain.

I arrived at Tokio on the morning of January 17th. That evening I had the honor of meeting the following Japanese gentlemen: Marshal Yamagata, the Minister-President; Viscount Aoki, Minister for Foreign Affairs; Marquis Saigo, Minister for the Interior; General Viscount Katsura, Minister for War; Admiral Yamamoto, Minister for Marine; Viscount Tanaka, Minister of the Imperial Household; Baron Sannomiya, Grand Master of the Ceremonies; Baron Kawaguchi, Vice-Minister of the Household; and Count Hirosawa, Private Secretary to the Minister-President. All these gentlemen were intensely interested in the trading and commercial future of China. They were quite open in their opinion as to the necessity for the great trading nations to combine together with the object of keeping the door open in China. Their expressions were most friendly to Great Britain, and the remark was frequently made: "England and Japan must work together in the East in order to secure the future development of their trade and commerce."

I elicited the opinion that the "Sphere of Influence" policy in China would be considered fatal to the trading interest of Japan. On asking why, it was pointed out to me that Japan had a large and increasing trade with Corea and Newchwang, and hoped shortly to develop a large trade at Foochow and Hankow; that if the Open Door principle prevailed Japan intended to push her mercantile enterprises in other parts of China. Opinions were often given that the integrity of China must be preserved if the principle of the "Open Door" was to obtain. I was further informed that the question of the reorganization of the Chinese Army was occupying the attention of those in authority in Japan, and with the object of helping China forward in this direction the Japanese Government had consented to receive thirty Chinese students into the military college at Tokio. Besides these students, while I was at Tokio, fifty-seven Chinese recruits arrived from China to be trained as non-commissioned officers. I asked the opinions of those officers who had been in command in China during the late Chino-Japanese War as to the soldier-like qualities of the Chinese.

JAPAN

Opinion was unanimous that they would make splendid soldiers if properly trained, properly treated, and properly led. Throughout my journey in Japan I heard the most friendly expressions towards the Chinese.

I was given to understand that the Mission sent to China by the Associated Chambers of Commerce was regarded with the keenest interest in Japan. The Japanese hoped that it would result in a closer relationship between the two nations, as the interests of each were identical.

On several other occasions I had opportunities of meeting high authorities, and the leading merchants of Japan. The expressions of opinion were always similar to those above narrated.

I again had the pleasure of paying several visits to the late Prime-Minister, Marquis Ito.

During my stay at Tokio the authorities took me over the various schools for military training—the District School, the Central School, and the Military School, where I saw all the classes at work, both in the lecture-hall and in the gymnasium and riding-school. Nothing could be more perfect than the system of teaching and training.

I also went over the arsenal and made myself acquainted with the pay, hours, and system of the establishment. There are 6000 men employed. No country turns out better work. The greater part of the machinery and tools are British, the remainder being German and American.

While at Tokio the Minister for War, General

Viscount Katsura, kindly ordered a parade of troops. Artillery, cavalry, and infantry were each quite excellent in organization, appearance, and discipline. The cavalry and artillery are mounted on a very good class of horse, bred in the country from Arab and American stallions. I also saw recruits in every stage of learning their drill.

The remarkable increase of the physical development of the men who serve in the army is well worthy of notice. It was so apparent that I questioned the officers as to the reason. They said that the fact was perceived with the greatest satisfaction throughout the whole Empire, and that it was accounted for by the physical exercises the men had to perform in their training, as well as the change of diet which had been inaugurated. Part of the men's rations now is bread (made with American flour) and meat, the same as that supplied to the troops of European countries. I tasted a ration and found it excellent.

The barracks which I saw are as smart and clean as is possible. I visited the stores of clothing, etc., for the reserve; each regiment is responsible for its own reserve clothing necessary for mobilization. The *esprit de corps* of the Japanese Army is very apparent. The Government allows a certain sum to each regiment for the clothing for the reserves. The colonels and officers by economies and even subscriptions increase the amount of clothing until the stores are really in excess of that laid down, which adds considerably

JAPAN

to the comfort of the men if suddenly called out.

The Chamber of Commerce at Tokio invited me to address a public meeting on the future development of trade with China. I did not think it would be courteous to refuse. The meeting was attended by Ministers, military and naval officers of distinction, the President and many members of both Houses, and all the leading gentlemen of the mercantile community. My remarks were translated for the benefit of those who did not understand English. I was informed that the views I expressed were in hearty sympathy with the audience, who thought they tended towards the development of trade with China, and also provided a peaceful solution of the problem in the Far East. It was conveyed to me that if Great Britain would only lead with a definite policy in China, Japan would most certainly follow.

Several Japanese merchants came to see me, and asked me to convey to the Associated Chambers of Commerce a matter which they declare hinders Japanese trade with Great Britain. They said that the merchants of Tokio had always to pay in advance for goods forwarded direct to Tokio, which was not the case with goods ordered for Yokohama.

I visited the new prison of Tokio, with the object of ascertaining whether any industrial works were carried on in the establishment. I found all prisoners were employed in working for private firms, who employed them by contract; nearly every industry was represented.

Before leaving Tokio I had an opportunity of paying my respects to his Majesty the Emperor. His Majesty was much interested in the objects of the Commercial Mission to China. His Majesty said: "I am very pleased you have visited my country. The development of trade with China must promote a stronger feeling of friendship between the peoples of Great Britain and Japan, the interests of both countries being the same. I am in hopes that the Mission you have undertaken may be the commencement of great trading enterprise in the East, in which my country must take a prominent part. Such enterprise will not only affect the East, but Europe as well, though Japan and Great Britain will be the countries that will principally benefit."

I arrived at Yokohama on the 24th of January, and was invited by the Minister for Marine, Admiral Yamamoto, to visit the dockyard and fleet at Yokoska. The Admiral placed H.I.M. cruiser *Takasago*, built at Elswick, at my disposal to take me from Yokokama to Yokoska. I went all over the ship, engine-rooms, boiler-rooms, etc. She was in as good condition as a man-of-war could be, and her ship's company were smart, well dressed, and well disciplined. There is a large torpedo depot at this place, where everything connected with torpedo warfare is kept under its own administration for care and maintenance—boats, mines, cables, batteries, torpedoes of all sorts, and all stores connected with torpedo warfare belong to this depot. This is an infinitely preferable plan to the British, where everything connected with torpedo warfare is only an auxiliary of the great dockyards. I saw here three of the Chinese ships captured by the Japanese in the late war, among them being the *Chen Yuen*. They were all being refitted for service in the fleet. I went all over the naval barracks, which were in the same complete state of efficiency that I found all naval and military establishments in Japan. I observed the same system carried out with the seamen's rations as is carried out with the military rations. The officers in command informed me that before the rations were altered to those in vogue in Europe—*i.e.*, meat and bread substituted for or added to native diet — the terrible disease of beri-beri was not at all uncommon in the Japanese Navy. Since the alteration of this ration the disease has entirely disappeared.

My visit to Japan impressed me that the political as well as the commercial classes are determined to maintain an "Open Door" in China, in those places where they have at present large commercial interests. The nation is arming slowly, but most effectively. There is a patriotism among all classes that is most discernible. The future well-being of Japan depends much more largely on the maintenance of the "Open Door" in China than is generally known in this country.

The population of Japan is increasing rapidly. Only one-twelfth of the whole Empire can be cultivated. Food will have to be imported. In a bad rice year now, food is imported in enormous quantities. In order to pay for this import Japan must have an export. China is the nearest market, and Japan requires that her export shall not be hampered by adverse tariffs on arrival in China. I have entered rather fully in this Report into the question of the organization and efficiency of the naval and military forces of Japan; because these forces will have to be reckoned with when solving the problems connected with the future development of trade and commerce in the Far East, and their efficiency must be almost as great a point of interest to Great Britain as it is to Japan.

XXIX

THE UNITED STATES

I ARRIVED at San Francisco on February 10th. I visited the great ship-building yard of the Union Steel and Iron Works. This yard turned out the famous battle-ship *Oregon* and the cruiser *Columbia*. The battle-ship *Wisconsin* had been recently launched here, and was being completed. This yard has the reputation of continually turning out men-of-war vessels at from one to two knots over the contract speed. While I was there the Japanese cruiser *Chitose*, built at the Union Works, undertook her contract steam-trial, the result being nearly two knots over her contract speed. I visited this vessel, and found her excellent in all details. Her armament was to be supplied by Elswick. This yard has patented a pair of electric engines for revolving the turrets of the heavy guns mounted on the *Wisconsin*. It is a cheap, light, and most efficient method. By invitation of the Commodore, I visited the Naval Yard at Mare Island, and saw some of the auxiliary ships sent out with the *Iowa* and *Oregon*. These consisted of five colliers, properly fitted for coaling, a distilling-ship, and a refrigerating-ship for fresh provisions. The provision-ship, the *Celtic*, bought from an English firm, can carry in her refrigerators fresh meat and vegetable rations for 10,000 men for four months. I visited her and saw all her fittings. The two battle-ships were entirely self-supporting during their long cruise from the Atlantic to the Pacific, owing to sailing in company with these auxiliaries. I mention this in the Report, as it is the first practical illustration of what can be done to enable a fleet to keep at sea, ready for action, and supplied with all necessaries —a matter very important for the protection of trade and commerce to a country with such vast maritime interests as Great Britain.

The San Francisco Chamber of Commerce asked me to address them on matters connected with the future development of trade in China. I accepted their invitation. Afterwards, many members of the Chamber informed me that they entirely concurred with the view that the "Open Door" was the only satisfactory solution of the problem of how to develop trade in China. They also said that they hoped the present friendly feeling between the United States and Great Britain would always continue, maintaining that if the two countries worked together it would not only benefit the trade and commerce of the world but also make for peace. All the mercantile community were intensely interested in the Eastern Question, pointing out that San Francisco would

THE UNITED STATES

naturally be the port for the great output of American trade when China was opened up.

I arrived at Chicago on February 17th, where, as the representative of the British Associated Chambers, I enjoyed the hospitality of Mr. McCormick, the President, and the Committee of the Commercial Club. These gentlemen invited me to visit the Board of Trade (the Produce and Stock Exchange of Chicago). On being introduced as the representative of the British Associated Chambers, the whole business of the great market ceased for the moment, an event, I was informed, absolutely without precedent, which showed the keen interest taken in the Commercial Mission of Inquiry which had been sent to China.

Every possible kindness was shown me, and I was enabled to visit the Great Bank (Illinois Trust), the operating room of the Postal Telegraph and Cable Company—one of the largest in the world—the printing works of one of the great newspapers, and other establishments of great interest.

I was entertained (February 18th) by the Commercial Club, where I met the President of the Club and also the representative merchants of this great city. The regular date of this entertainment was altered to suit my convenience, an unusual compliment only once before paid to an individual—viz., General Grant—a further proof of the interest taken in the Mission to China.

The speeches delivered, after the remarks I

ventured to make, seemed to indicate that the mercantile community of Chicago were intensely interested in the Chinese problem, and that they regarded the question of equal opportunity for the trade of all nations in China as being quite as necessary for the development of the American trade as it was for British trade.

I arrived at Buffalo on February 20th. I was invited by the Merchants' Exchange and the Independent Club to address a meeting on the commercial future of China. The sentiments generally expressed after my remarks were to the effect that the " Open Door " was essential for the further development of American trade with China. Some gentlemen interested in the great electric plant at Niagara kindly took me all over the colossal works. There is no reason why Buffalo and its vicinity should not become the greatest manufacturing city in the world. I observed that already the ground between Buffalo and Niagara was well occupied with manufactories built and building. I was informed that motive power—electricity—is supplied from Niagara to those who rent it at $5 (£1) per horse-power per month. Every one connected with this electric plant feels assured that a splendid future awaits their enterprise.

I visited Washington and paid my respects to the President of the United States, and was most hospitably entertained by Mr. Hay, the Secretary of State and late American Ambassador to Great

THE UNITED STATES

Britain, where I met many distinguished Americans, senators and others.

The British Commercial Mission to China was regarded with considerable interest by all whom I met.

I arrived at New York on February 23d. That night I was entertained by the American Asiatic Association, and I was asked to deliver an address. The American Asiatic Association was formed on the same lines, and with the same objects, as the British China Association, and, like the China Association, its objects are political. It watches over the American commercial interests in the Far East, and brings political pressure to bear in furtherance of those interests. A notable feature of this entertainment was an eloquent speech delivered by Mr. Whitelaw Reid, the great apostle of Protection in the United States, declaring that the "Open Door" policy was the best for American trade in the Philippine Islands and in China and, more, that the American Government intended to commit itself to this policy in the Philippine Islands.

The following day I was asked to address the Chamber of Commerce of New York. This meeting was quite as crowded and enthusiastic as the other meetings which I had been requested to address in the United States. At all these meetings I spoke on matters solely connected with trade as it at present exists in China, and on questions connected with its future development and security.

THE BREAK-UP OF CHINA

There can be no doubt that the subject excited a considerable amount of interest throughout the United States. This was shown not only by the manner in which the Press of the country discussed the matter, but also by the numerous letters I received from trading and commercial communities from all parts of the United States, and by the many telegrams inviting me to address public meetings throughout the country. Among these latter were several from the largest and most important cities of the United States, such as Philadelphia, Boston, Milwaukee, Louisville, Kansas City, Cincinnati, Baltimore, and many more, besides those I had the pleasure of visiting.

I visited the Naval Yard, where I was received with the greatest kindness and cordiality by the authorities. I went on board the *Massachusetts*, a most serviceable and heavily armed battle-ship.

I visited also the great steel cable factory, and observed the most interesting method of effectually lubricating the shaft; the shaft, with the six reels containing steel-wire strands, weighs 250 tons. It revolves at the rate of 106 revolutions a minute, on a bearing 9 inches in diameter. It is kept lubricated by means of an automatic hydraulic pump, of great power, charged with oil. I was informed that a hot bearing is unknown, although the shaft, with all its weight, rests vertically on so small a surface.

I travelled home through the United States, hoping to be able to obtain from the Chambers

THE UNITED STATES

of Commerce some definite opinions for the Associated Chambers of Great Britain. The interest in the Mission was intense, and I personally was received with the most unbounded hospitality, kindness, and cordiality. I was asked to give my views on China, and what opportunities existed for the development of trade (particularly American trade) in the East.

Since my return home I have continued to receive many letters of a similar tenor, three of which I here append to show the interest taken by the commercial communities in the United States in the Mission in which I was engaged.

"MASSACHUSETTS STATE BOARD OF TRADE,
    "LOWELL, Mass., *March* 21, 1899.
"Rear-Admiral Lord Charles Beresford, R. N.,
    "representing the
    "Association of Chambers of Commerce
    "of the United Kingdom,
            "London, England.

"DEAR SIR,—The Members of the Massachusetts State Board of Trade, composed of forty-two mercantile organizations representing the commercial and industrial interests of the State, beg to acknowledge receipt of your favor of the 21st ultimo, and also express their regrets that your limited time in this country would not permit an acceptance of the invitation to visit our Commonwealth.

"The Mission in which you have been recently engaged, under the auspices of the Associated

Chambers of Commerce, to ascertain the best methods for promoting trade and commerce in China, is one of more than ordinary importance to the American people, and the results of your investigation, as embodied in a report, will be read with great interest throughout the commercial and industrial world.

"The Massachusetts State Board of Trade is in hearty sympathy with any plan that will provide equitable national competition for the import and export trade of the great Chinese Empire, and believes that the earnest support and forceful influence of commercial bodies among the nations interested should be freely given in promoting and advancing national legislation in this direction.

"Please convey to the Members of the Associated Chambers of Commerce of the United Kingdom the most cordial greetings of the Massachusetts State Board of Trade, who deeply appreciate their earnest efforts to develop trade and commerce and advance the standard of civilization in the Far East.

"With the hope that a practical and beneficial commercial alliance may be the ultimate result of your endeavors,

"We have the honor to remain,
"Very truly yours,
"CHARLES E. ADAMS,
"*President.*"

THE UNITED STATES

"The Philadelphia Commercial Museum,
"233 South Fourth Street,
"Philadelphia, *March* 21, 1899.

"Lord Charles Beresford,
"The Admiralty,
"London England.

"My dear Lord Charles,—I have your very kind favor of March 3d, written on board the *St. Louis*, and appreciate very much your thoughtfulness.

"It was a great disappointment to me, and to Philadelphians generally, that you were not able to visit our city. I was especially sorry not to have had the opportunity of showing you in detail the workings of the Philadelphia Commercial Museum, especially in view of the efforts we are at present making to acquaint our people with the opportunities existing in the Far East—opportunities which you have so eloquently set forth as presenting themselves.

"I trust when the result of your observations in the Orient is laid before the Associated Chambers of Commerce in England, this Institution may be favored with a copy.

"Hoping that some time in the future you may find it possible to visit Philadelphia, and that I may then be fortunate enough to explain to you the efforts being made by our Institution to foster export trade, and trusting that our two countries

may always co-operate in the industrial and commercial development of the Far East, believe me,
"Most sincerely yours,
"W. P. WILSON,
"*Director.*"

"*February* 24, 1899.
"Right Hon. Lord Charles Beresford, M.P.,
"London, England:
"SIR,—I am directed by the President to acknowledge receipt of your valued favor 15th inst. It is a matter of great regret to us that your time was so limited in this country that you could not give us the pleasure of entertaining you.

"Your Mission is one of very great importance to this country, as well as the country you so ably represent. We take this occasion to express the thankfulness (which we believe is the feeling of every true American) for the very cordial relations existing between Great Britain and the United States. So long as cordial relations and active co-operation for the good of humanity exist, untold benefits must come to the world.

"It will give us very great pleasure to receive a copy of your Report.
"Yours faithfully,
"E. D. BIGELOW,
"*Secretary.*"

The principle of the "Open Door" is unanimously held to be the policy necessary for the in-

THE UNITED STATES

crease of the United States trade with China; but there the matter rests. I heard no sentiments expressed which conveyed to me any opinion on the part of any of the American Chambers of Commerce as to how the "Open Door" principle was to be insured, although I did hear many opinions expressed that the time could not be far distant when the Chinese Empire would be added to the list of those countries which had fallen to pieces from internal decay. Though the great trading classes of the United States, as far as I could gather, are keenly alive to the necessity of safeguarding the future of the United States' commercial interests, it was quite apparent to me that those in authority, and indeed the people as a whole, are, for the present, at any rate, going to allow Chinese affairs to take care of themselves. It was very satisfactory to me to be frequently told that the fact of the British Associated Chambers having sent a Mission of Inquiry to China would provoke an interest among the commercial classes of the United States with regard to the future of China. The attitude taken up by the commercial classes in Japan was totally different from that which I found in the United States. Both saw the necessity of keeping the Door open in China if full advantage was to be taken of the possible development of American or Japanese trade; but while on the Japanese side there was every indication of a desire to act in some practical manner in order to secure the Open Door, I could discover no desire on the part of the commercial communities in the United States to engage in any practical effort for preserving what to them might become in the future a trade, the extent of which no mortal can conjecture. On many occasions I suggested that some sort of understanding should exist between Great Britain and the United States for the mutual benefit of the two countries with regard to the future development of trade in China; but while receiving the most cordial support to this proposal, nothing of a definite character was suggested to me that I could present to the Associated Chambers.

Looking at the matter fairly, the public mind in the United States is occupied with an entirely novel policy, which, being an actual fact, must be more engrossing to the American public than matters which up to now even have not advanced into the region of discussion. I refer to the policy of expansion, as illustrated by the difficult problem which has to be solved in the Philippine Islands. Added to this, the actual trade between the United States and China at the present moment is a very small proportion of the whole foreign trade of that country, only 8 per cent. The American trade with China is, however, very much larger than appears in the import list contained in the returns of the Imperial Maritime Customs of the Chinese Empire. Taking the question of the import of plain cotton goods alone for the years 1887–1897 inclusive, referred to in this Report in the chapter

THE UNITED STATES

on "Shanghai," it will be seen that American goods during those ten years have increased in quantity 121.11 per cent., and 59.45 per cent. in value, while the British import of the same class of goods has decreased 13.77 per cent. in quantity, and 7.9 per cent. in value. In examining these trade returns the question of ownership and manufacture is an all-important one. At the time of import this cotton is owned by the British merchant and shipped in British bottoms, but the competition of the United States is directly with the Lancashire cotton manufacturer. I was much impressed by the good feeling and friendship towards Great Britain expressed by all with whom I came in contact in the United States. These kindly sentiments were particularly marked on all occasions when the health of her Majesty the Queen was proposed. I believe that a great deal of the enthusiasm with which I was received during my journey throughout the United States was actuated by the sentiments of kindly feeling towards the British.

There is a very large and increasing export trade of flour from America to China. The Chinese are appreciating this class of food more every year. There is also a great export of American machinery of all sorts to China. The whole of the Russian railway plant in Manchuria — viz., rolling-stock, rails, and sleepers—comes from the United States. There is also a large import of American machinery into Japan.

Although the American percentage of trade with China is only 8 per cent. of the whole, it is important to remember in what a comparatively short time this has been built up, and if to this percentage was added the proportion of British-owned trade in commodities of American origin, I am of opinion that it would be found that the actual American manufactured goods represent a very much larger percentage than is generally known. As it is, American trade represents 8 per cent., as against 28 per cent. of all other nations (excluding Great Britain) combined.

The only direction in which I found a falling off in American trade was in kerosene-oil, in which industry Russia and Sumatra are becoming America's chief competitors. A noteworthy fact that was brought to my notice by the Commissioner of Customs at Newchwang was, that American manufactured goods at that port now represent about 50 per cent. of the whole foreign import, showing that, at any rate in North China, American trade is increasing in volume and importance.

The problems connected with the future development of trade in China will be solved more easily if the powerful Anglo-Saxon races can come to some mutual understanding regarding them. As the interests of the United States and Great Britain are absolutely identical in China, an understanding must conduce to the benefit of both great nations, and certainly make for the peaceful

THE UNITED STATES

solution of the difficulties. Both nations are essentially trading nations, neither want territory, they both wish to increase their trade. With an equal opportunity throughout China, they would not only increase their trade but do much towards increasing the prosperity of the whole world.

XXX

OBSERVATIONS

IN reviewing this Report, several points become apparent:

1. The anxiety of British merchants in China as to the security of capital already invested.

2. The immediate necessity for some assurance to be given to those who are willing to invest further capital.

3. That this existing sense of insecurity is due to the effete condition of the Chinese Government, its corruption and poverty; and to the continual riots, disturbances, and rebellions throughout the country.

4. That the rapidly advancing disintegration of the Chinese Empire is also due to the pressure of foreign claims, which she has no power either to resist or refuse—all this leading to the total internal collapse of authority.

5. The terrible prospect of a civil revolution, extending over an area as large as Europe, among 400 millions of people, upon which catastrophe the thin line of European civilization on the coast, and a few ships of war, would have little or no effect.

OBSERVATIONS

6. The uncertainty as to what Government would follow, should the present dynasty fall, and our ignorance as to what policy any future administration would adopt respecting the contracts and concessions made by the existing Tsung-li-Yamen.

7. The fear of the traders of all nations in China that the home Governments of Europe, in their desire to conciliate the interests of those who seek trade with those who want territory, should drift into the Sphere of Influence policy, thereby endangering the expansion of trade, incurring the risk of war, and hastening the partition and downfall of the Chinese Empire.

8. The apprehension existing in all capable minds in China lest the Governments of Europe, after beginning with the bullying expedient of claims and counter-claims, and then drifting into the policy of Spheres of Influence, should end by hopelessly blocking the Open Door.

9. The undoubted loss of British prestige throughout the whole Chinese Empire owing to recent political events in the North.

From my own observation, I consider these fears and anxieties, put before me by the traders of all nations, and the Chinese, well worthy of the immediate attention of the Associated Chambers of Commerce. Upon the foregoing Points I beg to offer the following Observations:

Upon Point 2, I would observe that the more capital is invested in China, the greater the claims of the foreign traders upon the protection of their home Governments.

As to Point 3, I assert that the great bulk of the Chinese people are honest, acute men of business; that only the traditional method of government is corrupt; the honest mandarin has no chance under the system. Disturbances are due to the want of proper military and police.

With respect to Point 4, I feel most strongly that the pride and profession of Great Britain, to be the champion and chivalrous protector of weak nations, have been humbled and exposed by her acquiescing and taking part in the disintegrating policy of claims and counter-claims with which the Chinese Empire is being bullied while she is down. I hold that to break up a dismasted craft, the timbers of which are stout and strong, is the policy of the wrecker for his own gain. The real seaman tows her into dock and refits her for another cruise.

With regard to Point 5, in my opinion there is only one remedy, which is to maintain the integrity of the Chinese Empire, and give security to the trade of all nations, by a thorough reorganization of the army and police of the entire country. As this can only be done by outside help, and as those who are able to render the service are apparently afraid to step in, either from want of confidence in China's recuperative power, or from fear of their neighbor's opinion, I would, with all deference, offer the following sugges-

OBSERVATIONS

tion: Why should not Great Britain, which has the largest vested interest in the country, lead the way, and invite the co-operation of all interested parties, in the organization of China's military and police, in the same spirit as Sir Robert Hart has organized her Customs? If it is objected that some one nation might thereby seek or gain predominance in the country, and thus provoke jealousy among the rest, why should not this objection be anticipated by a clear understanding that those who co-operate from various nations to do this work shall be strictly the servants of the Chinese Empire, like General Gordon or Sir Robert Hart; and that the one and only end in view is to strengthen, support, and maintain the Government of China, and the lives and properties of the European traders?

If it be objected that some nations might refuse to co-operate, may it not be said in reply that Great Britain has met a similar objection before in Egypt; and that no number of such refusals can absolve the four great trading nations from coming to the rescue of the Chinese Government and their own traders in a moment of imminent peril?

If it be objected that China itself is effete and rotten, I reply that this is false. The traditional official system is corrupt, but the Chinese people are honest. The integrity of their merchants is known to every banker and trader in the East, and their word is as good as their bond. They have, too, a traditional and idolatrous respect for authority, and all they need is an honest and good authority.

If it be objected that this reform of the Chinese forces would be costly, I answer that the necessary reorganization could be effected by an honest expenditure of the moneys now allowed for defence, and need not cost a shilling of European money. I have proved to my own satisfaction that effective military and police forces could be organized on the funds now available for these purposes. The country is not over-taxed, it is badly taxed, and the Revenue is peculated wholesale. What the Sphere of Influence policy would cost, in loss through hostile tariffs and in expenditure of blood and money for defence, it is not possible to say. For who can estimate the difficulty and cost to European Powers of defending and administering huge sections of a country with bad roads, teeming with a population absolutely hostile to foreigners and foreign domination? The Chinese are conservative. They have behind them the traditions of 4000 years, and within them the prejudices natural to isolation.

The Spheres of Influence policy would certainly weaken all central authority in the Chinese Empire, and would transfer the responsibility for law and order to a disconnected and often antagonistic group of foreign settlers, who would find the work of peaceful administration wellnigh impossible.

Nominal Spheres of Influence, such as those of

OBSERVATIONS

Germany in Shantung and Russia in Manchuria, may exist as long as a semblance of Chinese authority remains, but once the people realize authority is powerless, anarchy, rebellion, and bloodshed must ensue. The breaking-up of the Chinese Empire into Spheres of Influence would also be certain to lead to war between the European nations. It is surprising that people can be found to talk calmly of the break-up of an empire of 400 millions of people, as if such a gigantic revolution could be accomplished by a stroke of a pen.

I may be told that we've got a policy made out of old treaties and agreements which we must continue. If that be so, I reply that the time has come when these treaties and agreements should receive a thorough revision, because arrangements made with safety when China was strong may turn into grave perils now China is weak. The effete condition of the Chinese Government entirely alters the mutual relations of her foreign neighbors. It has been said that the danger connected with weak nations comes from the jealousies of the neighbors who are waiting to divide the property among them. These jealousies may for a moment be smoothed over by small mutual concessions paid on account; but such temporary expedients can have no finality, and will only serve to bring about the fatal policy of Spheres of Influence, creating gigantically expensive European military frontiers in the Far East, with no strong Chinese buffer between them.

With respect to Point 8, I cannot repeat too

often the profound conviction held by every trader in China that the policy of the Open Door, or equal opportunity for the trade of all nations, is the one and only policy possible for the development of trade and commerce. It is, however, no use theorizing over so vital a question. We must declare in some practical manner how the policy is to be carried out. Neither is it any use keeping the door open without insuring that the room on the other side of the door is in order. To keep the door open the integrity of the Chinese Empire must be maintained. To preserve that integrity, the organization of her military forces for police purposes is necessary. Whatever fiscal policies may be projected by the stay-at-home diplomatists of European States, let this be clearly understood, that the traders of all countries in Chinese territory are absolutely unanimous in their belief in the policy of the Open Door. The Chambers of Commerce in China are composed of all nationalities, and it will be seen that the resolutions of these Chambers cordially support the views of the China Association, which is purely British. Politicians and traders have not always the same ends in view, nor the same plans for getting what they want. The politician may wish only for an apparent advantage, and get it by bluff, but in doing so he may seriously endanger the peace and progress necessary for the development of commerce. Nations weak in trade but enterprising in diplomacy may seek territorial aggrandizement, and by their action

OBSERVATIONS

ruin the commerce of countries strong in trade but feeble in policy.

Another point of importance is the probable demand of China to increase, under a new Treaty, the tariff levied on foreign goods. If this be acceded to some *quid pro quo* must be given to the European Powers. Again, if the European Powers, by joint action, agree to maintain the integrity of the Chinese Empire on the lines I have indicated, some *quid pro quo* must be given by China in return.

The European nations should insist on a series of reforms in Chinese administration and finance, which are as necessary to China herself as to her foreign traders. These reforms may be epitomized thus:

1. An Imperial coinage.
2. Reform in the method of collecting the land tax.
3. Removal of restrictions on the export of grain.
4. Modification of the laws governing the salt monopoly.
5. The right of foreigners to reside in the interior for purposes of trade.
6. The registration and protection of trademarks and copyright.
7. The removal of the remaining restrictions on inland water navigation.
8. The abolition of the likin, or reforms which would insure that likin should be collected once only.

9. Greater facilities to be given to *bona fide* foreign syndicates to work minerals.

10. The establishment of bureaus for the regulation of finance, railways, waterways, roads, posts, and telegraphs, and a bureau to deal with all questions connected with trade. All of these are urgently needed, particularly for the postal and telegraph services, which are at present managed under a legalized system of squeeze. The foreign merchants constantly complain that the existing service is so untrustworthy that no letters between the ports are safe unless registered. The present telegraph service is so bad that a letter from Tientsin to Shanghai has been known to arrive before a telegram sent at the same time. The *Times* Correspondent at Peking told me that his telegrams very often cost as much to send from Peking to Shanghai as from Shanghai to London.

11. One other bureau is urgently needed, and that is a Trade Intelligence Department, to deal with scientific and practical questions relating to the natural products available in China for commercial purposes. What is an insignificant export to-day may become a valuable article of commerce to-morrow. There should be a scientific classification of the products of China on the same lines as the classification of products in India.

I would also like to point out to the Associated Chambers the desirability of impressing upon the British centres of commercial education the neces-

OBSERVATIONS

sity for teaching the Chinese language to British youths who are to seek employment in that country. This has been undertaken already by German and American traders.

The question for the future, to my mind, is this: Are the great trading nations of the world going to allow the Powers that seek only territorial aggrandizement to blockade the wealth of China, and shut the Open Door in their faces?

With regard to British Commerce in China, it is true that we have lost no ground so far as existing trade is concerned, but our commercial supremacy is seriously threatened by competition. We could not expect to enjoy always the advantageous position we have held in the past. We cannot hope to have everything, but with equal opportunity to all we shall do well.

If it be said that my policy for the reorganization of the Chinese army and police is a warlike policy, I reply that it is the only plan yet suggested which gives any guarantee of peace. Great Britain's strongest guarantee of peace has been the reorganization of her fleet. Without peace commerce must perish. To keep the peace, authority must be properly equipped. Our choice with regard to the Chinese Empire is simple—we may choose to wreck or we may choose to restore.

APPENDIX

REFERENCE EMBODIED IN A LETTER
FROM THE
HON. SIR STAFFORD NORTHCOTE, BART., M.P.,
President of the Associated Chambers of Commerce of Great Britain.

"*August* 1, 1898.

"DEAR BERESFORD,—You know the deep interest which the Associated Chambers of Commerce take in the development of British trade with China.

"As President of the Association, I feel bound to do all in my power to promote our commercial interests in that Empire.

"It appears to me that one most important question for the Associated Chambers is to obtain accurate information as to how security is to be insured to commercial men who may be disposed to embark their capital in trade enterprise in China.

"It is generally admitted that there is a great possible field for business undertakings; but I, personally, feel some doubt as to whether the organization of the Chinese civil and military administration is sufficiently complete to insure adequate protection to commercial ventures.

"I believe it would be of immense advantage to the commercial classes of other countries if they could obtain a comprehensive Report on this question from a competent authority.

"I want to get, for the benefit of the Associated Chambers, a report from a non-official source.

APPENDIX

"At the same time, it is necessary that our Commissioner should possess certain qualifications.

"He must be of sufficient position to warrant the expectation that he will be able to secure ready access to all sources of information.

"And I should like to have the services of an officer of naval or military experience, since, as I have said, I believe much turns on the question of British merchants being able to rely on adequate protection for their enterprises from the Chinese Government; and I should wish to know how far such protection can be regarded as effective.

"I have, therefore, to ask whether your engagements would permit of your visiting China at as early a date as may be convenient to yourself; and if you would kindly furnish me with a Report on these matters, and upon any other subjects you may think would be of interest and advantage to the Associated Chambers of Commerce.

"Believe me,
"Yours very truly,
"H. STAFFORD NORTHCOTE,
"President of the Associated
"Chambers of Commerce.

"To Rear-Admiral
"The Lord Charles Beresford, M.P."

CHINA ASSOCIATION, SHANGHAI

Meeting of October 6, 1898

"MY LORD,—On behalf of the Committee of this branch of the Association, I have much pleasure in welcoming your Lordship on your arrival in China, not only in view of the object of your visit, which we understand is directed towards the general advancement of British interests in this country, but also on the score of your Lordship's personality, which will give weight to the opinions which you may form, and to

APPENDIX

the representations which you may make on your return home.

"We believe that prior to your Lordship's departure from England you were in communication with the London Committee of this Association, and you are no doubt acquainted with the objects to which our work is directed—namely, to represent, express, and give effect to our views and opinions on matters affecting British interests in China, whether political or commercial; and you are no doubt also acquainted with the more important questions which are at present occupying our attention. In asking for this interview, we have thought that you might not be unwilling, prior to your visit to Peking, to receive some expression of this Committee's views regarding current matters of interest.

"It is unnecessary to say that at the present moment the further development of recent events in Peking is being looked for with the keenest interest. We are still without information sufficient to enable us to judge of what is likely to result from the change which has taken place in the Peking Government, but on the face of it it would appear that the results can hardly be favorable to British aims and interests in China. The facts before us appear to be that the new party in China, a party which had for its object progress and reform, and with which party the interests of Great Britain surely lay, has, for the time being at any rate, been crushed, and that the old *régime* which we connect with stagnation and corruption has been re-established. In such case it is difficult to say what may not be the effect upon the Empire generally, for undoubtedly the doctrines of the 'new movement' are now widely spread over the country, and are not only favorably received by a very large section of the people, but have also been embraced by very many intelligent officials in high places; that the spirit of rebellion may be stirred seems to us only too likely—indeed, there is already rebellion on an alarming scale in the Southern provinces, and, seeing that it is the Cantonese element in the Peking Government that is suffering chiefly from this Manchu reaction, it seems fully probable that the

APPENDIX

rebellious movement in the South will be largely strengthened. It is unnecessary to dwell upon the disastrous effects which internal troubles must have upon commerce, in which Great Britain is so vitally interested.

"A question of great commercial interest at the present time is the pending revision of the Tientsin Treaty of 1858, more particularly as it will be China's object in the revision to obtain a substantial increase in the present Customs tariff. The principle of a revision of the tariff in favor of China has long been admitted by foreign merchants in the country; but at the same time it has been, and is, consistently held that if increased duties at the ports are granted to China, ample safeguards must be taken that merchandise, having once paid these duties, shall receive in the interior the protection from irregular and illegal taxation which it nominally enjoys under the Treaties, but which it has never received. It is impossible at this interview to enter into detail as to this vexed question. Volumes have been written on the subject, and it is one which has no doubt been studied by your Lordship. It has been, and is still, urged that internal fiscal reform is the first step necessary towards remedying the evils complained of, but how this reform was to be brought about has been the question which has for years baffled those who have made a study of the matter. There is not only the difficulty caused by the wholesale corruption of the provincial Governments, which the restricted nature of foreign intercourse with China has made it impossible to check, but there is the further difficulty arising out of the practically autonomous nature of the Governments of the provincial units; interference with the existing irregular taxation in the provinces means a loss of provincial revenue, and in the event of an increase in the Imperial duties, which we contend must be dependent upon the abolition of internal 'squeezes,' means must be devised for satisfying legitimate provincial needs out of the Imperial collection. This consideration has not been lost sight of in suggestions which have been put forward by the Association. The question of dealing with the difficulties upon which we have touched has, however,

APPENDIX

assumed a new complexion in view of the changes which have taken place in China during the past few years. Now that the Chinese bubble has burst, and China is forced to pledge her resources to meet her financial needs, there seems to be better opportunity for insistence upon foreign interference in her internal affairs. It has been urged by this Association that the reforms required before an increased tariff be conceded should include:

"(1.) Extended rights of residence and trade.

"(2.) The opening up of internal communication by means of railways, and by the opening of all inland waters to free navigation.

"(3.) Guarantees to be taken for the immunity of merchandise from further taxation after it has paid the duties fixed by Treaty.

"With regard to these, some measure of progress has already been made towards opening up internal communication, and the success of her Majesty's Minister in securing the freedom of inland navigation is heartily acknowledged. It is, however, still contended that this freedom of navigation must, to be effective, carry with it the right of inland residence; there must be freedom to establish stations under foreign control for the effective handling, and for the protection of the merchandise which is carried in foreign vessels; without this right the freedom of inland navigation will be limited to a mere extension of the facilities for passenger traffic. The case of railways is somewhat similar. At the present time financiers from Europe and America seem to be jostling for so-called 'concessions,' but concessions without control and management are likely to prove disappointing! Chinese management of railways is scarcely likely to be less corrupt in this respect than in others, and foreign control, either sole or in conjunction with a minority of natives, should be insisted on, in addition to the Imperial guarantee for ultimate redemption of loans and payment of interest thereon. In this connection

APPENDIX

there again arises the necessity of the right to reside inland, and such right is also essential for the protection of goods which the railways carry. Would-be concessionaires who visit this country, hoping to obtain something that they can float at home with immediate benefit to themselves, may rest assured that those who have long local experience are alive both to opportunities for gain or loss in this as in any other pursuits. In connection with the third condition which the Association puts forward for an increased tariff—namely, guarantees against any taxation of goods beyond that fixed by Treaty—it has been urged that such guarantee can best be found by extending the sphere of the operations of the Imperial Maritime Customs—the only honest source of revenue that China possesses. In this direction an important beginning is being made in the Yangtse Valley provinces, where the collection of likin is being undertaken by the foreign Customs; it is earnestly to be hoped that the area of operations will be extended, and particularly that it may be found possible to supervise likin collection in the provinces of Kwangtung and Kwang-si, where the Treaty rights of goods have been so notoriously ignored. To sum up this part of the question, we are convinced that until extended rights of internal residence and trade are conceded; until guarantees are given for the management of the vast sums of money that are being invited for investment in China, and until reforms can be effected in the provinces which will secure merchandise from irregular taxation, the claim of the Chinese Government to an increase in the Customs tariff should not be acceded to.

" For the furtherance and protection of British commercial interests, it has again and again been urged by this Association that the appointment of a commercial attaché, or of attachés, is essential. It is felt that the multifarious duties of the Consular body, and the fact that these are only exercisable at fixed stations, render it impossible for the members of that body to give the care to commercial matters which the magnitude of British interest requires; and, moreover, in con-

APPENDIX

sidering this question the exceptional difficulties which surround all matters in China are specially to be remembered. Our representations on this subject have been apparently admitted to be sound in that a commercial attaché has been appointed, but, seeing that the office is merged in that of Consul-General at Shanghai, the appointment is useless. Our conception of the position and duties of a commercial attaché has been several times expressed; he should be of definite rank sufficient to enable him to command the respect and attention of the high provincial officials; he should be free to move about the country at will, unhampered by other work, and he should be in continual touch both with the Chinese officials and with his own nationals. In a communication from this branch of the Association, dated two years ago, we stated that our object in pressing for the appointment of a commercial attaché was 'not limited to the petty details of official obstruction, but comprehended a system of reform calculated to raise and strengthen the Chinese Empire and simultaneously promote the welfare of British commerce and British interests.' These views we repeat to-day, but, seeing the enormous difficulties which attend the procuring of reliable information in China (difficulties which seem to have become very plainly apparent during the changing events of last year), we would now go further and urge the establishment of a complete service which would continue the duties of the special case of commercial matters with those of obtaining intelligence. So far as we are aware, the British Government, despite its vast interests in this Empire, is without anything approaching an Intelligence Department, and we believe that the establishment of such a department would immensely strengthen the hands of her Majesty's Minister in Peking.

"In an interview such as this it is impossible to do more than touch on the veriest fringe of the many reforms which have constantly been urged as essential for the benefit both of China herself and of foreign interests in the Empire; the corruption which saturates every department of government throughout the length and breadth of the country makes fiscal reform a

APPENDIX

first necessity. The Reports published recently by Mr. Jamieson and Mr. Brenan contain official record of the vastness of this corruption, and though had China been able to maintain her exclusive position, she might have continued for decades longer unchanged, yet her altered circumstances cannot fail to bring disaster, unless she sets her house in order on lines consonant with the ideas and wishes of the Western nations from whom she cannot now detach herself. Among the reforms which have been advocated may be mentioned: The necessity for a national coinage; reform in the method of the collection of the land-tax; the removal of the restrictions on the export of grain; modification of the laws governing the salt monopoly; registration and protection of trade-marks, and the establishment of a law of copyright; also the establishment of railway and mining bureaus, placing these enterprises on a uniform and organized basis.

"We do not propose on this occasion to occupy your Lordship with any expression of our views on the broad question of the political situation which has arisen in China, nor to criticise the action of our Government in connection with it. This much, however, we may say—namely, that there seems to us to have been a regrettable want of stability in the policy which has been pursued. We seem to have left the policy of the 'Integrity of China,' and, walking through the 'Open Door,' to have arrived at the policy of the 'Sphere of Influence.' We think that the long neglect of Chinese affairs by our Government, a neglect probably due to a mistaken feeling that British influence in the Far East reigned supreme, coupled with a fallacious belief in the power of China herself, has been the cause of an indecisive policy which has apparently allowed us to fall between two stools. Great Britain's 'Sphere of Influence' should be wherever British trade preponderates, and with the 'Open Door' for other nations all peoples would have equal opportunity; but this ideal can never be attained without resolute determination on the part of the British Government to *lead* and not to follow in the councils at Peking. On these matters, however, your Lordship will, no doubt, form your own

APPENDIX

conclusions during your visit, which we trust will be enjoyable to yourself, and will achieve its object of benefit to British interests in the Far East.

"L. J. DUDGEON, Chairman.
"To the Right Honorable
"Admiral Lord Charles Beresford, C.B., M.P.
"SHANGHAI, *October* 4, 1898."

CHAMBER OF COMMERCE, SHANGHAI

Address of October 7, 1898

"MY LORD,—On behalf of the Shanghai General Chamber of Commerce the Committee have the honor of welcoming you.

"As a General Chamber of Commerce representing all foreign nationalities, we greet you as representing the Chambers of Commerce of Great Britain, and we can all do so without hesitation, for under the Favored-nation Clause no one nation benefits more than another in their commercial treaties with the country in which we now are.

"On this principle the Shanghai Chamber of Commerce is established, and has for many years been a factor.

"We will not weary your Lordship with retrospect more than to remark that, had Treaties been observed in the past, we should have heard less of likin and loti shui, and that no revision of Treaty, be it based on the many reports this Chamber has already fathered, or on any inquiries yet to come, can be permanently of advantage unless it combines conditions, and indeed exactions, that its terms shall be adhered to, not only technically, but in a common-sense interpretation.

"Our views on existing Tariffs are recorded in Reports of Sectional Committees drawn up in 1896, which our Secretary, Mr. Drummond Hay, will hand you; but though then complete as far as we could see, they may now need revision, and in view of the probability that the Minister for Great Britain

APPENDIX

will be the first Minister seriously engaged in such work, we have mentioned to his Excellency that, until this Chamber has some knowledge of the views held by the Consular and Customs officials on the Reports we took such labor to compile, we can say no more than to suggest that a round-table conversation of a few Consular, Customs, and mercantile representatives might pave the way and clear the atmosphere of many cloudy bedarkenings.

"That all nationalities will agree to a more productive scale of Import Duties, *provided* there are proper and really binding guarantees of an end to inland 'squeezes' and irregular impositions, is, I think, certain, but *that* is a condition, and it is well we should all understand this.

"On the other hand, if China's true interests are to be considered, considerable amelioration of Inland and Export taxation on Exports is a *sine quâ non*.

"Taking the political aspect, which we, as an International Chamber, do not attempt to define, we may, in the interests of all nationalities, contend that in a commercial sense we know no geographical 'Spheres of Influence,' but advocate equal rights and equal opportunities for all who have integrity and perseverance necessary to carry their initiative to successful ends.

"We have little time to discuss political matters with your Lordship, but while alive to the fact that political issues may outweigh the commercial, and necessitate here and there depots of nourishment for those forces on which we, as foreigners, are compelled to rely in countries which we sincerely regret are now retarded in adopting Western civilization and usages, we see no reason for commercial jealousies; and when you consider that for several decades of years this International or General Chamber of Commerce has on these lines done service, all will admit that proportional tradal influence demands consideration.

"Dealing thus generally with the points we have alluded to, your Lordship will bear with us while we mention one or two more local.

"You will have heard, my Lord, of the Woosung Bar.

APPENDIX

Though the number of our ships has greatly increased of late years, many millions have been exacted from foreign shipowners in the shape of tonnage dues! This Chamber has raised and spent money in formulating proposals by which it is hoped that this important Treaty port may maintain its waterways, the Yangtse and Whangpoo Rivers; but the improvements, remedial and novel, cost money, and we see no reason why those who pay the piper should not name the tune. We therefore demand a Conservancy Board here, on which mercantile and shipping representatives should adjudicate and direct, along with Consular and Customs officials, the expenditure of money which is solely derived from the foreign merchant and ship-owner. In short, in this, as in the question of tariffs on goods, we maintain that politics, whether Tory or Liberal, and whether British, German, American, Russian, Japanese, or any other country, have no part, for the fact remains in our minds that Taxation and Representation are inseparable.

"My Lord, we may say another word to strengthen our position in regard to expenditure of tonnage dues derived from foreign ships, when we tell you that for years three-tenths of these receipts have been diverted to purposes other than those we believe were obviously intended by Treaty. We admit that departmental expenses of harbor administration, etc., and funds for light-house purposes, are proper charges, but, apart from these, moneys received *from* shipping should be used *for* shipping, and conservancy expenses might easily be met were this principle admitted and adopted.

"In a somewhat similar light we, as representing all foreign nations, have taken up, at the request of our Municipality, the overshadowing, important subject of the *extension of our settlement*. A settlement defined fifty years ago as, perhaps, one and a half miles wide and a mile and a quarter deep, is no use for us. We—that is, foreigners—have extended four or five miles each way, and yet in the area in which we live and move and have our being there are drains and stinks innumerable, though we spend money in making roads.

"The Chinese reply ('that if we had kept for foreigners

APPENDIX

alone the area assigned to us') is all nonsense. If we had done so, we should havé had no country roads, no country houses, no nothing!—merely a place like Shameen, at Canton, a *prison for* foreigners, surrounded by masses of natives living *on* foreigners, but in slums worse even, far more numerous and larger, than those we now assert are a danger both to health and order. Not only out in the Bubbling Well and Yangtzepoo districts do we want the extension, but also over at Pootung, where from Tungkadoo to down below the harbor limits foreigners have built wharves and docks and factories, which, it is almost inconceivable, are not within our municipal jurisdiction! We held a public meeting on this 'extension' subject in June last, and the printed Report, with the sanitary medical news it contains, will, we hope, not be too long for your Lordship to study.

" CHARLES ALFORD, Chairman."

CHAMBER OF COMMERCE, TIENTSIN
Resolution of October 24, 1898

"That this meeting of the Tientsin Chamber of Commerce welcomes the mission of Rear-Admiral Lord Charles Beresford, from the Associated Chambers of Commerce of Great Britain, and unanimously desires to record its conviction that the policy of preserving the integrity of China, with a guarantee of an 'Open Door,' a fair field, and increased trading facilities for all countries, is the best and most sound for all foreign trading communities in China, and hereby desires Lord Charles Beresford to convey the resolution of this Chamber.

(Signed)   " W. W. DICKINSON (Chairman).
                   " JOHN H. OSBORNE (Hon. Sec.).
                   " M. MARCH.
                   " E. HEGH.
                   " J. N. DICKINSON.
                   " CHARLES H. ROSS.
                   " D. H. MACKINTOSH.
                   " R. LURRY."

APPENDIX

NEWCHWANG MEETING

Address of November 7, 1898

"MY LORD,—I have great pleasure in handing you herewith two copies of a series of resolutions passed unanimously, after full and free discussion, at a meeting of British residents this morning.

"Further, I am instructed by the meeting to request you to be good enough to communicate one copy of these resolutions to Lord Salisbury, with such comments as you may consider advisable.

"I am, Sir,
"Your obedient servant,
"J. J. FREDK. BANDINEL,
"Chairman of the Meeting.
"To Rear-Admiral
"Right Hon. Lord Charles Beresford, C.B., at Newchwang.

"COPY OF RESOLUTIONS

"Unanimously adopted at a meeting of British Residents at the Port of Newchwang, North China, on the 7th November, 1898.

"We advocate:

"1. Obtaining a British concession on the north bank of the river—that is to say, on the side opposite to the present town.

"2. Forming the East end of the town within the walls into a foreign (not necessarily British) settlement.

"3. The right of owning land in the interior, and establishing there filatures and other similar enterprises worked by foreign machinery.

"4. The right of working mines in any part of the three provinces where Chinese or other foreigners may or do work them, and on equally favorable terms.

"5. The maintenance of our right to inland navigation, with

APPENDIX

power to stop at any town or village on the banks, equally with those enjoyed on any river in China.

"6. That the rights and property of the Protestant missionaries and their converts should be maintained intact as heretofore according to the rights existing by the Treaty of Tientsin and the Edict of 1891.

"7. That a British Consular Agent be permanently stationed in Kirin, as formerly in Chungking.

"8. We deprecate most strongly the annexation of this port, and of any of the three provinces, by any foreign Power, and we rely on the British Government to maintain the 'Open Door.'

"9. We object to the right claimed and exercised by the Russians of landing railway material without examination or payment of duty, especially as this diminishes the security on which money has been loaned by British subjects to the Chinese Government.

"10. We view with apprehension the establishment of Russian military posts throughout the provinces as at Kirin.

"11. That the Russian Government should be requested to appoint a Consul at this port, in view of the large and increasing Russian interests, and the possibility of complications arising which would demand immediate conference between Consular officials on the spot.

"12. That a copy of these resolutions be sent by the Chairman to Lord Charles Beresford, also another copy with the request that he will communicate the same to Lord Salisbury, and that another copy be sent to her Majesty's Minister at Peking. J. J. FREDERICK BANDINEL,
"Chairman of the Meeting."

SHANGHAI GENERAL CHAMBER OF COMMERCE

Address of November 16, 1898

"MY LORD,—I have the honor to inform you that the Committee of this Chamber have passed the following resolution,

APPENDIX

which is in general confirmation of the views verbally expressed at their recent interview with your Lordship:

"'That in the opinion of this Committee the interests of both China and of the Foreign Powers having commercial relations with her require that the equality of rights as secured by existing Treaties be strictly safeguarded against any changes of an exclusive or preferential nature in favor of different nations in any part of the Empire; and, further, that it is desirable that, in order to effect this end, a *general agreement* be entered into between the Powers interested, guaranteeing the equality of commercial rights and privileges to all nations alike.'

"I have the honor to be,
"Your Lordship's obedient Servant,
"DRUMMOND HAY, Secretary.
"Rear-Admiral Lord Charles Beresford,
"R.N., C.B., M.P., etc."

HONG KONG GENERAL CHAMBER OF COMMERCE
Meeting of November 19, 1898

"MY LORD,—I have the honor to transmit to your Lordship copy of a series of resolutions unanimously adopted by the General Committee of this Chamber at a special meeting held on the 19th inst.

"The resolutions embody the views and recommendations of the Chamber in connection with the present situation, *vis-à-vis* China and the new policy latterly developed by the Treaty Powers.

"I have the honor to be, my Lord,
"Your most obedient Servant,
"R. M. GRAY, Chairman.
"To Admiral Lord Charles Beresford,
"M.P., etc., etc."

APPENDIX

"With reference to the Mission of Lord Charles Beresford to China, this Chamber, having considered the situation, political and commercial, wish to record the following opinions and recommendations:

"1. In the interests of commerce it is vitally necessary that the position of the Colony of Hong Kong, as the natural outlet and focus for the trade of the Two Kwang Provinces, should never be lost sight of in considering any claims to 'Spheres of Influence' that may be put forward either now or in the future.

"2. Hong Kong, through a line of railway, connecting first with Canton, and eventually with Hankow and her sister cities Wuchang and Hanyung, is in a position to directly tap the very heart of commercial China.

"3. The trade of Hong Kong, now roughly estimated at some fifty millions sterling per annum, may, when the riverways of South China are opened and the railway to the Yangtse Valley becomes an accomplished fact, reasonably be expected to expand immensely.

"4. The geographical situation of Hong Kong, lying, as it does, half-way between India and Japan, on the very borders of one of the most populous provinces of China, and at the mouth of one of the greatest systems of inland navigation in Asia, is of supreme importance to British trade, and any scheme or policy that loses even partial sight of its unique advantages ought not to commend itself to the attention of the British Government.

"5. That, however important the trade of the United Kingdom with Central China, it must not be forgotten that the key to British influence and prestige in the Far East reposes in the Colony of Hong Kong.

"The Chamber, therefore, respectfully urge that while it is of the utmost importance to secure an 'Open Door' for British and foreign trade in the Yangtse Valley and in the North of China, it is imperative that—

"(a) Trade throughout China should be freed from all

APPENDIX

inland imposts, one tax payable at the port of entry sufficing to frank goods to their destination.

"(b) That the dual system of Customs should be abolished, and a contribution to the Provincial treasury be made out of the revenues of the Imperial Maritime Customs.

"(c) In view of the lawless condition of the Two Kwang, it should be strongly impressed on the Chinese Government that vigorous measures be promptly taken to put down brigandage and restore order throughout the provinces.

"(d) That, as part of the grand scheme for throwing open to foreign trade the entire waterways of China, means be at once taken to secure the opening of the West River above Wuchow-fu and also the North and East Rivers along their entire navigable courses."

CHINKIANG CHAMBER OF COMMERCE

Resolutions of November 22, 1898

The following are the recommendations of this Chamber:

" 1. Strict and immediate enforcement of the inland navigation rules.

" 2. Right of foreigners to reside in the interior, unfettered as regards trade, and to buy land in the vicinity of Treaty ports.

" 3. Amelioration of condition of certain barriers in Kiangsu, notably that at Huai-kuan on the Grand Canal.

" 4. Revision of the Yangtse Regulations.

" 5. A more hearty and willing co-operation on the part of H.M.'s Consuls for the furtherance of trade and protection of British interests."

KIUKIANG MEETING

Address of November 25, 1898

" MY LORD,—As Chairman of the deputation and other British residents appointed to wait upon you, I beg to present to

APPENDIX

your Lordship this expression of the pleasure your visit to this port affords us, and to invoke your powerful influence at home, both in Parliament and with the Government, with a view to the extension of the privileges of British residents in Central China.

"British subjects desire:

"(1.) Full liberty to establish in the interior manufacturing and other industrial concerns, particularly in tea-growing districts.

"(2.) To open and work mines on equally favorable terms with the natives.

"(3.) That the rights of Christian missionaries and their converts in the interior and elsewhere be fully recognized.

"(4.) That ample protection be accorded British subjects in all legitimate enterprises in China.

"(5.) That special attention be given to the French and Russian activity in Central and Western China, especially in view of the fact that an armed French force is at present in the West, and that a railway is now being constructed opening up direct communication between Central China and the Russian sphere in the North.

"(6.) That a British naval force be stationed permanently in the Yangtse as a demonstration of the intention to protect her interests.

"(7.) That Hunan be opened to trade and missionary work, which shall have the fullest protection throughout the province, and that a British Consul be appointed to reside at Changsha, the capital.

"(8.) That an understanding be arrived at with the United States of America by which both nations may take concerted action against the closing of any doors to missionary work and trade now open in the Empire, and that the two nations reopen any doors that may have been closed.

"The British community resident in this part of the Yang-

APPENDIX

tse Valley, in the centre of the section of the Empire specially guaranteed by China to Great Britain, urge a close attention on the part of the British Government to the development of this important 'sphere of British influence,' for its possibilities and resources are almost unlimited.

"The deputation confidently anticipate that the result of your Mission to the Far East will promote a still more rapid opening up of this part of the Empire of China to Christianity, and all forms of Western civilization.

"I am, my Lord,
"For and on behalf of the Community,
"Your obedient Servant,
"EDWARD S. LITTLE,
"Chairman of the Deputation.
"To Rear-Admiral
"Right Hon. Lord Charles Beresford, C.B."

HANKOW MEETING
Resolutions of December 5, 1898

"MY LORD,—I beg to hand you herewith a copy of resolutions passed unanimously at a meeting of the British Mercantile Community of this concession, and to request that you will call the attention of her Majesty's Government to the subjects mentioned therein, which are of the greatest importance to all residents and traders here.

"I am, my Lord,
"Your obedient Servant,
"C. E. GEDDES,
"Chairman of above Meeting.
"To the Right Honorable
"Admiral Lord Charles Beresford,
"R.N., C.B., M.P."

"Resolutions passed at a meeting of the British Mercantile Community, held at Hankow on the 3d December, 1898:

"1. We believe that it is largely in consequence of the lack

APPENDIX

of firmness on the part of her Majesty's Government that this country is now plunged into such a state of political turmoil that the Chinese merchants have practically ceased to do business. The Local Governments in this part of the Empire, impoverished by the loss of revenue derived from likin, are no longer able to control the people, and the general feeling is that it is only the want of a leader that prevents an uprising of a dangerous character. And inasmuch as the native authorities are not in a position to afford us security and protection to carry on our trade in the future, as we have done heretofore, we call upon her Majesty's Government to extend to us the protection to which we are entitled as British subjects.

"2. We consider it of the utmost importance that the further opening up to trade of the waterways of the Yangtse and its great tributaries, the Tung Ting Lake, etc., on the principle of the 'Open Door,' free to all, should be carried out with as little delay as possible, and permission obtained for foreigners to trade direct with and reside in the large cities within this district on similar terms as with the existing Treaty ports. We would suggest that the establishment of a Consulate at Changsha, and the opening of that city as a Treaty port, would be a measure of great importance towards securing a standing in the province of Hunan.

"3. Since the establishment of the Treaty port of Hankow, in 1861, British subjects have, from time to time, bought land outside the limits of the British concession under Chinese titledeeds. These deeds have been duly registered, and bear the Consular stamp of her Majesty's Government. Since the war with Japan proved the weakness of the Chinese, advantage has been taken by the French and Russian Governments to seize upon such property as above mentioned, to the loss and detriment of British subjects, claims to the ownership of land lodged with the French and Russian Consuls having been rejected and declared invalid without explanation or the possibility of appeal. The result of this has been to lessen in Chinese opinion the value of the British Consular stamp on a deed, a fact which will have a most serious effect on British

APPENDIX

interests here; and the native officials now refuse to register deeds sent in by her Majesty's Consul, to which they offer no objection if the application is made through the French or Russian Consul.

"C. E. GEDDES, Chairman."

FOOCHOW CHAMBER OF COMMERCE

Resolution of December 22, 1898

"That the General Chamber of Commerce of Foochow desires to avail itself of the opportunity of your Lordship's visit to place before you its endorsement of the views already expressed by the other Chambers of Commerce in China, viz. :

"1. That the 'Sphere of Influence' policy, so called, would be fatal to the interests of British Trade and Commerce in China.

"2. That we earnestly hope that the declaration of her Majesty's Government with regard to the maintenance of the 'Open Door' will be strictly adhered to.

"3. That in order to keep the 'Open Door' for the trade of all nations, it is necessary that the integrity of China should be preserved."

AMOY GENERAL CHAMBER OF COMMERCE

Address of December 23, 1898

"MY LORD,—I have the honor to transmit to your Lordship the following resolutions, unanimously carried at the meeting of the British Members of this Chamber, held this morning, at which your Lordship was present:

"'1. That this Chamber is of opinion that British trade at Amoy would be considerably enhanced were the right of residence in the interior allowed, and likin either abolished or compounded in one payment.

APPENDIX

"'2. That the best thanks of this meeting are offered to the Associated Chambers of Commerce for having sent out a Mission to inquire into British Trade and Commerce, and that it is hoped that the Mission to China will result in considerable benefit to British merchants.'
"I have the honor to be,
"My Lord,
"Your most obedient Servant,
"J. J. DUNNE,
"Secretary.
"To Rear-Admiral
"Right Hon. Lord Charles Beresford,
"C.B., M.P., etc., etc."

SWATOW MEETING

Resolution of December 24, 1898

"That this meeting trusts that her Majesty's Government will see the necessity for taking more vigorous measures to maintain and promote British influence in China."

CHINA ASSOCIATION, HONG KONG

Meeting of December 28, 1898

At a meeting of the Committee of the Hong Kong Branch of the Association, held at the City Hall, on the 28th December, 1898—present, J. J. Francis, Q.C., in the chair, the Honorable C. P. Chater, C.M.G., Thomas Jackson, C. S. Sharp, E. W. Mitchell, and F. Henderson (Hon. Sec.)—the following resolutions were unanimously passed:

"Resolved—
"1. That unless some definite policy is adopted by the British Government in connection with affairs in China, and

APPENDIX

unless prompt action is taken to give effect to that policy, British trade and British influence in China are in serious danger of diminution.

"2. That the policy embodied in the term 'Spheres of Influence' tends to the eventual dismemberment of the Chinese Empire, can only lead to war, and ought to be set aside.

"3. That the policy embodied in the phrase the 'Open Door' ought to be clearly defined and strictly enforced, even at the risk of war.

"4. That the policy of the 'Open Door,' in our opinion, means that all rights and privileges obtained by any one Power, under treaty or convention with China, should be common to all Powers and their subjects throughout the Empire of China; that the action of any nation in endeavoring to obtain from the Chinese Government any exclusive rights or privileges should be deemed an unfriendly act, and that Great Britain should call upon the Chinese Government to refuse to grant any exclusive rights to any Power, and should support China, by force if necessary, in her refusal.

"5. That if any nation has any reasonable claim to exclusive influence in the Southern provinces of China—Kwangtung, Kwangsi, and Yunnan—that Power is Great Britain; but that Great Britain claims no such exclusive privilege, and will permit no other Power to exercise any exclusive right.

"6. That the Revenue system of China is the greatest of all obstacles to the improvement of trade, to the increase of manufactures, to the opening of mines, and the construction of railways in China, and that the British Government should bring all its power and influence to bear on the Imperial Government to compel the unification of the finances of the Government, Imperial and Provincial, in the hands of a Special Service, entirely manned by Europeans and worked on the plan of the Imperial Maritime Customs.

"7. That with the unification of the collection of revenues in the hands of a special department, as above, there will necessarily be conjoined an immense improvement in the

APPENDIX

policing of trade routes both by land and water; and greater additional security for investments in China.

"That these resolutions be transmitted to Lord Charles Beresford, and that copies thereof be sent to H.M.'s Minister in Peking, the Shanghai branch of the Association, and the Committee of the Association in London.

"F. HENDERSON,
"Hon. Secretary.
"JNO. J. FRANCIS,
"Chairman."

CHINESE MEETING, HONG KONG

Resolutions of January 22, 1899.

Resolutions passed at the meeting of Chinese merchants and traders, and other Chinese gentlemen resident in Hong Kong, interested in trade, held at the Chinese Chamber of Commerce Rooms on Sunday, the 22d January, 1899, at noon.

On the motion of Mr. Ho T'ung, seconded by Mr. Leung Shiu-Kwong, it was resolved:

"1. Having closely followed with great and attentive interest, and carefully considered what Lord Charles Beresford has said and done in China in connection with his recent Mission on behalf of the Associated Chambers of Commerce, we, the Chinese community of Hong Kong here assembled, are in accord with and heartily support the policy the noble Lord proposes in regard to the 'Open Door' as regards commerce, and also with regard to the reorganization of the Chinese Army under the British.

"2. That we recognize the combined proposals, if carried out, will benefit China quite as much, if not more, than England, and other nations, in her trading interest, and we therefore hope that Lord Charles will be intrusted by the British Government with the carrying out of the views

APPENDIX

he has so closely enunciated, as we, the Chinese people of Hong Kong, observe that his efforts are directed to the benefit of both his country and our country, and to the benefit of the trade of China and the trade of England.

" 3. That we recognize and make our cordial acknowledgments for the sympathetic manner with which he has approached our country; and

" 4. That we desire to emphatically express our full confidence in Lord Charles Beresford, whose ability, integrity, and zeal we are sure peculiarly fit him to successfully carry out the proposals he has made for the furtherance of trade and the preservation of the Chinese Empire.

(Signed)   "Lo Chi Tiu, Chairman.
"H. O. Fook, Secretary."

GENERAL FOREIGN COMMERCIAL COMMUNITY, SHANGHAI

Resolution of January 8, 1899

"That our cordial thanks be tendered to Lord Charles Beresford for the service he has rendered to the foreign communities in China by personal investigation into the conditions of the various interests we represent."

Memoranda showing views of British merchants are also to be found under "Canton," "Wuhu," and "Chefoo."

SUMMARY OF TRADE STATISTICS

The following is a summary of the trade statistics given under the headings of the different places mentioned in this Report. I was unable to get reliable figures for 1898, as I left China in the early part of January, 1899. I was also unable to obtain trustworthy figures at each place of the proportionate value of British trade, so I have preferred to omit it alto-

APPENDIX

gether, as the tonnage of shipping gives a fairly approximate idea of the British preponderance of trade in China, which amounts to 64% of the whole foreign trade. The American percentage is 8% of the whole, and the remaining 28% is divided among the other foreign nations, Japan having the larger share, and Germany coming next.

Towns	Estimated Population	Total net value of Trade, 1897	Total tonnage of Shipping entered and cleared, 1897	Total British tonnage entered and cleared, 1897
		Haikwan taels		
Tientsin . .	1,000,000	55,059,017	1,326,663	574,177
Newchwang	60,000	26,358,671	730,964	363,922
Chefoo . .	32,876	22,051,976	2,385,301	1,327,559
Hankow. .	800,370	49,720,630	1,783,042	1,109,853
Kiukiang .	53,101	14,865,563	2,656,552	2,004,298
Wuhu . .	79,275	8,888,361	2,867,485	2,159,307
Chinkiang .	135,220	24,145,341	3,535,739	2,353,702
Shanghai .	405,000	101,832,962	7,969,674	4,591,851
Foochow .	636,351	13,556,494	641,795	470,239
Amoy . .	96,370	12,973,616	1,727,251	1,417,135
Swatow . .	40,216	28,398,001	1,917,027	1,655,864
Canton . .	1,600,424	49,934,391	3,718,064	3,000,571
Wuchow .	50,000	1,912,711	52,188	41,402
Hong Kong	246,880	£50,000,000	15,565,843	8,268,770
Nanking .	150,000			
Peking . .	1,300,000			
Wei-hai-Wei	4,000			

DEFINITIONS OF CHINESE WEIGHTS, ETC.

16 taels = 1 catty.
1 catty = 1⅓ lb. avoirdupois.
100 catties = 1 picul.
1 picul = 133⅓ lbs. avoirdupois.
75 catties = 100 lbs. avoirdupois.

Six mou = 1 acre.
3.3 li = 1 mile.

In 1897, 1 Hk. (Haikwan or Customs)
tael = 2s. 11¾d. English.
" = $0.72 American.

INDEX

ADDIS, C. S., Report on relation between copper and silver cash, 370–377.
Albumen, 167.
Alcock, Sir Rutherford, Convention of, 399.
Allen, Mr., British Consul at Newchwang, 51.
American Asiatic Association, 437.
American interests in China: Car couplings, 29; Firms in Shanghai, 93; Flour trade, 95; Kerosene, 95; Locomotives, 26; Lumber, 95; Machinery, 445; Piece goods trade, 92; Railway material, 49.
Americans, Opinions of, on Lord Beresford's Mission, 439; Opinions of, on Open Door policy, 436–437, 443.
Amoy, Report of Chamber of Commerce, 479; Visit to, 182.
Antimony, 165.
Armies (*see* chapter on "Chinese Armies and Navies," 267).
Army, Chinese, Inefficiency of, 280; Reorganization of, essential to future prosperity, 7, 11, 96, 107, 110, 139, 143, 157, 174, 231, 450; Japanese, 427; Russian, in Manchuria, 286.
Arsenal, at Osaka, 421; Shanghai, 294; Tokio, 427.
Arsenals, 290–302.

BALDWIN engines, 28, 45.
Bank, China and Japan, 89; Tientsin, 16.
Banker & Co., Case of, 238–247.
Banks, List of China, 388.
Bean mill, 63.
Bean oil, 57.
Beancake, 34, 57.
Beans, 34, 40, 57.
Belgium, Railway interests of, 305.

Beri-beri, Disease of, 431.
Bradley & Co., 180.
Buffalo, Visit to, 436.
Butterfield & Swire, 33.

CANAL, the Grand, 318, 328.
Canes, Canton trade in, 235, 260.
Canton, Arsenal of, 301; Exports of, 259; Piracy of, 248–258; Trade statistics of, 198–202; Visit to, 232–263.
Capital, Anglo-Saxon, Opportunity for, 170; Demoralization of, 17; Need of, 38; Tientsin Bank, 16.
Cassia, Canton trade in, 260; Wuchow, 265.
Catholics, and Yu Man Tsu, 141.
Cavalry, Chinese, 275; Japanese, 428.
Cereals of Manchuria, 35.
Chamber of Commerce, Amoy tea, Report on, 183–184; Chinkiang, Report no, 121, 131; Shanghai, Address to author, 88; Tientsin, 14.
Chambers of Commerce, Reports of (*see* Appendix).
Chao-Chao Fu, 178.
Chefoo, Convention of, 240, 244, 247, 401; Development of, 66; Goldmines of, 68; Trade, 65; Visit to, 65.
Chicago, Visit to, 435.
Chihli, Viceroy of, 292.
China, Administration of, 211; Alienation of, 20; American interest in, 433, 447; British trade with, 198, 203; "Break-up" of, effect of, 20; Policy should be changed, 84; Population of, 194; Revenue system of, 225; Trade compared with Japanese, 417.
China Association, Report of, 480.
Ching, Prince, Interview with, 2.
Chingfui tax, 405.

INDEX

Chinkiang, British merchants' report on, 133; Chamber of Commerce, 121-475; Trade statistics of, 120-135; Visit to, 120.
Ching-tu, Arsenal of, 302.
Chu-kiang River, 232.
Chung Chi Tung, Interview with, 156; Army of, 276.
Chungking trade with Newchwang, 33.
Coal, Chefoo, 66; Hunan, 164; Kwangnin, 25; Kwangtung, 188, 262; Nan-Paian, 24; Mining of, 61; Newchwang, 40; Shansi, 313; Statistics of, 30; Wuhu, 116.
Coinage, Report on relation of silver and copper, 371.
Coins, 368; Analysis of, 371-379.
Coke, not manufactured, 31.
College, Visit to Imperial Naval, 110; Visit to Military, 112.
Commerce, British, Protection of, 211-230; Chambers of (*see* Appendix); Piracy, No security because of, 248-258; Protection lacking, 280.
Commercial attaché, 351.
Company, Japan Sugar Refining, 421; Mitsu Bishi, 419; Taku Tug and Lighter, 18; Union Steel and Iron, 433.
Consul, the British, in China, 348; Complaints against, 349-358; Russian needed at Newchwang, 37.
Consular representation, 128.
Consular system, Defects of British, 349-357.
Convention of Chefoo, 240, 244, 247, 401.
Copper, Used in coinage, 370.
Corea, Japan trade with, 426; at Russia's mercy, 55.
Corn, waste of, 188.
Cotton, American export of, 445; Newchwang trade in, 58; Quality of Chinese, 91; Taxation of, 410; Shanghai trade in, 90, 93, 294.
Cruisers, English and German built, 284.
Currency, (*see* chapter on), 359; Defects of, 387; Gold, 383; Opinions on, 382-386.
Customs, Opium, Report on Hong Kong, 208 (*see* Tariffs, 389).
Customs House, Regulations of Shanghai, 77; at Kowloon, 204.

DEBT, of China, 363.

Deer-horns, 60.
Dickinson, W. W., 14.
Dockyards, of Mitsu Bishi Co., 419.
Duck feathers, 260.
Duties (*see* chapter on "Tariffs," 389), Ad valorem, 415; Opium, on Hong Kong, 204-210; Preferential, 236; Railway materials exempted from, 45; Shanghai Customs House collection of, 80; Tientsin, 15; Transit, agreement of Chinese Government concerning, 401.

ELECTRIC PLANT of Kioto, 423, 424.
Emperor, Interview with the Japanese, 430.
Evans & Pugh, 147.
Exchange, Declining gold, 384.
Exports (*see* tables, 198, 203, 391), American, to China, 445; Canton, 235, 259, 260; Chinkiang, 136; Newchwang, 33, 57, 60; Value of Newchwang gold, 62; Taxes on, 410; Tea, 184; Tientsin, 15; Wuchow, 265.

FEATHERS, 167.
Felt, 60.
Fergusson, Mr., property case of, 69.
Finance (*see* chapter on, 359), Spheres of Influence and, 367.
Fire-crackers, Canton export of, 260.
Fleming, murder of, 140.
Flour, American export of, 445; Fluctuation in price of, 375.
Foochow, Arsenal of, 300; Report of Chamber of Commerce, 479; Trade statistics of, 169; Visit to, 169.
Forests of Manchuria, 35.
Forts (*see* chapter on "Forts and Arsenals," 290).
France, Chinese interests of, 99; Hanchow interests of, 144; Silk trade of, 259; Sphere of influence of, in Kwangsi and Kwangtung, 235, 260; in Yangtse Valley, 325; Treaty rights of, 82.
Furs, Tientsin trade in, 18.

GERMANY, Canton silk trade of, 259; Chefoo controlled by, 65; England's relations to, 21; Kiao-chow occupied by, 67, 74.
Gingal, 280.
Ginseng, 60.
Glass, Opening for manufacture of, 40, 390, 418.

486

INDEX

Gold, at Chefoo, 66; Currency, 383; at Hunan, 166; at Newchwang, 62; in Yangtse Valley, 345.
Gordon, Chinese, 6.
Grand Canal, Condition of, 131; Peculation of officials of, 326.
Great Britain, China trade, extent of, 6; Canton silk trade of, 259; China trade with, 192 (*see* tables, 198–203); Confidence of China in, 231; Fergusson case, action in, 69; Manchurian trade, 47; Right of, to establish shops in Canton, case of Banker & Co., 238–247; Russia, fear of, 158; Spheres of Influence, policy in regard to, 3, 4; Subjects, inadequate protection of, 212–214.
Greaves and Giddes & Co. case with French Consul, 145.
Grieg, Dr., 52.

HAIHOW, Value of trade of, 198–202.
Halliday, Mr., 111.
Hankow, Arsenal of, 299; Geographical importance of, 168; Report of Chamber of Commerce of, 477; Visit to, 139.
Hanyang, 150.
Harbor of Wai-hai-Wei, best in Northern China, 72.
Hart, Sir Robert, 6, 12; Administration of, 175.
Hemp, 40.
Hides, Tientsin trade in, 18.
Hisaya, Baron, 420.
Ho Kai, Address to Lord Beresford, 211–231.
Hoi Chou, Pirates of, 250.
Hong Kong, Report of Chamber of Commerce, 473; Visit to, 191–231.
Hosie, Mr., British Consul at Wuchow, 264.
Hsü Jung Kwei, Viceroy of Foochow, Interview with, 173.
Hsu Ying Kwei, Army of, 278.
Hu Yen Mei, Interview with, 11.
Huang Chin, Interview with, 98.
Hunan, Manufactures of, Mineral wealth of, 164; Soldiers of, 271.

ICHANG, Trade with Newchwang, 33.
Imports (*see* tables, 92, 198–203, 391), Cotton, Comparison of, for 1887 and 1897; Newchwang, 33, 57; Oil, American, 59; Tientsin, 15.
Iron, in Hankow, 153; Kwangnin, 25; Kwangtung, 188; Manchuria, 39, 61.
Ito, Marquis, Interview with, 95, 416.

JACKSON, Mr. P., 359.
Japan, Electricity as a motive power in, 424; Exports of, compared with Chinese, 60; Open Door in China desired by, 431; Trade of, compared with Chinese, 417; Visit to, 419.
Jardine and Matheson Steamship Company, 33, 149.
Junks, Description of river, 323.

KAIPING, Cavalry camp at, 275.
Kang Yu Wei, Interview with, 191–195.
Khanpingkhan pass, 18.
Kiangzin, Army at, 277; Visit to, 138.
Kiaochow, Visit to, 73; German occupation of, 73.
Kioto, Electric plant of, 423.
Kirin, Hospital at, 52; British Consul needed at, 36, 44.
Kiukiang, Report of Chamber of Commerce, 475; Population and trade statistics of, 117.
Ko Chun, Pirates of, 250.
Kobé, Visit to, 421.
Kowloon, 204.
Krupp guns, 290.
Kwangnin coal and iron, 25.
Kwangsi, British trade with, 198–202; French Sphere of Influence in, 235; Silk exports of, 259.
Kwangtung, British trade with, 198–202; French Sphere of Influence in, 235; Mineral wealth of, 188; Piracy on waterways of, 248–258; Silk exports of, 259.
Kwei Chun, Interview with, 97.
Kwei Yun, Interview with, 261–263.

LABOR, Cost of native, 27; need of skilled, 38.
Lake Poyang, 346; Tung Ting, 345.
Land, Russian policy in purchase of, 57.
Lang, Captain, 7.
Lead, 39, 165.
Li Hung Chang, 12; Proposition of, 84.
Likin, Evils of, 170, 178, 184, 189, 234, 238, 241, 333, 406.
Lin Kwen Yi, Army of, 277; Interview with, 106.

487

INDEX

Lo Tak Fat, Statement on piracy by, 254.
Loans, 363 ; Present prices of, 368.
Locomotives, American, 26, 29; Dubs's, 26 ; Baldwin's, 28, 45.
" Loto Shui," 410.
Lumber, 95.

MACDONALD, Sir Claude, 8, 68; Letter in Banker & Co. case, 238.
Machinery, American, 26, 49, 445 ; German, 70.
Maize, 40.
Manchu, Armies of, 268.
Manchuria: Annexation, Effect of Russian, 55 ; Army of, 275; Forests of, 35 ; Foreign trade of, 57 ; Importance of, 42 ; Missions in, 52 ; Port of, 34; Resources of, 35, 61 ; Russian army in, 32, 34, 36, 47, 287 ; Russian and British trade with, 48.
Mandarins, Illegitimate gains of, 219–225.
Mansfield, R. W., Consul at Canton, Letters in Banker & Co. case, 238–244 ; Reports on piracy at Canton, 249–253.
Manufactures : Bricks, 185; British, openings for, 418 ; Cannon, 294; Cotton goods, 422 ; Matches, 422 ; Munitions of war, 294; Powder, 293 ; Rifles, 294; Salt, 179 ; Steel and iron, 154 ; at Tongshan, 25.
Matches, Newchwang trade in, 57.
Matting, Export trade of Canton in, 235, 260.
Mauser rifles, in use in Chinese Army, 271, 276, 112.
Maxim guns, Chinese Army equipped with, 271.
Millet, 40.
Min River, Navigation of, 170–171.
Minerals : Wealth of Hunan in, 165 ; of Hupeh, 154 ; of Kwangtung, 179, 188, 262 ; of Manchuria, 61–62; of Newchwang, 39.
Mining Rights desired, 38.
Mint, at Tientsin, 293.
Missions: Catholic, at Hankow, 142 ; at Hunan, 165 ; Jesuit, at Shanghai, 104 ; Protestant, in Manchuria, 52.
Mitsu Bishi Co., Visit to docks of, 419.
Mongolia, Absorbed by Russia, 55 ; Army in, 275.

NANKHOW Pass, 18.
Nanking, Arsenal of, 298; Treaty of, 237, 238, 395 ; Visit to, 106.
Nanyang, Squadron of, 284.
Navigation Laws, Anglo-Saxon trade affected by, 77 ; Inland, 122.
Navy, Report on Chinese, 284 ; on Japanese, 419, 430.
Needles, 40.
New York, Visit to, 437.
Newchwang, Port of, 33–40; Visit to, 32; Report of Chamber of Commerce, 471.
Nieh, Army of General, 274.
Ningpo, Riots at Joss-house of, 100.
Northcote, Sir Stafford, 1, 459.

OFFICIALS, Corruption of Chinese, 216–225.
Oil, 40 ; Canton export of, 235, 260; American export of, 446.
Open Door, American trade, essential for future of, 437, 443; Benefits of, to all nations, 96, 103, 115; Canton merchants on, 261 ; Desire of Chinese for, 19 ; at Foochow, 172 ; at Hong Kong, 196, 211 ; Report of Hong Kong merchants on, 211–231 ; Japanese trade, imperative for future of, 423, 426, 431 ; at Kiao-chow, 67, 74; Necessity of, 41 ; Only rational policy, 454 ; Tientsin Chamber of Commerce on, 470 ; In Yangtse Valley, 317, 393.
Opium, Hong Kong duties on, 204–210.
Osaka, Visit to, 421.

PAKHUI. (See table, 198–202.)
Paotung, French claim to, 102.
Paper, Wuchow trade in, 265.
Pavloff, M., Russian Chargé d'Affaires, 1.
Pease, Trade in, 34.
Peking, Field force of, 275 ; Government of, 83–86; Visit to, 1.
Petroleum, Newchwang trade in, 59.
Peyang, Squadron of, 284.
Pigs' Bristles, Canton trade in, 260 ; Newchwang trade in, 62.
Piracy, at Canton, 234 ; Accounts of, at Canton, 248–258.
Police, Inefficiency of Chinese, 4 ; Necessity for reorganization of, 450.
Population. (See Statistics.)
Port Arthur, 1.

488

INDEX

Ports, of Manchuria, 34; Wei-hai-Wei, 71.
Powder (*see* Arsenals) Manufacture of German smokeless, 302; Quality of Chinese, 290; Tientsin factory, 293.
Preserves, Kwangsi and Kwangtung exports of, 257.
Prison, Visit to Tokio, 429.

RAILWAYS (*see* chapter on, 304): Burmah Extension Railway, 314; Chefoo, 66-69; Hankow-Canton Railway, 312, 167; Kiao-Chow-Yichow-Tsinan Railway, 73, 312; Lu-Han Railway, 306; Pekin Syndicate Railway, 29, 313; Russian Manchurian Railway, 309; Shanghai-Nanking Railway, 314; Shanhaikwan Extension Railway, 23, 314; Shanhaikwan-Newchwang Railway, 308; Soochow-Hanchow-Ningpo Railway, 314; Stretensk-Vladivostock Railway, 309; Swatow and Chao-Chao Fu, 180; Taiyuan-Fu-Chengting Railway, 311; Tientsin-Chinkiang Railway, 312; Tonquin-Nanning-Fu Railway, 313; Trans-Manchurian, 44, 48; Wuchow and Chungking, 265
Railways, Essential for development, 11; British interests in, 305; German interests in, 305; Gauge of, 316; In course of construction, 306; In operation, 304; Projected, 310; Russian interests in, 305.
Reform, of Chinese Government, 211-230.
Reforms, suggested by author, 455
Reports of Chambers of Commerce. (*See* Appendix.)
Residence, No liberty to foreigners for purposes of trade, 83; In interior, 126.
Revenues, Corruption of Chinese, 220-225; Amounts of, 362; Newchwang, 56.
Rice, 187; Wuchow trade in, 265; Fluctuation in price of, 375.
Rifles, in use in Chinese army, 279; Factory at Hankow, 299.
River, Reports on, Han, 343; Liao, 342; Pei Ho, 341; Siang, 345; Wangpoo, 340; West, 329; Yangtse, 320; Yellow, 337.
Rivers. (*See* Waterways, 318).
Roads, 346.

Russia, Army of, in Manchuria, 286; British interests affected by, 145; Manchurian trade of, 47; Policy of, 13, 18, 36, 51.
Russian courtesy to author, 156, 52.

SALARIES, Official, 220-225; Evils caused by small, 364.
Salt, Effects of illegal taxation of, 411; Swatow manufacture of, 179; Monopoly of, 186.
Salt Fish, Trade in, 185.
Samshui. (*See* table, 198-202.)
Schools, Japanese military, 427.
Seaweed, Newchwang Imports of, 57.
Shanghai, Report of Chamber of Commerce, 472; Visit to, 76.
Shansi, Mineral wealth of, 313.
Shantung, Soldiers of, 271.
Sheng, Director of Chinese Railway, Interview with, 161.
Shipbuilding, Japan, 419; San Francisco, 433.
Shipping, British, 41.
Shiung Yo, Trouble at, 48.
Siberia, Position of Russian army in Eastern, 286.
Silk, Export of Canton, 235-259; of Wuchow, 265; Taxation of, 410.
Silver, 39; Relation between copper cash and, 370.
Singapore, Emigration to, 189.
Skins, Tientsin trade in, 18, 60
Soon Ching, Army of General, 273.
Spheres of Influence, Canton merchants protest against, 259; Evils of, 215-217; Finance affected by, 367; French in Kwangsi and Kwangtung, 235; In Yangtse Valley, 325; Hong Kong, 196; Result of, 452; Shanghai Chamber of Commerce report on, 468; Yangtse Valley in, 317.
Spirits, Trade in, 40.
Statistics (*see* Summary of Trade), 483; Amoy trade, 182; Canton trade, 232; Chefoo trade, 65; Chinkiang trade, 120; Foochow trade, 169; Hankow trade, 139; Hong Kong trade, 191; Imports cotton into all China, 92; Kiukiang trade, 117; Newchwang, export, 58; trade, 32; Peking, 1; Shanghai, cotton imports, 90; trade, 76; Swatow trade, 177; Tables, 198-203; Tientsin, 14; Tongshan coal, 30; Work-

INDEX

shop and locomotive, 25; Wuchow trade, 264; Wuhu trade, 115.
Steel, Hanyang Mills, 164; Opening for British manufacture of, 418; used in Shanghai arsenal, 296.
Stuhlman, Dr., Report on copper cash, 377.
Sugar, Staple trade of Swatow, 177; Export of Wuchow, 265.
Summary of trade statistics, 483.
Sung, Army of General, 273.
Swatow, Visit to, 177-181. (*See* table, 198-202.)
Szechuan, In French Sphere of Influence, 325.

TABLES, Analysis of Coin, 371, 379; British trade with China, 198; Canton exports, 259; Cotton imports into all China, 92; Currency, 360; Newchwang imports, 83; Summary of trade statistics of, 483; Tongshan, Workshop and locomotive statistics, 25.
Tael, Commercial Standard of, 368.
Taku Tug and Lighter Company, 18.
Tan, Viceroy of Canton: Letters in Banker & Co. case, 238-244.
Tan Chung Lin, 261; Army of, 278.
Taotais, Officers of International Board of Trade, 171, 181.
Tariff, Revision of, 413. (*See* chapter on, 389.)
Tax, Chingfui, 405; Evils of likin, 170, 178, 184, 189, 234, 238; Area of exemption from likin, 241; Hai Kow, 405; Land, 411.
Taxation, Evils of illegal, 124, 410; Chinese feeling about, 157.
Taxes, Illegal, 405.
Taylor, F. E., Report on depreciation of silver, 376.
Tea, Amoy trade in, 182; Foochow, 170; Formosa, 184; Oolong, 183; Swatow, 177; Wuchow, 265.
Tientsin, Arsenal of, 292; Banks of, 16; Mints of, 293; Trade of, 15; Treaty of, 242; Report of Chamber of Commerce of, 470; Visit to, 14.
Tin, Trade in, 165.
Tobacco, 40.
Tokio, Visit to, 425.
Tongshan, Coal-fields of, 25; Manufactures of, 25.
Torpedo Boats, German built, 224-285.

Trade (*see* chapter on, 389), American, with China, 444; with Shanghai, 92; Amoy, 182; Anglo-Saxon, Dependent on Russia's good-will, 53; British extent of, 5; With Manchuria, 47; Protection of, 2; In Hankow, 139-168; Canton, Effect of piracy on, 248-258; Chefoo, 66; China compared with Japan, 417; Chinkiang, Discussion of, 121; Russian occupation of Manchuria, effect on, 36; Foreign, Reason for limited, 79; Hong Kong, 191 (*see* tables, 198-203); Development of foreign, 205; Opium, 204; International Board of, 171; Manchuria, Effect of Russian occupation on, 36; Newchwang, Value of, 40, 41, 56; Review of 1898, 63; Shanghai, 76; Cotton, 90, 93; Summary of statistics of, 483; Swatow, 177; Tientsin, 15; Wahu, Importance of trade of, 115.
Trade Intelligence Department, need for, 456.
Transit Passes, Enactment of Chefoo Convention, 401; Enactment of Tsung Li Yamen, 403; Free, 87, 234, 356; Utter failure, 81.
Treaty (*see* chapter on 389); Chefoo, 401; Nanking, 395; Tientsin, 17, 19, 177, 242.
Tseng, His Excellency, 245.
Tsung Chee, 171.
Tsung-li Yamen, 2; Obstacles to plan of, 159; Interview with, 2.
Tug and Lighter Co., Taku, 118.
Tung Fu Chan, Army of, 274.

UNION Steel and Iron Works, San Francisco, Visit to, 433.
United States, Competition of, in cotton trade, 92, 94; Visit to, 433.

VALUE, Standard of, 368.
Vladivostock, Russian dockyards at, 289.

WADE, Sir Thomas, Opinion on likin, 409.
Washington, Visit to, 436.
Waterways, 318.
Wei-hai-Wei, Population of, 71; Harbors of, 72.
Wheat, 187, 188.
Wong Chi Tong, Visit to, 163.

490